PHalarope Books

PHalarope Books are designed specifically for the amateur naturalist. These volumes represent excellence in natural history publishing. Each book in the PHalarope series is based on a nature course or program at the college or adult education level or is sponsored by a museum or nature center. Each PHalarope Book reflects the author's teaching ability as well as writing ability.

D0958039

BOOKS IN THE SERIES:

THE
WILDLIFE
OBSERVER'S
GUIDEBOOK

Charles E. Roth

A SPECTRUM BOOK

PRENTICE-HALL, INC., Englewood Cliffs, New Jersey 07632

Library of Congress Cataloging in Publication Data

ROTH, CHARLES EDMUND   (date).
   The wildlife observer's guidebook.

"A Spectrum Book."
"PHalarope books."
Bibliography: p.
Includes index.
   1. Wildlife watching.   I. Title.
QL60.R67   590'.72   82-389
ISBN 0-13-959536-8   AACR2
ISBN 0-13-959528-7 (pbk.)

To Charles E. Mohr:
naturalist, teacher, friend.

© 1982 by Charles E. Roth
All rights reserved. No part of this book may be reproduced in any
form or by any means without permission in writing from the publisher.
A Spectrum Book. Printed in the United States of America.

This Spectrum Book can be made available to businesses
and organizations at a special discount when ordered in
large quantities. For more information, contact
Prentice-Hall, Inc.; General Publishing Division, Special Sales;
Englewood Cliffs, New Jersey 07632.

Editorial/production supervision
and interior design by Eric Newman
Art production by Marie Alexander
Cover design by Honi Werner
Manufacturing buyer: Cathie Lenard

10 9 8 7 6 5 4 3 2 1

ISBN 0-13-959536-8

ISBN 0-13-959528-7 {PBK.}

PRENTICE-HALL INTERNATIONAL, INC., London
PRENTICE-HALL OF AUSTRALIA PTY. LIMITED, Sydney
PRENTICE-HALL CANADA INC., Toronto
PRENTICE-HALL OF INDIA PRIVATE LIMITED, New Delhi
PRENTICE-HALL OF JAPAN, INC., Tokyo
PRENTICE-HALL OF SOUTHEAST ASIA PTE. LTD., Singapore
WHITEHALL BOOKS LIMITED, Wellington, New Zealand

CONTENTS

FOREWORD

The human species is a wandering type—an adventurous and coloniz-
ing one. Adventure needs the stimulation of discovery, and discovery
needs diversity. Without it we will stagnate and degenerate. That crucial
diversity consists of varied habitats, other species, and other human
communities, since both animal and plant species and other human
groups evolved in response to differing environmental circumstances,
both physical and biological.

We need, therefore, to value the great diversity that nature has
produced over the millenia. It is a godsend. We need, for example, to
remember and practice the arts—both practical and academic—handed
down to us by those who devised them and used them in coping with
their particular circumstances. It is not so much that we will need these
for our own survival (though that is by no means assured), but that we
can appreciate the accomplishments of our many ancestors only if we
know the resourcefulness they exercised.

For North Americans, especially, the skills in wildlife observation
brought to perfection by American Indians and a few pioneer colonists
are both intriguing and worth mastering. They have what Aldo Leopold
once called "split rail value" because they provide historical continuity.
More than that, they are basic skills for the never-ending exploration of
nature's intricacies. The world is more complex than we will ever know,
but that is a challenge to those of us who see life as an adventuring in
time.

Chuck Roth, the author of this guidebook, is one of the most
thoughtful of the current generation of nature interpreters, and has here
brought together a broad array of helpful clues to seeing, recognizing,
and appreciating the things we find afield even in the much man-

handled suburban landscape. It will extend your senses to test these old arts and crafts of the Indian, the *coureur de bois,* and the mountain men.

ROLAND C. CLEMENT

President,
Connecticut Audubon Society

PREFACE

Many wildlife books are available today that tell the reader about the wonderful ways of animals, but almost none that give the reader help on how to discover the ways of animals for himself. This book is one that does.

Wildlife observing is both an art and a science. Unfortunately for many people today, there is a mystique to science engulfed in white lab coats, contorted glassware, and complicated electronic devices. It is a sad perception. The marine biologist Dr. Kenneth Norris puts a much truer face on the nature of science when he says: "For me science is a deeply human endeavor. It is simply human curiosity channeled toward the truth, with our normal human tendency toward fish tales and exaggeration weeded out." This book is devoted to bringing that kind of science to all who would observe wildlife.

Science is a process of exploring the world that is available to all who retain something of their childhood curiosity and who are willing to search for information that others can verify. There is no mystery. Truth is truth no matter who reveals it.

There is a remarkable amount yet to be learned about animals that exist in vacant lots and back yards as well as those that dwell in the wilderness. If you are armed with a mindset that joy is to be found in studying the other life forms about us, along with some tools for ferreting out the facts about these creatures, endless hours of pleasure and reward lie before you. The devoted naturalist never seems to age, for there is so much new to discover each day that one lifetime is too short to uncover it all, and *boredom* becomes a meaningless word.

This book is built on the cumulative experiences of hundreds of students of wildlife, both amateur and professional. Some of its ideas are easy to trace to the work of a specific observer, but many more are so much a part of the field itself that only the most rigorous scholar could pinpoint their source. By my not giving a reference for every source there is no intent to deny anyone credit, but only to get out information on techniques to as many as possible in a reasonably readable fashion. The intent is to provide broad access to the tools of discovery in the area of live animal biology. If a reader invents a new technique or improves on one presented here, or if errors are discovered, please communicate and share it with others through revised editions of this guidebook.

Acknowledgments

To Sam Stack, long since gone to his reward, and to my boyhood field companion Duane Adams, this books owes much, for their influence on observational skills was at work long before any formal academic influence blinded some of my sensitivity. They helped me learn to read nature. Certain teachers of my academic years had potent influence, helping me learn to organize random experiences into coherent patterns of understanding. These also fostered learning from nature as well as books—Charles E. Mohr, Hobart Van Deusen, Ralph M. Wetzel, Richard B. Fischer, and William Dilger.

Of course any such book owes a great debt to the pioneering work of such people as Konrad Lorenz, Niko Tinko Tinbergen, C.R. Carpenter, L.S.B. Leakey, Aldo Leopold, and the generations of students they have stimulated in the fields of ethology, primate field studies, and wildlife management. It is they who have generated many of the successful techniques for studying living animals in the wild. They have helped make biology truly the study of life, not merely the study of dead specimens. As one early student of bears remarked: If you want to find out about how an animal lives, you watch it live and not watch it die.

From these students of wild animal ways has arisen a large literature on the subject. Some is noted in the Further Reading sections of the chapters and also at the end of the book. Some of these works have been quoted directly, and I gratefully acknowledge the kindness of the following in granting permission to reprint passages from their publications:

The quotation by Horace Kephart on page xv is reprinted with permission from his *Camping and Woodcraft* (copyright 1916, 1917 by Macmillan Publishing Co., Inc., renewed 1944, 1945, Laura M. Kephart).

The quotation from Charles Elton on page 19 is from his *Exploring the Animal World* (1933) and is reprinted with the permission of George Allen & Unwin (Publishers) Ltd.

The quotations on pages 32 and 36 are from *The Tracker* by Tom Brown, Jr., and William Jon Watkins and are reprinted with the permission of Prentice-Hall, Inc. © 1978 by Tom Brown, Jr., and William Jon Watkins.

The quotation on page 109 is from Niko Tinbergen's *Social Behavior of Animals* (1953) and is reprinted here with the permission of Methuen & Co., Ltd.

The quotations from Bil Gilbert's *Chulo* on pages 48, 142, and 144 are reprinted with the permission of Alfred A. Knopf, Inc. © 1973 by Bil Gilbert.

The quotations by George Schaller on pages 90 and 150 are from his *The Serengetti Lion* (1972) and are reprinted with the permission of The University of Chicago Press.

The quotation by Alfred S. Romer on page 138 is from his *The Vertebrate Story* (1971) and is reprinted with the permission of Holt, Rinehart and Winston.

The excerpts from Shoshana Satter's "The Nutty Professors" on page 143 is reprinted from the February/March 1978 *Animal Kingdom* (published by the New York Zoological Society) with her permission.

I also want to express my deepest appreciation to Dr. John Fitch for his patient reading of a draft of the manuscript and for the cogent advice he gave. I am also in debt to Tom Tyning and Elissa Landre for their insights on the amphibian and bird banding sections, respectively. Thanks also to Roland Clement for his support through the years and for contributing the Foreword.

Mary Kennan, Eric Newman, and the editorial staff at Prentice-Hall have been most patient and helpful through the development of this project. They have provided ongoing encouragement and their technical skills have helped unsnag many of the rough edges. Charlotte Smith faithfully maneuvered the rough script into a creditable final typescript with boundless good cheer.

In the long run, writing this book was possible only because of the patient love of a wife and children who suffered the neglect and picked up the domestic pieces that are inevitably engendered by the lonely vigil of author at typewriter. Fortunately for me, this is a family that shares my love of wildlife and has been willing to endure the tribulations related to the care and feeding of an author.

As for book-learning in such an art, it is useful only to those who do not expect too much from it. No book can teach a man how to swing an axe or follow a faint trail. Nor is it of much account to one who merely learns by rote, without using his own wits and common sense as he follows the pages. Yet a good book is the best stepping stone for a beginner. Without it he might bog and flounder a long time without aim or method. It gives a clear idea of general principles. It can show, at least, how *not* to do a thing—and there is a good deal in that—half of woodcraft, as of any other art, is knowing what to avoid.

HORACE KEPHART, 1917

CHAPTER 1

INTRODUCTION

WILDLIFE HOLDS A DEEP FASCINATION for a great many people. Even in our highly urbanized society where day-to-day contact with wildlife is sharply limited, large numbers of people retain an inner yearning for involvement with other forms of life. Ever since the dawn of our existence humans have interacted with other animals. Some species fed us; some species killed us; and some stirred our sense of the aesthetic. The birds and beasts were our neighbors—some were friends and allies, some were enemies, and a great many more lived out their lives totally unnoticed by mankind.

For most people today contact and interaction with wildlife is remote and confined largely to vicarious involvement via television, movies, paintings, books, or the symbols of our mechanical wildlife—Cougar, Falcon, Bobcat, Mustang, Eagle, and the like. Even these latter are giving way to X-19s, B210s, and similar abstract numerical designations. For the majority, wildlife observation, like athletics, has become a spectator sport. Most of us rely on the devoted work of professional wildlife biologists, film makers, and artists.

It need not be so. There is still considerable opportunity for direct interaction with various types of wildlife that may begin close to home and expand farther afield as interest, skill, and commitment develop. Wildlife observation is great fun; it stimulates the human mind, body, and often, the spirit. Almost anyone can participate in wildlife observation. With a little training, practice, and perseverance one not only uncovers a great deal of pleasure but also contributes to the fund of human knowledge.

From the variety of currently available books on wildlife and the number of wildlife films on television one might conclude that our knowledge of wildlife is complete. But nothing could be further from the truth. To be sure, some species are reasonably well known, but even with these the more we learn about them the more new unanswered questions arise. On the whole, the range of our ignorance about the vast majority of this planet's life forms is overwhelming. Currently hundreds of species of life, particularly those in the tropics, hover on the brink of extinction. They have been brought to the edge of existence largely by the massive manipulation of habitats by modern man and his extensive and overwhelming technologies. It is profoundly saddening to realize that most of these species will become extinct with no human knowledge of them beyond occasional museum specimens and locality labels. We will only be able to speculate on what they ate, how they reproduced, what their behavioral repertoire was, how they interacted with neighboring species—indeed, anything about their lives.

What may be much more surprising is that we know very little more about even the most abundant creatures around us unless they happen to be economic pests. For example, the tiny spring peeper, whose amazing spring chorus that for several weeks comes to the attention of millions of people across the eastern United States each year, has managed to have its summer activities and wintering sites go essentially unrecorded. As a youngster I couldn't find any adults who could tell me what made the sound. I was told birds. I was told turtles! When I discovered for myself that the creatures were actually inch-long frogs, nobody in my neighborhood would believe me until I brought some home in a jar and demonstrated for all who would listen. These delightful little tree frogs concentrate by the thousands at the breeding pools each spring, yet they are seldom seen at all during the rest of the year. How far do they wander from the breeding pools? Do they haunt the tree tops; low shrubs; or forest litter? Do they move around a great deal or stay on a relatively small territory? What creatures are their major enemies? What are their favorite foods? Where do they go to hibernate? They have such weak toes and no toenails; how do they dig below the surface? Do they go below frostline? How do they get out to the breeding grounds when the ground is often still frozen? How far do they travel to the ponds in spring? Or do they move in close to the ponds to hibernate in the fall? Do they hibernate singly or in clusters? If the latter, do they associate in single- or mixed-sex groups? The questions roll on but the answers remain elusive.

Such questions are unlikely to be answered by professional scientists. Most formal scientists are deeply involved in what are considered more profound questions and the funding for scientific research under current government- and foundation-granting priorities is not likely to be spent on such mundane issues. These questions are asked by people who are restlessly curious about the other animals that share their environment, and if they are to be answered at all, it will almost certainly be by dedicated amateurs having the times of their lives.

The jaunty blue jay—beautiful, raucous, all too obvious at some times of the year, and quite abundant in most of the heavily populated eastern suburbs—is another near neighbor that holds many mysteries. For example, these birds can frequently be seen in groups going through a head-bobbing or pumping display. In what context do they do this? What does it mean? Only one scientific paper exists that offers even a hypothesis.* What percentage of the local jay population remains in a given location year-round; what percentage migrates? How far? How do other wildlife species respond to jay alarm calls? How stable are blue jay social groups? Are such groups random collections of individuals or kinship groups? And so it goes. There is much to be discovered. And again it is most likely that dedicated lay people will make the discoveries. Margaret Morse Nice made the classic and definitive study of the song sparrow as a housewife raising her family and making observations between a myriad of other chores. Likewise, the basic life history and behavioral repertoire of the common house or English sparrow was unraveled by a British physician, D. Summers-Smith, during spare moments of observation made amid the demands of a busy medical practice.

In reading a spate of natural history books, particularly those that summarize the basic life histories of various species, we find a great many definitive statements. Dig into the scientific literature upon which the authors drew for their statements and some interesting things come to light. All too often the statements are based on the rather restricted observations of a very limited number of observers and often these observations were made many years ago. Frequently, a particular observation is handed down through several generations of authors without its ever being looked at again to confirm, expand, or alter the original observer's information. The facts are that the data base is very limited upon which to make so many broad, almost dogmatic, statements about what a species does or does not do. The opportunities are at hand for new generations of observers to confirm, expand, and enrich the data base about almost any species.

In the last twenty years there have been a number of superb field studies carried out in various parts of the world. The primates and the large predators—particularly of Africa—have received the lion's share of attention, but there have been others. The result of these long-range, in-depth studies has been not only to expand our knowledge but also to multiply our areas of ignorance. The more we learn, the more we dis-

---

*J. W. Hardy, "Studies in behavior and phylogeny of certain New World jays," *Univ. of Kansas Sci. Bull.*, 42 (1961), 13–149.

cover there is to find out, but until certain discoveries are made we don't know enough to identify some of these areas of ignorance. Such intensive and long-range studies serve to point up how tentatively we must take the information in many of our existing natural history books. We need to have more interested people observe and collect information about almost every species in a wide range of habitats.

Researchers working on the behavior of the spotted hyena did detailed work on the population in Ngorongoro Crater. They carefully pieced together the species' basic behavioral and ecological relationships. Later, working on the Serengeti Plains, only a few hundred miles distant, they found the spotted hyenas behaving in significantly different ways. The heavily studied chimpanzees at the Gombe Stream Reserve demonstrate a number of unique behaviors not always found among the chimp populations in other habitats. In other words, behavior can adapt to different environments just as anatomy may. Only a large number of studies in areas representing the full spectrum of a species' habitat, particularly with the so-called higher organisms, is likely to provide a truly comprehensive view of what that species is all about—its capacities and limitations.

Among species closer to home we know that woodchucks hibernate, but the times, intensity, and length of such hibernatory behavior seem to be quite different at the southern end of its range from such behavior in the northern sectors. How different? Much remains to be learned. Among native birds researchers have found that our crows have a broad repertoire of calls and that these are further differentiable into regional "dialects." Crows of one regional dialect often do not respond appropriately to the recorded calls of a different regional dialect. How many other species show such local variations in vocal patterns and other basic behavior?

From microbes to whales, there are millions of species of wildlife on this planet. And there are still more remaining to be discovered by humans, particularly in the tropics and the depths of the seas. For most, particularly the smaller ones, we know little more than what they look like and the scientific binomial name assigned to them. There are forms of wildlife in every place that humans inhabit as well as in many places that they only visit. There is no lack of material for the hobby of wildlife watching.

One needs only to learn that every species is interesting in its own way and that the more we learn the greater the interest. There are those who wish to study such spectacular species as wolves or grizzly bears, and so they read with envy of the studies of Dave Mech, Durward Allen, and the Craighead brothers. But others will learn that there is fertile ground for investigation among many much smaller creatures. Fabre, Wheeler, Evans, and von Frisch, for example, spent productive lifetimes studying insects.

This book is for all those who would be serious wildlife observers. Some of you will already have begun by watching birds at backyard feeders or on bird walks. Or perhaps you are a hunter who has become fascinated not only by the behavior of your favorite quarry but also by the antics of other wild creatures. The purpose of the book is to acquaint you with the necessary skills and tools to become fully involved in the challenging hobby of observing wildlife and bringing home the trophy of increased knowledge and understanding. It will also help you record your observations for later sharing with others.

As a hobby, wildlife observation can be physically challenging and mentally stimulating. It demands a honing of the full range of our senses. It can be done either with the basic sensing equipment with which you were born or with sophisticated technical equipment. (For example, Frank Craighead used a communications satellite to relay radio signals from the radio collar on a free-ranging grizzly bear to his field laboratory.) Wildlife observation is not limited to any season, time, or geography; it is a lifetime pursuit. Furthermore, it helps us maintain close touch with our planetary roots. All in all, wildlife observation is not only an ideal hobby for many people, but it also carries with it the added bonus that the recorded observations may potentially contribute to the aggregate of human knowledge.

Although there is great potential for group discussion of findings and even for some kinds of team observation, wildlife observing is basically a hobby for those who desire at least periodic solitude. Most wildlife is wary, and it is difficult enough for one person to exercise the needed self-control and caution to move slowly and stealthily through wood and field without trying to coordinate such activity with others. Also, two or more people have strong desires to communicate verbally when in association for any length of time. This too may interfere with serious observation.

However, it is good fun and good growth to discuss your field observations regularly with others, either informally or in a club. Bil Gilbert and his boys undertook a study of coati-mundi, or chulo. He remarks in his book *Chulo* how much the evening discussion of everyone's daily observations not only helped share information but also helped challenge—and thus improve—everyone's observational technique and accuracy of field observations, which set the stage for the next round of observations. Search around. Find some cronies or form a club. Humans are social creatures—even those who like solitude.

In the chapters ahead we will explore a variety of techniques to make you a better field observer. There will be some beginner's techniques, a great deal of intermediate-level approaches, and some advanced techniques. My assumption is that you will have already demonstrated some basic interest or you wouldn't have picked up this book in the first place, and that if you want really advanced materials you will have entered the ranks of the professionals. In deciding what to exclude, I have confined the material basically to field observations with limited captive observational techniques. I have also essentially limited the techniques to those that do not require special permits or truly professional training and expertise. I encourage studies that nonprofessionals can undertake with reasonable competence and whose data could be compiled and synthesized by professionals if that is desirable. In a world where so much of recreation is purely frivolous, it is a joy to be able to recommend some recreational activity that is fun and yet contributes to a broader purpose.

Clearly, we need to gather a great deal more information about almost every species. Unfortunately a great many species are being pushed to the brink of existence. By the time the plight of any one species is widely recognized there are usually too few left for their continued survival. Most of those that have become extinct in recent years are gone with our having only the most minimal description of what and who they were. It is also quite clear that much of what data is collected will have to be collected by dedicated amateurs because little professional research money is available for such work. The more information that is gathered during the near future, the more likely it is that fewer species will be pushed to that greatest of finalities—species extinction. It also means that we may be able to better understand the success of certain other species, like the blackbirds, that have rapidly been expanding their numbers and habitat.

CHAPTER 2

THE ART OF SEEING

To THOSE NOT BLIND, seeing seems so obvious that to devote a substantial portion of this book to the art of seeing may appear frivolous or inane. However, seeing in its broadest sense is absolutely basic to wildlife observation and is neither simple nor obvious. Like common sense, it is a scarce commodity; many people who think they have the ability don't.

As its primary definition, Webster's Dictionary says that *to see* is "to get knowledge or an impression through the eyes and the sense of sight; to perceive visually." Then it goes on to expand that definition: "to get a clear mental impression of; to grasp by thinking; to understand; to learn, discover, to find out." Quite a spectrum for such a little word! The art of seeing comes from moving beyond the mere intake of sensory stimuli to making sense of the messages they carry, which is where the word *perceive* enters this word game because it means "to grasp mentally."

Seeing is an essential part of *observing*, which, to the lexicographer, is "noticing or perceiving something; examining scientifically." Further word play indicates that a *watcher* is "one who undertakes close observation for some time to see or find out something," while *observation* is "the act or practice of noting and recording facts and events, as for some scientific study." These terms all end up flowing into one another in subtle ways. However, we may note that some enjoy watching just for aesthetic pleasure but that a true observer is not satisfied merely with the aesthetics; the real observer wants to see in the fullest sense of the word.

Unfortunately we are often unaware of the extent of our general ability to see. From childhood I have been a devoted wildlife watcher and during my college years fancied myself quite competent in the art of seeing. And compared to some of my generation that was probably true enough. However, during my first semester at graduate school I had the opportunity to attend a special film lecture on the behavior of herring gulls by the world-renowned, and now Nobel Laureate, Niko Tinbergen. On the screen the audience watched as gulls bobbed and weaved about, uttered strange calls, and carried things about in their beaks. Throughout, Tinbergen delivered a triphammer discourse on the meaning of each of the bobs and weaves and other movements. I must admit that I left the lecture extremely skeptical. I was looking at the same birds as Tinbergen but I was not seeing. However, I didn't realize that at the time.

The next semester I took a course in ethology—the study of animal behavior. At the time I registered for the course I didn't realize that it was also to be a literal "eye opener," one that would help me not only to look but also to see. I remember vividly the first class when the professor put on a film of the courtship behavior of some tropical fish and asked us all to write down everything we observed. When all was done our pages contained only a very few notes. He then gave us our lab assignment for the semester; it was deceptively simple. We each were given an aquarium setup and our choice of a pair of one of the species of anabantid fishes (gouramis, bettas, and paradise fish). Our assignment simply was to discover everything we could about the behavior of these fishes.

At first it seemed that all we saw was the fish swimming back and forth. It was rather boring. But look we must! Before long it became apparent that the fish responded to one another and that each held its fins differently when in the presence of the other. We went on to discover an entire "fin language." We saw that they would shove water at each other's lateral line organs, flare their gills, and on and on. After a few weeks we were spending hours in front of our tanks discovering more and more about all that had been going on right in front of our eyes but which we had not been able to see earlier.

On the last day of class we were again shown the film we had viewed the first day and asked to write down what we saw. We could hardly write fast enough and filled several pages with our observations. What a change! I couldn't help but think back to my impressions following the Tinbergen lecture and realize how truly blind I had been in spite of my previous years of field study.

Actually, the ability to really see and observe is something most of us have as young children but that our culture inadvertently trains out of us. However, it is a skill almost everyone can regain if they wish and once it is regained, it is like crossing a one-way threshold—you never see the world again in quite the same way. You not only see more clearly, you change all your perceptions of the world.

I have taken groups of youngsters to watch native ducks on a pond in late winter and spring, a time when ducks exhibit courtship behavior. I ask the youngsters to write down everything they see. In general they indicate that they see ducks swimming and taking baths. I then ask them to pick out one duck and follow it everywhere. What other ducks does it chase? Which ducks chase it? What does it do when it approaches another duck or when another duck approaches it? Are there motions that it always, or usually, uses in certain situations? What are these motions? What are the situations? After exploring and answering questions such as these, most observers begin to see definite patterns. By comparing one's observations with those of others, the patterns become even stronger.

After a couple of hours of observation these youngsters become much more aware of subtleties that seem to have meaning for the ducks although they hadn't previously had meaning to the youngsters. Eventually they begin to "see like a duck" and realize that there is a great deal more going on at the pond than swimming and bathing. Once that happens, they never see ducks on a pond in the same light again; they have begun to learn how to really see ducks. Such a process need not be limited to youngsters.

The major problem is that humans are among the most easily habituated creatures; that is, they learn to turn off messages reaching their brains that don't have immediate value to their lives. Our environment is sending vast quantities of information all the time and our sensory receivers pick up a high percentage of them. If our brain were to respond to each of them we would clearly suffer from circuit overload. As young children, we are generally much more responsive, but we increasingly learn to filter out those units of information that we determine are unimportant to our lives. These filters tend to differ with each person's culture and lifestyle.

We are not the only creatures that habituate; most higher creatures do to one degree or another. You may have noticed that baby hamsters or gerbils jump at the slightest noise and when they become slightly older run for cover at the slightest motion. There clearly is survival value in this, but if they continued this way throughout their lives they would quickly wear themselves out. As they mature they learn which sounds and motions do not bring danger, and they ignore these. Taming them involves habituating them to the sound, smell, and motion of at least certain people.

Our urbanized human environment is especially enriched in environmental messages; the sensory overload is tremendous. We learn to habituate ourselves to many of them in order to retain some semblance of adult sanity. To become good wildlife observers we must remove some of the blinding filters and regain responsiveness to environmental signals we have learned to ignore. There are some exercises you can do to improve your ability to see and observe. Some are very elementary;

others a bit more advanced. Not knowing where you are personally in your development of the art of seeing, I will offer a series of increasingly more difficult activities. Begin with the one most suitable for you.

EXERCISE 1

One of the most basic exercises is "Kim's Game," so called because it was used to train young thieves in Rudyard Kipling's story *Kim*. In essence, a number of items (four or five at first, increasing to many more with developing skill) are placed in a box that is covered with a cloth. The exercise is done with two or more participants. One person arranges the objects in the box without the other's knowledge and covers it. He then snaps away the cloth for a fixed period of time (start with thirty seconds and work backwards with developing skill) and the others write down as complete a description of the items and their placement in the box as possible. Repeat the procedure over and over, each time changing the number, type, or placement of objects in the box. It's not a bad party game, but take it seriously if you want to become a good wildlife observer.

EXERCISE 2

You can follow up on Exercise 1 by visiting the home or office of either friend or stranger, or by going to an unfamiliar public building, vacant lot, or similar unfamiliar place. Walk through at a casual pace and leave, then see how completely you can describe the place either on paper or to a friend. Return and study the place more carefully. How much did you miss? Were there whole categories of objects that did not register with you? Repeat until you feel you are really getting the whole picture when you set your powers of observation to work.

EXERCISE 3

Visit a variety of different habitats. What are the biggest things you notice right away? What are the smallest? What other basic impressions do you receive besides visual clues? What animals do you see? How did they come to your attention? What movement, color, sound, tactile sensations, smells do you notice? You will discover that full seeing is more than just visual stimulation; it is the assembling of a variety of sensory clues.

EXERCISE 4

Practice looking at your world using your peripheral vision. First focus your eyes on some object directly in front of you. Without changing your point of focus, put your finger out in your center of focus and move it slowly to the side until it just disappears from view. Hold the finger at the point of disappearance. That angle represents the limit of your peripheral vision. With the stereoscopic vision that humans possess, the breadth of peripheral vision is much less than with some animals whose eyes are located more to the side of their heads. With their eyes focused straight ahead most people have a field of vision of about 140°, but by moving the eyes that field may be increased up to 180°. Of course not everything within this field of vision is clearly in focus.

Once you have determined the extent of your peripheral vision, work on developing your ability to define objects near the outer limits. Move your finger forward from the side of your head just into the range of your peripheral vision. Then hold up different numbers of fingers. Develop your skill through practice until you are seeing the numbers correctly. You can also test yourself with dominoes. Reach into a pile and pick up a domino without looking directly at it. Bring it into your peripheral vision and determine the number of spots.

Heightened use of peripheral perception is very useful in field observation when you are sitting motionless and an animal is approaching you from either side and you can't risk frightening the creature by quickly moving your head. Also, many animals take a straightforward look, or stare, as a threatening act from which they will flee (or occasionally attack). To prolong an observation of such creatures, you may have to watch them using some peripheral vision while your direct gaze appears to be fixed elsewhere. Don't expect too much improvement in peripheral perception because the human eye can generally only discern colors and shapes well within an angle of 50°—and a 20° scope is about right for sharp accuracy.

EXERCISE 5

You are probably familiar with the "What's Wrong With This Picture" puzzles often used with young children. This exercise is a variation on that theme. It is best done as an exercise with two people. The first observer sits and carefully studies the area around him. He then closes his eyes and the second observer quickly makes a change in the area (moves a stone or log or bends a branch, etc.). When that is done, the first observer opens his eyes and sees how quickly he can spot the change. They then reverse roles. They can continue this indefinitely, seeing just how small and subtle a change their partner can note.

A number of animals have developed to a high degree the skill of spotting things out of order in their normal surroundings. They are minutely familiar with their territory and the smallest change is noted and treated with suspicion. Thus they may take weeks to accept the presence of a blind in their territory and quickly note the presence of a trap or even the well-camouflaged shape of a motionless observer. As wildlife observers we often must learn to "see" in the same manner as the objects of our own observations would see the same territory.

EXERCISE 6

Although it is not as directly useful, another interesting exercise is to make several pairs of eyeglass frames from cardboard and paste in lenses of various transparent colored cellophanes or gels—red, blue, green, yellow, and so on. Walk around an area and observe it while wearing the different colored lenses. Notice the way different objects stand out or disappear.

Humans are among the relatively few animals that possess good color vision. Most creatures apparently see only in black, white, and shades of gray. Many things that are highly visible to us because of contrasts in color are not distinctly separable from the rest of the surroundings when viewed as shades of gray, particularly if the object is motionless. Learning to think black and white in your colored world helps when it comes time to conceal your presence from color-blind species of wildlife—that is, most things other than birds.

This may also be a safety feature because colors such as bright yellow and blaze-orange are quite visible as colors but blend into the surroundings as shades of gray. Hunters can spot and avoid you while you remain obscure to other animals.

EXERCISE 7

No creature is an island. It is part of a web of life. It is always anticipating, if it is not actually interacting with, others of the same or different species. It is such actions that generally motivate a particular animal's behavior. Only when the animal is asleep does this not hold basically true. Thus when one is watching an animal one must look not only at the animal itself but also attempt to determine the others, seen and unseen, which are affecting that behavior. Is it alert for predators? Is it seeking food? Is it seeking another of its own kind? Is it caring for another of its own kind? Is it avoiding an enemy? Is it alert to the alarm calls of other species?

If we see only the one creature and don't think about these other questions as we observe, we may miss the significance of the behavior being transacted. We need to practice intermittent concentration. Focus for a few moments on the object of our primary observation; then scan the whole surrounds that set the context; then back to the primary object; and repeat. Too total a concentration on the one object may give us less, rather than more, information. This is very much related to the skills developed in Exercise 5.

Each creature has its own ways of sending and receiving communication signals. Sounds, scents, and bodily movements are the major ones. As fixed on verbal language communication as most adult humans are, we often have lost our skill at reading the other signals. I say lost because most children are quite skilled at interpreting subtle body language; but this skill fades with fuller use of verbal language proficiency. Refresh your skill at reading human body language—raised eyebrows, facial positions (such as smiles, smirks, frowns), taut muscles of people under stress, eye movements and positions. Observe how each of these is used in transactions among people. As you gain skill at this, observe neighborhood cats and dogs and their movements—tail positions, body orientation, facial movements, and the like. Notice what transactions occur during each movement and how the different participants differ in their signals. For further insights investigate Desmond Morris's book *Man Watching*.

As you develop skill in seeing and interpreting such behavior in its environmental context, you will be ready to observe more closely the behavior of shyer wild creatures. You will realize that each species has its own lexicon of body movements and signals and a "grammar" of movement sequences and intensities. As you become more proficient in learning these basics for each species—what the anthropologists Tiger and Fox call *biogrammar*—you will be able to "see" much more of the lives of the wildlife you observe.

Developing such perceptual skills is not an overnight task. One would not expect to pick up a basketball for the first time and go out and get into a full-blown game. There are fundamental skills to be learned, equipment to master, and rules to be learned. Wildlife observation is no different in this regard and as you have probably determined by now, true seeing requires an active use of the mind as well as the senses.

CHAPTER 3

TRAPPING OBSERVATIONS

THE WILDLIFE OBSERVER WITHOUT NOTES is much like the fisherman telling about the big one that got away. Human memory is remarkable when it is trained and kept in condition, but the human capacity to forget seems to be even more remarkable. Any trial lawyer can attest to how unreliable eyewitnesses can be when pressed for details about an event and, of course, the longer the time span between the event and the trial, the greater the likelihood of error and confusion. The same is true of wildlife observations and often the potential importance of an observed detail does not become apparent until long after the actual observation.

As a high-schooler I was very interested in bats and regularly explored the caves and mineshafts in the vicinity of my home. I enjoyed learning the habits of these curious little flying mammals that so seem to terrify a number of people. Several different species lived in my area and utilized as winter quarters the shafts of a local lime quarry, one of my favorite haunts. One fall, when the shafts hosted a large number of one of the smallest varieties, and one not usually common in the area, I had the opportunity to watch a great deal of mating activity. I was particularly excited when many of these pipistrelles remained in the mineshaft to hibernate.

The following year the pipistrelles were back and in even greater numbers. There must have been several hundred. I spent many hours observing them. Then one winter day I visited the mineshafts only to find a scene of massive and disgusting vandalism. Others had entered the shaft with flaming torches and incinerated the scattered clusters of bats. Only a few of those that had sought their shelter deep in cracks and drill holes survived that holocaust. The pipistrelles were essentially destroyed. Only an occasional lone individual would be spotted in succeeding years.

In those younger years, of course, I never kept any field notes. I kept everything in my head. Many years later I was to learn that such a large concentration of pipistrelles in our area was very unusual. I was pressed (by a professor of mine) for details on a variety of questions relating to those pipistrelles. Specifically, how many were there? What was the sex ratio? What time of day did most of the breeding behavior occur? I had observed these things and more about the creatures but six or more years later I could not recall the details. I had seen so much but it was of little use to anyone except in the pleasure it had given me at the time. Too much water had crossed the memory dam since those original hours of observation and had washed away many details that would have been very useful in building a greater understanding of the biology of this species.

If your observations are to have any broader value than providing you with joy and amusement, you will have to work on trapping them in one way or another. For many people, myself included, this isn't easy. It takes self-discipline and some effort. However, when conscientiously worked at, note taking can become habitual and it is one of the best habits a serious wildlife observer can develop.

Although at times note taking may seem like work, reading over field notes can be great fun and trigger memories of many fascinating times afield. There is an added excitement when, as you review both old and new notes, bigger patterns begin to emerge from the jigsaw puzzle of repeated observations over time. Going over field notes is like mining; there is always a mountain of tailings for every bit of rich ore you find. On the other hand don't write off the apparently unproductive observational tailings. Going over them later with a different prime interest as a perceptual filter may reveal a whole new wealth of information just as going over old mine tailings with a new method may offer up a wealth of associated minerals that now have value.

The key to valuable notes is making them copious. The biggest mistake most people make is not taking sufficiently expansive notes. Usually this means not recording enough about the environmental context of the primary observation. Later, when after repeated observations an insight is building about the function of the behavior or its causality, we all too often turn back to earlier notes to see if the same factors were present only to discover in frustration that we didn't record the necessary corollary data. It always seems to be one of Murphy's Laws that what seems unimportant to put in the notes today turns out to be of critical importance tomorrow.

The trick is to routinely record certain basic environmental data and then not only to write up what is happening, but also to record as much as possible of the context in which it is happening. That is, to the best of one's ability, notes should be made of everything else that is going on in the observation arena at the time of the prime observation. This is a skill that comes only with time and practice.

WRITTEN NOTES

Although modern technology has given us additional ways to take useful notes, handwritten ones are still the most common and often the most convenient and least expensive. They demand the least amount of specialized equipment and are reasonably flexible. For practical purposes we can divide handwritten notes into two basic formats—field log and file card systems. Each has its strong points and drawbacks.

Field Logs

Field logs hold the notes of all observations in running order according to the sequence of observation dates and times. Some people use small bound notebooks and file them according to the calendar period covered. Others use a looseleaf notebook system and when a book is full they may choose to file their notes by dates, as with the bound journals, or they may keep each set of observations on separate pages so that they can be filed by category, such as by species or by habitats.

For many people the sequential field log provides the best method for recording general wildlife observations. One enters the date and time of observation; ecological data for the site; basic observations and any contextual information. Thus beautiful banks of raw information are compiled. The problem with these field logs is the difficulty of retrieving data at a later date. This problem can be somewhat alleviated by also maintaining a second type of log called a summary journal upon which we will elaborate a bit later.

If a field log system is being used, it is wise to assign serial numbers to each successive log book and be sure that every page of every log carries a page number. Since you may make several observations in a given day and each of these at different sites, it is valuable to assign each separate observation a sequential observation number. This will prove useful for later cross-indexing and correlating with photos and specimens. Any field specimens collected at a site of an observation would be assigned that sequential observation number.

There are probably almost as many ideas of what is the best type of material for a field log as there are log keepers. However, there are some key factors to keep in mind when choosing:

1. The paper should be of good quality because these notes may well be kept for many years. Acid papers will yellow and become brittle with age. Rag papers, though more expensive, have a longer life expectancy.

2. The binding should be durable so that the pages don't become dislodged and lost. Good stitched bindings or plastic or steel spiral bound books are a good investment. Many prefer the spiral bindings because they can be opened flat for ease of writing. If a three-ring binder and paper inserts are chosen, be sure to use gummed reinforcing rings around each hole in the paper so that the pages don't tear out and get lost.

3. Choose a convenient size that can easily be stashed in coat pockets or day packs. Six-by-nine inches has been a widely used size. There is now available a belt pack designed for two field guides and pencils. I use this pack for one field guide and a field log and find it very convenient.

4. If your style is primarily to use words, you will prefer a lined paper. A marginal line is often an advantage so that you don't end up losing notes in the binding. If you like to use a great many sketches in your note taking and can learn to write efficiently without benefit of lines, an unlined page is to your advantage. I find artists' six-by-nine inch bound sketch books to be most useful as field logs. Stationery stores frequently carry slim, bound books called *Journals*. Although many versions possess multiple vertical columns for keeping ledger figures, there are editions that are lined with only one vertical marginal line. These have also proven durable as field logs; some of mine are still in good shape after twenty years.

5. The writing instrument is as important as the book. Some people prefer a medium-hardness pencil because graphite doesn't run as does most ink; others argue adamantly that only waterproof ink will do. Certainly nothing is much more frustrating than seeing your notes dissolve as raindrops mix with nonwaterproof ink, or similarly, if the book falls into a puddle.

Ballpoint pens can be used if you are very sure of the indelibility of the ink in the particular variety chosen. Some people still prefer a fountain pen with Higgins Eternal or Higgins Engrossing Ink. I generally use a Rapidograph or Castell Drawing Pen with one of the newer nonclogging drawing inks, but I always carry a pencil to use in damp wet weather or if the pen runs out of ink.

The File Card Method

There are a number of people who prefer to use 3″ × 5″ or 4″ × 6″ cards to record their notes rather than a log book. They carry a packet of cards and record each observation of a species on a separate card, assigning each card a serial observation number. Then when they return home they can quickly file each card under an appropriate species or project heading. This can be very handy. Of course one must be continuously on guard against losing observation cards in the field and religiously use the summary journal as described later.

Many people print up their own cards with a checklist of basic data desired for each observation (such as time, temperature, date, locale, etc.). Depending upon your special interests you can devise coded checklists for a variety of special pieces of data such as vegetation types or behavioral types. You may find the relatively inexpensive multi-stamp, mimeo card printers useful for preparing such cards. Preprinted field data cards are available from commercial firms such as the Wildlife Supply Company, Saginaw, Michigan. Such cards come in perforated pads of several cards that will fit on a clipboard. The notes can be kept in the field, then the cards torn apart and filed separately upon return to home base. For certain types of projects these commercial cards are very convenient, useful, and relatively inexpensive.

Some people not only use the file cards for field notes but also as part of the summarizing process for field notes to be outlined later.

WHAT TO RECORD

First the formalities: Every page should have uniform headings that note your name and date in the upper left-hand corner along with a blank for an observation number and a space to designate a classification for the observation. How I regret not doing that in my early years as I turn back now to materials that have gotten separated and which I cannot certainly place in proper chronological sequence. Always write the date using the word or abbreviation for the month (June 15, 1982, or 15 June 1982). Never use just a sequence of numbers since different countries use different conventions for that number sequence and even in this country people vary in the sequence they use (6/15/82 or 15/6/82 may be intelligible, but what is 6/3/82 or 3/6/82?). Such inconsistency breeds confusion if the notes are to ever have a value broader in scope than just for the original observer. The heading should also consistently carry the location.

Apart from a key word to indicate location for repeated observations at a given site, the overall notes should carry a clear, concise description of the location such that a person unfamiliar with the area could readily locate it on a map. The description should give concise, yet precise enough, information that the site could be pinpointed within one square mile. Property regularly changes ownership, so combine personal references such as McDonald's Farm with more precise referents—4.5 miles west of Littleton on Rt. 110, Middlesex Co., Massachusetts. Always include county and state in the U.S. and similar subdivisions or geographical referents in other countries. Use only standard abbreviations: Co., mi., E, NE, WSW, etc. As one of my old professors used to say: "Assume that someone who speaks another language, lives in another country, and is unfamiliar with the area will use your notes a century from now—try to make it easy for him."

Now let's focus on the real meat of what to make notes about. For many beginning field note takers this is a stumbling block. The written word creates a permanence that brings out our self-consciousness and frightens us into writing far too little. Not wishing to appear foolish by writing down the trivial or obvious, very little gets recorded.

The pioneering ecologist Charles Elton addressed this reticence: "Most people, I find, are too humble about their natural history observations, although they are usually quite positive about the truth of their theories. That is to say they think that because they are not scientists nothing they see can be of importance to science. Now, this is of course true up to a point: especially where the technique and special training are difficult and complicated. But it is not by any means always true."

The point is that the more you note the more valuable the material becomes. Don't hesitate to repeat the same information over and over, even if it doesn't immediately seem important. Sometimes it is even valuable to note what you didn't see but thought you should have. Usually only review of notes collected over a considerable time span reveals the patterns that may ultimately prove significant.

Every creature is an individual as well as a member of a particular species. Some of what it does is idiosyncratic; some is species specific. Only a collection of observations over time will help to separate the one from the other. So write down everything you can every time you see it. Don't try to decide at the time if it is important or not. You can always edit material out later; don't trust anything to memory.

The essence of good field notes is to describe accurately the setting or context of your observation (weather, habitat, time, lighting and other physical conditions as well as other animals present of the same or different species) and to carefully delineate answers to questions of: what, when, where, for how long, how many, how often. In the field while observing, ignore the questions of why and how. They usually can only be answered by studying and contemplating the answers to the other questions and by setting up experiments to test various hypotheses.

Describe the animal you are watching carefully, particularly if you are at all unsure about its identity. Don't worry that you are not sure about its exact species; that can be verified later if you have described the creature carefully and accurately. What is important is to have the "specimen of behavior"—your record of what you saw it doing and in what context.

Be sure to *look* before you write. But don't wait long after your observations to write them down. Unfortunately you can't write and watch behavior at the same time. While watching, count and measure whenever possible. Keep track of the frequency of certain movements, songs, and so forth, and estimate distances as accurately as possible. Note distances between you and the thing you are watching and distances between the observed and other things with which it is interacting. It helps to include approximate margins of error, for example, the family of woodchucks was basking on the earth mound 100 +/− 10 yards from my blind.

There are a variety of behavior categories to look for during your observation but we will leave discussion of them to a later chapter.

Often a sketch can convey a great deal more information in less space than a verbal description. Don't hesitate to use sketches freely. Keep your writing terse and telegraphic but legible. If you use a number of shorthand-type symbols or abbreviations, be sure to add a glossary of them. For example, MO ♂⌇♀—→♂∧♀⌇ is unintelligible to others unless a key is supplied. Indeed, even the observer may later forget what some of his own symbols meant. Here is a list of word translations for the symbols in the afore-mentioned shorthand note:

MO = Macrodon opercularis (paradise fish)

♂ = male   ♀ = female

⌇ = parallel body positions head to tail

——→ = moves to

∧ = gill flare

⌇ = submissive position

The note might then be translated: Male and female paradise fish take up parallel body positions head to tail, then move into a mode where the male gill flares and the female assumes a submissive posture.

The shorthand conserves space and time but could be a useless set of lines if the key is lost or forgotten.

If you collect specimens during an observation session such as scats, feathers, opened nuts, track casts, or even photographs, assign each one a field number that also includes the sequential observation number. Record in the notes that the specimens were collected and record their numbers.

Figures 3.1 and 3.2 show examples of field notes in several different styles.

Figure 3.1

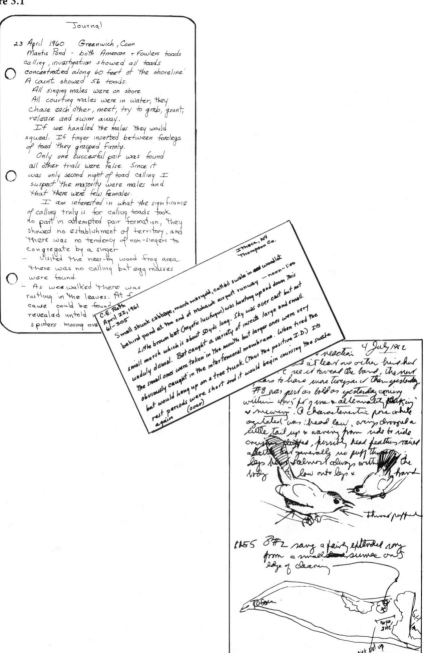

Figure 3.2

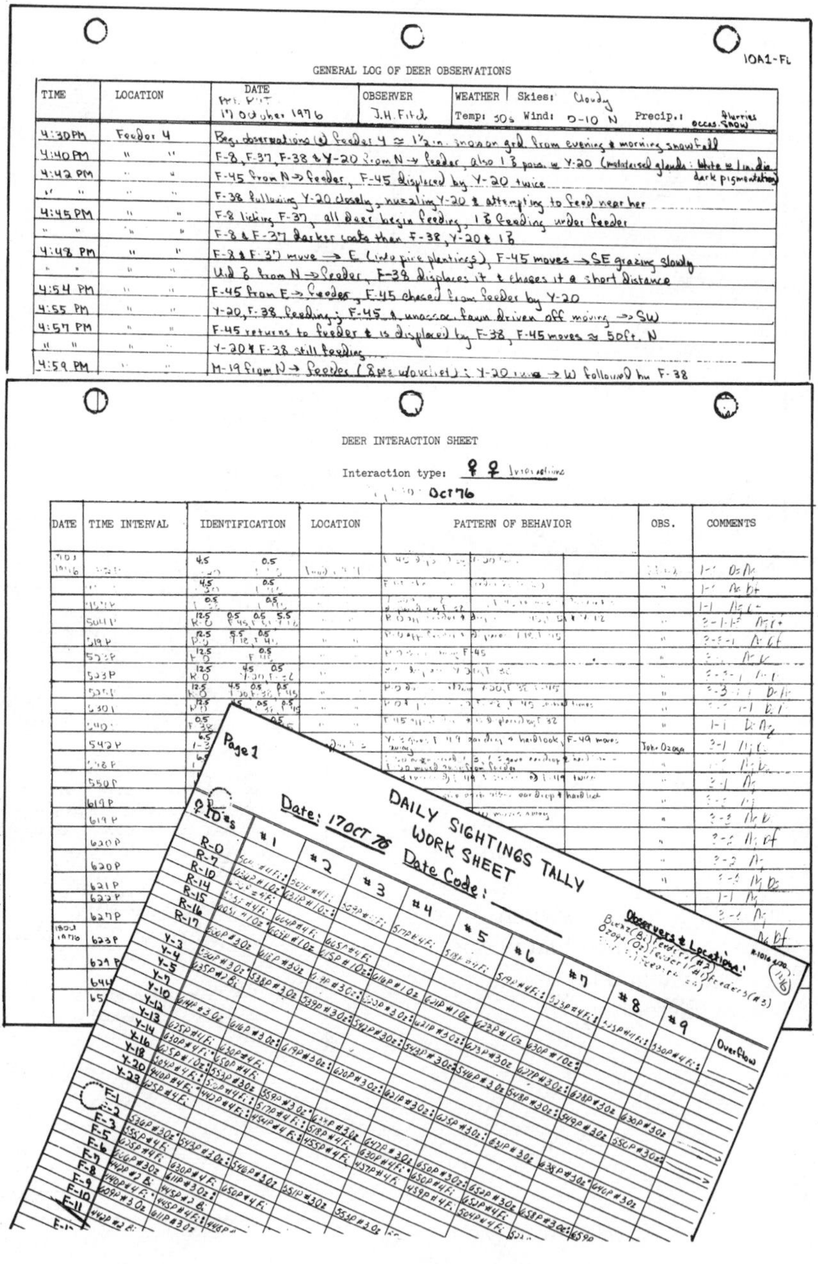
10A1-Fi
GENERAL LOG OF DEER OBSERVATIONS
TIME
LOCATION
DATE
17 October 1976
OBSERVER
J.H. Fitch
WEATHER
Skies: Cloudy
Temp: 30s
Wind: 0-10 N
Precip.: occas. snow flurries
DEER INTERACTION SHEET
Interaction type:
DATE
TIME INTERVAL
IDENTIFICATION
LOCATION
PATTERN OF BEHAVIOR
OBS.
COMMENTS
Page 1
DAILY SIGHTINGS TALLY
WORK SHEET
Date: 17OCT76
Date Code:
Observers & Locations:
Overflow

VERBAL NOTE TAKING

Cassette tape recorders have provided a new dimension to field note taking. In situations in which silence is not a requisite for observing, it is possible to dictate your notes, thus permitting commentary while keeping your eyes fixed on what is happening. The cassettes can be numbered and filed for retrieval and marks can be made on most cassettes to indicate the beginning and end of an observation sequence. The length and general nature of the observations is then noted on a sheet in the plastic storage box for the cassette. Some tape recorders have a meter to indicate how much tape has passed. Noting the beginning and end numbers for an observation aids in keeping track of specific observations, for example, wood duck courtship (20–23); white tail deer feeding (34–80), and so forth.

Of course, there are limitations to the use of recorders. They represent a relatively high initial investment. In addition you will probably want one or more special microphones. Cassettes are more expensive than notebooks, particularly in relation to the number of observations that can be recorded on each of them. Another drawback is the reliance on verbal descriptions without sketches or diagrams and the fact that machines may become inoperable if banged around under field conditions. Also, batteries lose power quickly when used heavily, which may affect the quality of your recording even when the machine appears to be functioning. In addition to carrying extra batteries, it is always wise to carry a notebook for emergency backup. Unless you also wish to record natural sounds with your equipment you need not invest in a machine with a broad-range sound spectrum. It need only be well within the range of the human voice, which will allow the use of a less expensive machine. For most purposes a small recorder suitable for the average businessman is adequate. Many prefer a model that can be carried from a shoulder sling or be hitched to a belt. Either a hand-held microphone with a built-in on-off switch or a clip-on microphone in combination with a separate switch that plugs into the remote jack and then be taped to your binocular may be used. Recording machines with a built-in condenser microphone are of little use in the field unless they are quite small and can easily be held up near the mouth. At best such machines are awkward to maneuver.

At first glance, the new mini-recorders with micro-cassettes would appear ideal for taking field notes. All controls are handled in one hand and the machine can be held up to the mouth for quiet dictation. However, the cassettes are simply too small to hold the data of prolonged observations. The cartridge must constantly be flipped or a new one added. This may well result in information gaps and frustration, to say nothing of expense.

Standard cassette machines are bulkier but more practical for our purposes. Cassettes are available in 30-, 60-, and 90-minute packages. Thus with a 90-minute tape you can record for 45 minutes without having to flip the cassette or insert a new one. Unfortunately, these cassettes tend to be somewhat less reliable than the 60 or 30 minute ones.

Always carry a set of fresh replacement batteries with you in the field and periodically, during a lull in observations, play back a bit of your most recent notes. If you begin to hear any slowing down or slurring of the voice, change the batteries. Few things are more frustrating than trying to listen to or decipher a badly slurred set of notes. Regularly check the capstans to see that no dirt has gotten on them to slow them down and create a similar slurring of the recording.

Because magnetic tapes are vulnerable to accidental electronic erasure, some people still prefer to transcribe the tapes rather than simply to store them. Today this is somewhat easier than in the past since many secretarial transcription machines accept standard cassettes. Of course, once transcribed the tapes can be reused. It is largely an economic decision whether the cost of transcription or the purchase of new tapes is the least expensive and most effective way of trapping observations.

If photography is a key part of your field observation procedure, you may wish to use a cassette recorder in combination with a lavelier microphone. This permits free use of the hands during recording. The trade-off is that the tape must be left running and will have large gaps of silence between comments unless you use the separate switch in the remote jack as mentioned earlier.

PHOTOGRAPHIC NOTES

Still photographs are an excellent adjunct to written or verbal field notes. They have high value because they provide much context as well as the prime subject. Field note photos may be artistic, but only as a bonus, not as the prime intent. Even photos that are not properly exposed may be valuable as a record. Whenever possible, field note photos should include objects that can be used as scale referents. You should also record the type of lens you used because different types of lenses distort reality in a variety of ways that may cause significant error when comparing sizes of objects or estimating distances.

Yet, in making behavioral notes, still photos are of somewhat limited value because they preserve only a momentary piece of an action. Added value can be gained by securing a sequence of stills in rapid succession with an autowind or motor drive accessory to a 35mm single lens reflex camera. Stills are most valuable in recording tracks and signs, dens, habitat, and other clues to an animal's lifestyle and behavior.

For recording such static clues, instant cameras (such as those of Polaroid and Kodak) are quite useful because you can determine within a matter of minutes whether or not you have secured your record. The drawback is the cost of film and the amount of debris created. Please be sure to pack the debris out if you pack the film in.

For all-around use, a single lens reflex camera is generally the best because of its relatively small size, its ruggedness, and its versatility. Most good name brands offer a wide range of interchangeable lenses ranging from ultra-closeup to extreme telephoto. New technology has reduced or eliminated the need for additional light meters and their built-in light metering systems greatly ease the task of securing proper exposures. The biggest problem is the range of choices and the limitations of your budget. For general wildlife observation recording, the basic options for a single lens reflex camera would be a 50mm Macro lens, a strobe light, an autowind, and a 200mm telephoto lens. As interests become more focused other items will seem important.

Good cameras and accessories represent a sizable investment and a time commitment in order to learn how to use them as effectively and automatically as possible. If you have to focus a great deal of concentration on the mechanics of taking the picture, you generally miss much of what is happening around you at the time. You may get a picture but miss much of what you actually meant to observe. In inexperienced hands a camera can be more of a hindrance than an aid to good observation.

When it comes back from the developer, each slide should be marked with date taken and the observation serial number. Today clear plastic slide holders are available that are of three-ring notebook format and each holds twenty slides. They provide excellent protection for the slides as well as easy access and convenient filing for retrieval.

For serious note taking on animal behavior, nothing matches a good motion picture, because with that you really have a specimen of behavior that can be viewed and analyzed over and over again. This permits focusing on separate pieces of the total behavior or viewing for the full context in which the behavior occurs. Until recently almost all good-quality footage had to be shot on 16mm film, which was very expensive, indeed prohibitively expensive, for most amateurs and even for professionals without research grants. The availability of Super 8mm movie cameras with zoom lenses has changed that, and although the film is not inexpensive, it is within the range of many more amateurs. Again let us note that for behavioral record purposes the film need not be of exhibition quality.

Some of the newest Super 8mm movie cameras also have built-in sound recording capacity. This makes it possible occasionally to add call notes, songs, or similar behavior to a record and it certainly allows you to dictate your observational notes directly onto the film record, thus enhancing its value by putting it in an even broader context.

As home video cassette cameras and portapacks become increasingly affordable, videotapes of behavior will become an additional note-taking strategy and may even supplant the movie camera. Even now it is possible to have slides and 8mm films put on video cassettes at certain photo store chains for a reasonable price. In the future such electronic recording options will undoubtedly find increasing use.

It is important to note that motion picture records of animal behavior should be undertaken only after you have a good working knowledge of the general behavioral inventory of the species you are interested in recording. Taking movies requires concentration on technical detail and limits one's perception to the angle of view of the camera eyepiece. Much of the total context of the behavior can be missed. A number of nature photographers never really know what they have seen until they get their developed films back and they almost never know what they missed.

BENEATH THE WAVES

SCUBA* divers working underwater have special note-taking problems. They must cope with the water, turbulence, limited mouth movement, and the general cumbersomeness of their diving gear. Tape recording under water with custom-made equipment is possible, but in addition to being very expensive it is at best only marginally satisfactory.

Writing devices, although generally clumsy, are the best thing currently available. These all involve some combination of plastic or plasticized paper and grease pencils or graphite pencils. The most primitive form is a slate of heavy plastic and a grease pencil. More advanced models consist of underwater paper (ASCOT paper, Appleton Papers, Inc., Appleton, WI 54911) or sheets of frosted mylar bound into a pad with plastic spiral bindings, plastic rings, or clipped to a plastic clipboard. The frosted (roughened) surfaces of these materials permit the use of ordinary graphite pencils. The pencil needs to be tied to the note pad with nylon string or stuck into a rubber tubing holder permanently attached to the pad with silicone glue. All pads are somewhat clumsy and difficult to carry under water. They have a tendency to catch on corals, algae, or other underwater projections. Some divers find a

*Self-Contained Underwater Breathing Apparatus.

catch bag the most convenient way to convey them; others clip them to their weight belt.

Perhaps the most convenient underwater note-taking device to date is that developed by Michael S. Foster of California State University. This little device which Foster calls a mini-slate attaches to the forearm with a rubber strap from a dive knife. It consists of a plastic writing block over which a scroll of frosted mylar can be passed for note taking. The notes are then rolled up exposing a fresh strip of mylar. Frosted mylar can be written on and erased with a normal pencil. The pencil is attached with a sleeve of rubber tubing.

The device is illustrated in Figure 3.3 in exploded view so that you can see how to construct one for yourself. You would use .25-in. (.64cm) plexiglass glued together with ethylene dichloride. The rollers are attached simply by pushing them into the holes of the rubber stoppers. The mylar strips are attached to the rollers with electrical tape. To keep the mylar flat, it is passed through a .5mm space between parts K and A. The frosted mylar is available in most art stores. It comes in sheets and you cut it into appropriate strips for your use.

The materials for underwater note taking are generally more expensive than ordinary paper and thus are not usually filed away directly. The notes are transcribed to either logbooks or file cards soon after the dive is over and the original note sheets cleaned for reuse. The smooth plastic plates can be wiped clean with a cloth and mylar can be erased with a rubber eraser or wiped off with a damp cloth and kitchen cleanser.

Special housings are now available for photographing under water with either still or movie cameras. Underwater strobe lights are also available but this apparatus is still very expensive and housings cost about as much as or more than the cameras they protect. Because of the visual properties of water, different lenses are needed under water than above and new lighting rules must be learned. Wildlife watching under water is really in its infancy but is very exciting as a new frontier. We are now just scratching the surface of underwater wildlife observations and it is unfortunately still a relatively expensive hobby.

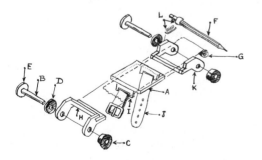

Figure 3.3. Underwater Mini-slate (after Foster, as modified by Roth). (A) plastic slate; (B) roller; (C) rubber stopper; (D) neoprene washer; (E) plastic disc; (F) pencil; (G) mylar scroll; (H) guide bar; (I) strap bracket; (J) strap; (K) plastic frame; (L) velcro.

HANDLING NOTES BACK HOME

Taking field notes is only the beginning of trapping observations. In many ways it is the most exciting and the easiest. Without organization, however, the notes become only so much accumulating junk. Doing the organizing often takes more time than the note taking and has a number of aspects that make it a chore—but then, every hobby has its chores. On the other hand, in the process of reviewing and classifying notes, the patterns and insights often emerge and this can be very exciting because it raises new questions to be asked during new rounds of observations.

The Summary Journal

A Summary Journal notes each major observation period, the date and location of the observation, the route of travel, hours of observation, weather conditions, habitats, topography, species observed, and any other pertinent remarks. It is followed by the sequential observation number of the log or field card or any other designation of the original field notes so that you can easily turn to them for reference. Indicate also retrieval data for any relevant specimens, films, or tapes of that observation period. In other words, the summary journal is a type of running index to your field notes and represents an ongoing chronological record of your explorations and discoveries.

The Species Account

Some people prefer to use a looseleaf notebook for species accounts, assigning a page or section to each species and using a marginal tab system to quickly locate a species. Others prefer a file card system. If you keep only verbal records, 3" × 5" size cards are probably adequate; if you make field sketches or diagrams, you will find 4" × 6" cards more desirable. Copy onto the card field data for each species observed. Use the same card for successive notes until the card is full, being sure to note the date for each successive observation and the original observation's sequential number. File the cards chronologically by species. Always start a new card for each new year. If an idea that seems worth future investigation comes to you as you are entering your data, write it down on a separate card, date it, and file it in the species account to serve as a memorandum to you at some later time when you are reviewing your data.

In establishing the order of the species in your species account files, it is useful to base it on some common referrent. Birders often use the American Ornithologists' Union checklist order and may assign A.O.U. checklist numbers to their bird slides or pictures for filing. Mammal watchers may use Desmond Morris's species order and numbers as noted in *The Mammals—A Guide to Living Species* (New York: Harper & Row, 1965). If your observations are going to be relatively limited geographically, you may want to use the species order of the best available field guide to that group and region. Whatever system you choose, be consistent and record the basis of your system in either your summary journal or your species account file or both. This assures that someone at a later date can accurately figure out your system.

Behavioral Inventory System

You may wish to summarize your field notes in terms of a behavioral inventory by species. In order to do this, prepare summary forms using the behavioral categories outlined in the chapter on behavior watching (Chapter 9) and Appendix A. Data from the field notes that pertain to a behavioral category are appropriately indicated along with the log identification numbers. This information is then filed under the appropriate species heading. Some people like to combine data from their reading about a species' behavior with their field notes, being sure to clearly identify, by means of color coding or a similar technique, their own observation from those gained through reading.

This combination of reading notes and observational notes does two major things: It lets you confirm things in print by comparison with your own observations, and it helps build a picture of what is known and not known about the full spectrum of a particular species' behavior. Periodic review of the summary cards indicates vacuums in the knowledge of a particular species and thus suggests observational projects. Gathering information to fill the gaps may well mean devising new techniques and/or strategies and provides real challenges to the dedicated amateur observer.

In Short

Wildlife watching for the sheer joy of it demands nothing but patience, skill, and more than a soupçon of luck. It can begin and end with the personal experience of observing the animals. But wildlife watching can be a great deal more, contributing to general human knowlege as well as to personal satisfaction. To do this requires trapping your observations in some fashion so that others can benefit from them. Regardless of the method or methods you choose from among those presented, or even if you invent a system singularly your own, it is important to develop the self-discipline to keep notes regularly and to undertake the chore of organizing them in ways that assure that the information they contain can be retrieved with relative ease.

As one who has all too frequently suffered frustration from not taking time to do the organization of his own notes, slides, and specimens, I can surely attest to the truism that it takes time to save time. Put some of that foul weather time at home to good use, keeping good field notes in convenient order.

FURTHER READING

BARTLETT, L.M. "A technique for recording rapid consecutive field observations," *The Auk*, 73 (1954), 193–202.

BUTLER, S.R., and E.A. ROWE. "A data acquisition and retrieval system for studies of animal social behavior," *Behaviour*, 57 (1976), 281–287.

EMLEN, J.T. "The art of making field notes," *Jack Pine Warbler*, 36 (1958), 171–181.

MOSBY, H.S. "Making observations and records," *Wildlife Management Techniques*, 3d rev. ed. (R.H. Giles, ed.), Washington, D.C.: The Wildlife Society, 1971.

RESMEN, J.V., JR. "On taking field notes," *American Birds*, 31 (5) (1977), 946–953.

STEPHENSON, G.R., et al. "The SSR system: an open format event recording system with computerized transcription," *Behavior Research Methods and Transcription*, 7 (1975), 497–515.

CHAPTER 4

CLUEING IN

WILDLIFE OBSERVATION APPEALS to the Sherlock Holmes in all of us. So often we find only clues to an animal's activity—tracks, scats, food wastes, and so forth rather than the animal itself. However, such tracks and scats will tell us what creatures are in the vicinity and where their main activity is concentrated. Even direct observations of animals are often of short duration, giving us only behavioral fragments, and we can use these other clues to round out our picture of the animal's activity. Thus one of the major skills that a wildlife watcher must acquire is learning to spot and read the clues and use the information in piecing together the various bits of information like pieces in a jigsaw puzzle to get a fuller picture of an animal's total behavior. This is particularly true in studying very shy or nocturnal species.

Success as a wildlife detective demands either a fantastic memory for small detail or careful notes collected over time. It helps to build a good reference collection of bits and pieces of plant and animal matter that can be used for comparison with clues found or the material in scats, food caches, bird pellets, and similar behavioral artifacts. Such carefully labeled collections might include the indigestible seeds of common fruits eaten by birds and mammals, guard hairs and fur from various parts of the body of local mammals, skulls and bones of birds and mammals, dried scat of various animals, indigestible parts of some insects such as beetle wing cases and grasshopper hind legs, nuts and seeds opened by specific animals, and the shells of local mollusks. While such collections may seem a bit morbid to some, they are exceedingly valuable when trying to determine food preferences from analysis of scat, or the material the creature seeks for its nest building, or what the animal is that has been going under your porch and got its hair caught on splinters, and so forth. For those with a bit of the collector bug in their soul, the compilation of the reference collection is good fun in and of itself.

TRACKS AND TRACKING

He gave us the questions that would lead us to our answers but he never told us an answer. He taught me to see and to hear, to walk and to remain silent; he taught me how to be patient and resourceful, how to know and how to understand. He taught me to see invisible things from the trail that all action leaves around itself. He taught me how to teach myself the mystery of the track.

TOM BROWN, *The Tracker*

Perhaps no aspect of wildlife detective work is more fun than tracking. It seems to awaken primordial feelings from our hunter-gatherer ancestors. There is something stirring about discovering a deer track in the mud with water seeping in indicating that it was made only minutes before and the animal is somewhere just ahead; or to follow the line-straight tracks of a fox in the snow until they cross a rabbit track and then see the tracks of both stretch out into a run and dodge pattern. You follow with excitement, wondering if the trail will end in blood and fur, or if the two tracks will diverge and each go its own way.

Learning to read tracks is not unlike learning to read a foreign language. You must first learn a basic alphabet—in this case the identification of the tracks made by each species. You then acquire the basic grammar—the patterns made by different gaits and activities, the related signs of activity such as gnawed branches, urine stains, scats, or dig marks. As you develop proficient literacy in track reading you learn about different soil and snow conditions and how tracks made in each are altered by time so that you not only can tell what animals had passed a specific site and what they were doing but also approximately how long ago they passed this way. As with a foreign language, tracking is not something you pick up overnight. It takes continuous study and practice. Also, like a foreign language, reading tracks and sign is a skill that quickly becomes rusty with disuse but, if well learned, is regained rather rapidly with renewed practice.

Figure 4.1 shows some tracks of common animals that illustrate the idea of the track alphabet. Figure 4.2 presents a few simple track stories for you to read. (The translations of these are printed in the captions for each.) You will notice that one track alone is seldom enough to unequivocally identify the maker. You generally need the pattern of all four feet and often at least two sets of the four prints to get the necessary

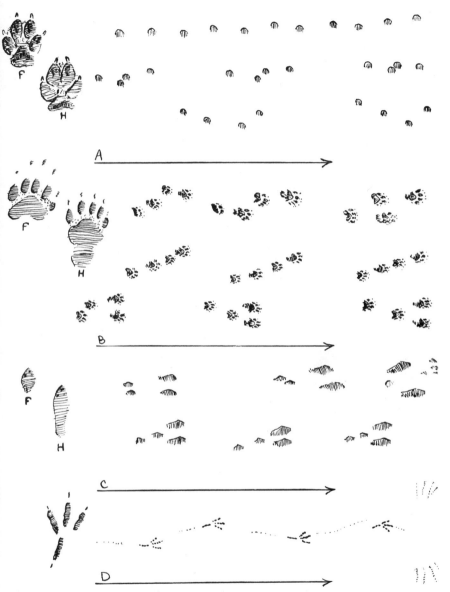

Figure 4.1. A beginning track grammar. (A) Red fox—top, walking; middle, trotting; bottom, running. (B) Skunk—top, walking; middle, trotting; bottom, running. (C) Cottontail rabbit—top, moving slowly (note at left where rabbit sat, leaving a tail or "sitzmark"); bottom, moving more rapidly. (D) Crow—note toe drag marks and wing tip prints when bird launches into flight (mainly from snow).

Figure 4.2

34

information. For example, cottontail rabbits normally offset their small forefeet while in motion, but when stopped these feet may be opposite each other. When so, the resulting single set of tracks is all too similar to a gray squirrel's paired tracks, particularly if the track is not fresh. However, a series of tracks usually shows the basically staggered pattern of the rabbit or the paired pattern of the squirrel.

Animals have a variety of moving gaits—walking, trotting, galloping, running, bounding, pacing, crawling. Each gait results from specific motions of the legs and degrees of exertion or thrust. Thus the resulting tracks are quite distinctive and form an essential part of the grammar of tracking. From the marks left we can assume the speed and, to a degree, the motivation of the track maker.

For animals with prominent tails, the tail mark is an important clue in reading the track. In slow motion the tail drags and leaves a mark. At higher speeds, the tail mark is sporadic or eliminated. A species like the cottontail leaves a tail mark only upon sitting.

Although wildlife watching is the ultimate goal, much can be learned about tracking by following the trails of domestic animals and even people. This is also good practice to keep the skills honed between wildlife outings. To be sure, nothing can substitute for seeing the species-specific marks that identify wild quarry, but many of the skills of interpreting the sign are very similar regardless of the species.

To learn to read the age of a track in various materials—mud, sand, snow, etc.—take a dog for a walk over those surfaces. Note carefully what the totally fresh track looks like. How crisp are the edges? How much material falls into the track? How moist does the surface of the track appear? Subtle changes can mean a lot, so be as precise and detailed in your observation as possible. Return to the tracks five minutes later; fifteen minutes later; one-half hour later; one hour later; three hours later; and a day later. Note carefully every change you see from what you observed in the fresh track. Don't be satisfied with looking at one print. Compare several prints to determine what changes are common to them all. The same process can be followed using a cat or a goat or even your own prints to get an idea of how different-shaped feet and different weights will be recorded in the same surface.

Remember that there are a great many different soil types across this country and that they are each different because of different properties. Each will handle tracks in a slightly different way. Try to gain

---

Figure 4.2. Using the track grammar, can you read these stories? *Top:* Cottontail rabbit is loafing along, moving from left to right. Fox comes running in from bottom and seizes rabbit, leaving blood and fur. Later a crow lands and circles the kill site and then leaves, having found nothing. *Bottom:* A rabbit has loped across the site. Later a fox, loafing along at a walk, crosses the rabbit track and turns to follow it. He is soon face to face with a skunk. After a brief confrontation the fox bounds away and the skunk ambles on in a slightly altered course.

familiarity with the track-making characteristics of the most common soil types of the region you plan to explore. The same is true for tracking in snow. There are many different snow types that depend upon the amount of moisture and the temperature. Tracks made in each type age differently. You will need to determine the effect of present sun and air conditions on the snow as you determine changes in an aging track.

When you trail an animal—that is, follow the tracks over a long distance—you may find long gaps between good clear prints. It is easy to become so focused in on searching for specific detail that the overall trail is lost. Use sun and shadow to good advantage. Animals passing through dewy grass leave a plain trail in the right light. Scuffed-up material from walking on a trail will also leave new shadows. Familiarize yourself with how all the surrounding ground appears. Study it until you feel sure you understand its normal appearance. Then begin looking for things that are slightly disturbed. If your quarry recently passed, chances are good that it is responsible for those disturbances. When trail sign is sparse, use what you find to try and project the direction of travel. Try as best you can to think like the animal; guess where it was heading and if it seems to be using any particular hunting or evasive strategy. Using such a combination of actual sign reading and intuition, it is often quite possible to remain on quite faint trails for a considerable period of time.

The ultimate key to good tracking is continued close observation. Tom Brown, Jr., in his book *The Tracker*, sums up the training of a good tracker in several key passages:

> We watched *everything*: animals, birds, plants, insects, weather, sunlight, stars, fossils, people, hundreds of things. We watched the animals first. We sat in swamps, in the woods, near lakes, by streams, along the river bank, any place where an animal might live. And we waited. When we were lucky, we saw something special. When we didn't we saw something else. . . . I had learned what track is made by that gesture the only way it can be learned, by watching a similar bird do a similar thing on the ground and then going over to see what the track looked like. By doing this time after time with bird after bird, animal after animal, person after person, I became a tracker. . . . I learned to track, not animals or men, but disturbances, things knocked out of place, minute and indistinct traces, the ghost of a print, a stone turned wrong side up, a fragment of hair on a branch.

Preserving Tracks

It is sometimes desirable to preserve animal tracks either for a reference collection or as a record of some observed behavior. Plaster casts are best for the former and photographs for the latter. Plaster casting is most effectively done if the track is in a firm medium such as mud or moist loam. It is more difficult to get a good print in sand but reasonable results are sometimes possible if you carefully dampen the track with a plant mister.

To make the cast, construct a simple collar of cardboard or tin that has been greased (see Figure 4.3). Set the collar in place around the track and push it slightly into the soil. Mix plaster of Paris and water—old plastic jugs are excellent mixing containers—to a smooth consistency like thick cream that will flow, not plop, and pour into the collar to a depth of at least one inch. When the plaster has thoroughly hardened (in a few hours), remove it from the collar and brush or rinse away any adhering soil. (You can speed up drying time by adding a pinch of salt to the plaster; slow it down with a little vinegar.) You will now have a positive cast of the foot as it made the track. You may wish to paint the foot part black to make it stand out more sharply from the white plaster background.

Tracks can also be cast with paraffin but this involves a double boiler to melt the wax. However, for emergency field conditions it pays to carry several large plumber's candles. Light one and drip the melted wax into the tracks. Reinforce with twigs and build up more layers of wax. It's a good trick for catching a track when you didn't come fully prepared.

Casting tracks in snow is a much more difficult and imprecise art that depends in large measure on current temperature and the type of snow. Dry powdery snow is almost impossible to take casts from; heavy wet snow offers a few more opportunities. The problem is that mixed plaster is warmer and wetter than the snow, causing the print to melt when the plaster is added.

In wet snow some success is occasionally possible using one of two methods. If the temperature is dropping and below freezing you can carefully mist the track with a plant mister that you have carried close to your skin. The mist will form a thin skin of ice inside the track. Plaster can then be quickly mixed and poured in. If luck holds, the plaster will begin to set before the ice layer melts and the track is seriously altered. In slightly warmer weather when the temperature is hovering around

Figure 4.3. Track casting. (A) deer track; (B) collar in place; (C) pouring plaster; (D) solidified plaster cast, finished.

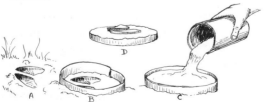

freezing, you can use clear Krylon spray to achieve an effect similar to the ice layer. Of course the Krylon won't melt either. Care must be taken to hold the spray far enough from the track so that the force of the propellant does not make the droplets alter the track. Only patience, practice, and good luck allow the making of good clear snow casts.

The simplest method of collecting track records is with the camera. Best results are achieved when the sun is relatively low in the sky so that shadows help give dimension and shape to the track. With snow trails it is important to carefully watch the exposure since reflection tends to produce more available light than what may seem apparent at first and overexposure is a common hazard with track photography. When using color film a skylight filter is a must to reduce excessive blue tones in the shadows. A polarizing lens is also a useful accessory to reduce snow glare.

A good series of photos can make an excellent set of notes; it is a permanent record of the actions you have followed that allows for later or further interpretation. Actually you shouldn't overlook the value of careful drawings of tracks made in conjunction with accurate measurements of the length and width of the individual tracks and the stride (distance between tracks).

SIGNS AND SCATS

Ingestion and elimination, that is, eating and depositing body wastes, are two very basic categories of animal behavior. All animals do both and their actions generally leave some form of evidence of the behavior.

Predators' various techniques for capturing and killing their prey often result in telltale clues that will reveal the identity of the predator to those who may later discover the remains of the prey. An insect wrapped in silk is clearly the prey of a spider; a mouse or small bird impaled on tree thorns or barbed wire is most likely the potential meal of a shrike; a cache of land snails, all paralyzed, bespeaks the short-tailed shrew; a mouse or chipmunk with the base of its skull bitten out is likely the victim of a weasel. A deer kill showing a broken neck and claw marks about the neck and shoulders is probably a puma kill while a similar deer with chewed hamstrings and/or ripped-open belly is more likely the work of dogs, wolves, or coyotes. The wildlife observer examines every kill and learns the distinctive patterns of the various predators. Such patterns may well reveal who the predator was when no tracks are visible. It is important, whenever possible, to corroborate your guess with more than one form of evidence.

Kills themselves should be examined for evidence of the age and physical condition of the animal at the time it was killed—look for signs of old age such as greatly worn down teeth, for excessive parasite load, for crippling injuries, or for youth and inexperience. Some predators secure most of their prey from the weaker members of the prey population; other predator species apparently do not. There is still some disagreement about just what percentage of a predator species' prey is from the weakest sector of the prey population. Only a few very large predators, such as the wolf and the lion, have been studied in detail. Much remains to be learned, particularly about predation in smaller species such as weasels, raptors, and predacious insects.

Some of the avian predators—hawks, owls, crows, herons, and gulls, for example—regurgitate the most indigestible parts of their prey in the form of pellets. By examining these pellets and teasing them apart you can often find enough solid evidence to identify the prey species. Your clues will come mainly from skulls and bone fragments along with hair specimens. A reference collection of small mammal, bird, and amphibian and reptile skulls and bones can be very helpful in the identification of pellet material, as can a collection of hair and insect parts. Skull keys such as those in Burt and Grossenheider's *Field Guide to the Mammals* or Bryan Glass's *Key to the Skulls of North American Mammals* may also prove very useful. Hair that has passed through a digestive tract is difficult to identify except by microscopic analysis of the hair scales. The determined investigator would find the hair keys of Leon A. Hausman useful for this purpose.

Often one pellet may give clues to a whole story (see Figure 4.4). A pellet from a barred owl that I recovered in a spruce bog in northwestern Connecticut contained parts of a gray squirrel skull and fragments of a red oak acorn. This evidence suggests that the barred owl had not had a successful night-time hunt and had stayed actively hunting until after dawn. The day-active gray squirrel was up and feeding in a red oak grove that was at least one-quarter mile away from the bog. The squirrel was caught while feeding and part of its acorn meal was ingested along with the squirrel itself. After feeding, the owl flew off to the heavy evergreen thicket in the bog to digest its meal. Here the owl was reasonably well hidden from predators and avoided the mobbing of crows. It regurgitated the pellet while in this retreat.

Regular examination of raptor pellets can provide a reasonable indication of the relative abundance of some of the smaller mammals of the area that serve as the basic food for the raptors. Raptors tend to catch

Figure 4.4.
Owl pellet (left, intact; right, dissected).

more of the more abundant species and less of the less abundant ones. Pellets may reveal a much higher population of some species than a trapping program in the same area. Some species are notoriously successful at avoiding traps yet they will fall to the hunting skills of the winged predators.

Predators are clearly not the only creatures that leave evidence of their eating. The evidence is everywhere—from nibbled leaf edges, to holes, to telltale tunnels between the epidermal layers of the leaf. There are sticky drops of sap where insects with piercing mouthparts have tapped the plant and hundreds of species of galls that shelter feeding insects in various stages of their life cycle. Aquatic snails leave winding trails where their radula have scraped algae off the rocks and predatory relatives like the whelks drill holes in the shells of other mollusk relatives to eat their soft bodies.

Rodents gnaw bark and bones and leave gouge marks the width of their teeth; toothmark width can give clues to what rodent did the chewing. The height and pattern of such feeding is also part of the clue. Rabbits, squirrels, and deer all nip off twigs, but rodent teeth nip clean as if a set of clippers had been used, whereas deer, lacking upper incisors like the rodents, leave a characteristic torn or frayed piece of bark on one edge of the twig. Some mice cut grass seed heads at ground level and then keep nipping off sections of stem until the seed head finally drops down to a level where the mouse can reach it to feed. Squirrels have characteristic patterns of opening nuts that are fairly species specific. Many rodents create hoards of seeds and nuts. Shrews may store snails.

The list goes on and on: the branches jammed underwater in the mud by beavers, the feeding platforms of muskrats with their waste roots and mussel shells, the rows of holes drilled by sapsuckers or the different-shaped feeding holes of their woodpecker relatives. Indeed, there are few creatures that do not leave some distinctive clue to their feeding habits for those sharp enough to recognize and decipher them.

Scat

An animal's digestive tract removes much of the nutritive value from the food ingested and compacts the indigestibles for elimination. Among the wildlife people this solid waste is generally referred to as *droppings* or *scat*. Biologists in general refer to it as *fecal material* or *feces*.

As the fecal material passes through the lower digestive tract the rhythmic contraction of the muscles in the colon wall pinches the material off into units. In a healthy animal the fecal material is relatively firm and each unit tends to assume a rather characteristic form that can be used to classify the depositor at least to its major group. See Figure 4.5.

Figure 4.5. Scat. At upper left, cottontail rabbit; lower left, snowshoe hare; center, porcupine; upper right, whitetail deer (summer); lower right, whitetail deer (winter).

In combination with other clues such as the site of deposition and tracks, even more specific identification can be made.

As the material leaves the lower digestive tract under the extruding pressure of rhythmic contraction of the colon wall muscles, it is periodically pinched off by closure of the anal sphincter muscle. In many species (particularly among mammals) this molds the fecal material at the end into something of a point. Seen at the site of deposition, this point generally indicates the direction the animal was facing when elimination occurred. Frequently this also indicates the animal's direction of travel.

There are few guides to animal scats. The best one currently available is Murie's *Field Guide to Animal Tracks;* it includes the scats of most species along with the tracks.

Scat form is not as precise a clue as tracks because a given animal's scat will vary with its state of health and the food it is eating. In winter deer scat, for instance, are classically like most of the illustrations—elongated pellets pointed at one end. But when the animals have been feeding heavily on greens and fruit in late summer or fall, their droppings may be loose and look much more like miniature cow droppings. Many carnivores will feed on fruit in the fall and their droppings will also become looser and lack patterns characteristic of firmer droppings. Rabbit pellets are typically compressed, flattened disks of cellulose and are smaller than those of their close relative, the hare. But cellulose is quite absorbent and after a few days of dampness a rabbit pellet may swell in size until it could be confused with a hare's pellet. In areas where the two animals overlap in range this can be confusing.

Scats can help determine the age of a trail once you learn to read the clues. In cool weather, scat that is still steaming signals a freshness of the trail that almost anyone can recognize. Fresh deer pellets that are a bit older will still appear shiny, dark, and moist. Break one open; if it's still somewhat moist inside it was probably dropped within the hour. If its texture is crumbly, pale, or dry you are probably dealing with droppings a day or more old. The scat of most meat eaters is very dark brown or black in color when fresh and turns white as it ages. The lighter the color the older the scat.

Analysis of scats will often reveal a great deal about what the animal is feeding on and fresh scats collected at different seasons can reveal a great deal about seasonal food opportunities and preferences.

Careful teasing apart of scat will often reveal indigestible parts of food eaten such as seeds, grass, hair, bone fragments, insect exoskeletons, and fish scales. The material can also be placed on a reasonably fine sieve and water flushed over it to wash away the soluble material and leave behind those insoluble food fragments. This technique often reveals items that simple mechanical teasing apart will not. Again, reference collections of potential food species will simplify identification of fragments in the scat considerably. However, accurate identification of much of the material you find will not be possible because digestive juices will have altered its appearance beyond recognition.

Bird droppings are much more difficult to identify by species and, due largely to the grinding action of the gizzard, little indigestible material gets through the digestive tract to the scat in any recognizable form. Since birds don't pass liquid urine but rather urea salts, they combine fecal and urinary wastes in one packet of dark fecal and white urinary material. It is the latter that leaves the characteristic whitewash effect of bird droppings. Actually some of our gallinaceous birds, such as pheasant and grouse, along with ducks and geese, do leave relatively large droppings that may be confused by the beginner with the scat of some mammals.

Areas splashed with whitewash droppings are often a good clue to a regular roosting site or a nest. When nestlings are small their droppings have a relatively tough mucous coating and the parents pick up this sac of feces and drop it some distance from the nest. As the young grow older, however, they learn to back up to the edge of the nest and eliminate their waste directly. It leaves a telltale clue on the branches or ground below.

Insects also leave droppings and some, such as that of the larger caterpillars, is quite recognizable. Insect scat is frequently referred to as *frass*. I have often been able to locate the caterpillars of the larger silk moths such as the cecropia and polyphemus by searching for the large round frass beneath a food plant and when it's found, searching carefully in the foliage above until the caterpillars are located.

Of course insect frass is only one component of what I call organic rain. You can learn more about it, and the amount of insect activity in your bushes or trees, by spreading a white cloth beneath the plants for a few hours or days. Examine carefully all the plant and animal debris you find. You may be very surprised. This material is an essential part of the natural system of recycling. Observe what creatures utilize this material and in what ways. It's an interesting aspect of wildlife watching in miniature.

There are other signs related to waste elimination that may give clues to an animal's behavior. Most tree dwellers eliminate wherever they happen to be and the waste, be it food coverings or scat, disappears from the animal's awareness. Since some, like squirrels, may have favored dining areas, considerable midden heaps of cone scales and the like may accumulate in select places. Some ground dwellers, however, take great pains to conceal their scat. Woodchucks and the cats are prime examples. Others, such as the voles, have definite side runways at the end of which they regularly deposit their scat. Porcupines regularly deposit at their den entrance and over the years large mounds of dung accumulate. Since the scat and urine reveal a great deal about the general health and sexual state of an animal to those that can read scents like we read words, there are some species, particularly among the dog and weasel families as well as many of the hooved animals, that deposit their scat and urine quite prominently as scent posts that mark territories and transmit complex messages on the status of the depositor. Locating such scent posts around an animal's territory can sometimes be enhanced by exploring with a dog. The dog will usually pick up and explore these scent posts of other animals as well as those of other dogs. Once a scent post has been located for you, you can usually find visual clues to its existence such as stains on leaves or slightly trampled areas. Of course, in snow the yellow stains are a quick clue to the existence of a scent post.

In the case of the dog and cat families an important clue to look for is scrapes. Dogs, after they defecate, and sometimes after urinating, will take a step or two and then kick dirt in the general direction of the waste. This leaves a series of scratches from the toenails. Cats not only bury their scat, but they also create scrapes when they urinate. Normally they crouch down and reach out to dig a shallow pit with the front paws. This results in a small mound at the rear of the pit and the cat moves forward until the mound is between its hind legs and then urinates on the mound. It then steps forward, often leaving a footprint in the depression. The pit and the mound together are called the *scrape* and the *pit*, and they usually indicate the direction in which the cat was traveling.

OTHER SIGNS

Tracks, scat, and pellets are far from the only types of sign to look for during tracking excursions. Animal homes are an important category and the variety is extensive—bird nests, mammal nests and dens, woodpecker holes, crayfish turrets, ant hills, caddis fly cases, spider webs, plant galls, and fish nests and redds are all among the many clues to examine. Note carefully the location of the homes—their elevation, the direction any exits and entrances face, and the microclimate they are located in or create. Note the material of the home. Did any of it have to be brought any distance? Where is the nearest source of the materials?

For many species homes are constructed and used mainly for rearing the young. Thus the condition of the home can give clues to the stage of the reproductive cycle the animal is in. Around many animal homes may be found debris from feeding the young, which helps build a picture of the feeding habits of the species. A number of animals broaden the scope of their normal food preference when faced with feeding active young.

Many mammals have regular runways that they maintain free of obstruction. Mapping these runways can be very informative in gaining an insight into that species' world. Following such runways often means you must assume some awkward, indeed even ridiculous, postures and poses but you will acquire information available in no other way. Animals, like humans, are not averse to doing things the easy way when the opportunity presents itself, thus many of the runways are utilized by many creatures other than the ones that constructed and maintain them. Animals are seldom randomly distributed over the landscape and runways indicate what parts of the area are being most heavily utilized. Examine the runways carefully for signs of recent activity. Many pathways get seasonal use because the animals exploit different resources of their home range at different times of the year.

Insects also may have distinct runways. Some beetle larvae chew out elaborate tunnelways under bark. Leaf miners eat out intricate pathways between the epidermal layers of leaves. Some caterpillars, such as the eastern tent caterpillar, lay down trails of silk wherever they go so that they can backtrack to their hiding place. Ants clear regular paths near their hills and leave pheromone scent markers as they explore more remote sites. Rub your finger across one of these trails to smear the scent and witness the ensuing confusion.

At the seashore amid the mudflats you can follow the trails of a number of the worms and mollusks that live there. Of course the next tide will erase the evidence. Earthworms often leave trails in the mud following a rainfall and, of course, you can search for their little mounds of pellet-shaped castings among the grassroots jungle or between your garden rows. Land mollusks, both snails and slugs, leave slime trails that can be followed. If mapped they often reveal the range and feeding of these animals. Many sea mollusks rasp algae of rocks for food as they move about and this, too, leaves a followable trail.

A number of birds and mammals enjoy taking dust baths. Apparently, this is useful in discouraging external parasites whose breathing mechanisms get clogged by the fine dust. These dusting areas are usually bowl-shaped depressions in areas of fine dry soil. Shed feathers are a clue to look for; even the down feathers of the pheasant and grouse family have a small second, or aftershaft, and this family of birds are frequent dusters. Mammals may leave a few telltale hairs or tracks.

Some species have preferred feeding sites to which they take food. Usually these are sites that provide reasonable shelter but also a good viewpoint that prevents unobserved approaches by enemies. Muskrat and beaver have flattened down areas along the shore or in sedge clumps that are usually surrounded by feeding leftovers. Scat is usually found on or near these platforms. Beaver also make special little mounds that they smear with their special scent, castoreum. This is for sexual and territorial advertisement. The squirrel family frequently has feeding platforms on stumps, stonewalls, or favorite branches. The individual characteristics of the different species in opening nuts or eating cones helps tell whose feeding platform you are observing. Hawks often have favorite plucking sites where they take their avian prey to remove the feathers.

Gray squirrels tend to bury individual food items, whereas chipmunks and deer mice may create considerable caches of seeds and nuts in underground chambers. In some parts of the country ants may have large underground treasure troves of seeds. Chickadees and other titmice, nuthatches, and some woodpeckers, as well as jays, hide nuts and seeds in crevices in tree bark or holes of their own making. Shrews may hoard paralyzed land snails.

Some large predators store excess meat by covering it over with ground litter and usually marking it with their urine to identify their claim to it. They may return to the cache several times. If you find a cache that seems to be attractive yet scavengers such as crows and ravens are about but keeping their distance, be alert; the predator is probably laid up in the brush quite near by. Bear, cougar, wolves, and lynx, are all among our native species that may make such a cache.

Check out likely tree trunks for scratch marks from the claws of climbing animals. Heavier animals, such as young bears or raccoons, will leave deeper marks than squirrels. If you find scratches examine the bark carefully for any hairs that may have caught on a rough spot and that can provide back-up evidence to identify the climber.

In lawn, field, and forest one often finds little dead-end diggings. These are usually the work of squirrels burying or digging for nuts, or of skunks digging up beetle grubs or yellow jacket nests. Raccoons will also make such divots in their food searches.

At the shore, particularly along mudflats, there are a number of clues to animal activity to be sought. In addition to tracks you will find round holes where shorebirds have probed the mud for worms and mollusks. You may find the burrows of a colony of fiddler crabs. You may find many round pockmarks in the mud where flounder have been sucking up mud to strain out organisms. There can be little spouts of water near where you walk from clams buried beneath the surface.

Several broken clam shells on a rock outcropping indicate that gulls have been clamming. Indeed there is a whole different world of clues to be explored.

At the shore or inland one should not ignore the clues of castoffs—the shed skin of a snake, the molted shell of a crab, the larval shell of a dragonfly, shreds of velvet from a deer's antlers, molted feathers, clumps of shed fur—all are tips to the presence and activity of various forms of wildlife.

Call Notes and Song

The tracker should not ignore such ephemeral clues as songs and call notes. Most birds sing mainly when they are on their territory. A great many regularly use a few well-defined perches in their territory from which they do most of their singing. Locate the bird aurally and you can usually move in to where you can spot it visually. Locate the song perch and wait. If you are patient enough the singer will usually return after a while. Following frog songs will usually bring you to a breeding site where calm patience will usually turn up a number of the singers.

In almost every habitat certain species serve as sentinel species. Their alarm notes or mobbing calls are heeded by many other species. In most areas jays, crows, squirrels, chickadees, and kingbirds function this way. It pays to know their various alarm notes. Frequently it is you, the observer, that they are announcing, but if you are sure it is not you then you too should take heed because they are serving notice that some creature, most likely a larger predator, is nearby.

Nor should one ignore the clue of sudden silence. A frog chorus that suddenly shuts down indicates that something has disturbed it. Sometimes you can follow the animal's progress as pockets of silence move through such a chorus. A group of chittering sparrows may suddenly go silent as a shadow—perhaps that of a hawk—passes overhead. The alert wildlife watcher heeds such clues and sees more.

THE VALUE OF NUMBERS

A single clue is seldom more than a tantalizing hint of what might be. It takes a number of clues tied together to build any sort of satisfying picture of who is about the area and what they are doing. By carefully collecting and recording the clues, basic patterns begin to emerge that will help you understand what animals are present, in roughly what number, and where in the area they tend to concentrate their activity.

Big-game hunter Jim Corbett developed a useful formula to determine how many animals are using a trail. It says: The number of animals using a trail equals one-half the number of footprints in a section of trail equal to the distance between the species' fore and hind feet. For example, in my area deer average about three feet between fore and hind feet. If a three-foot section of trail shows twelve hoofprints, then six deer have used the trail. This is, of course, only a crude estimate. Since the last time the prints were wiped out, six deer could have used the trail or one deer could have used it six times or three deer could have used it twice. To make the estimate more accurate, you can regularly clear areas of trail of previous prints and then record those made during known time intervals. It helps to make your print registration area a place along the trail that naturally focuses activity over the site and discourages animals from walking around it.

Scat counts over a study area can also indicate trends of relative abundance. To be most useful the area must be gone over carefully so that few, if any, scats are missed. For best estimate of a target species make one sweep of the study area and remove all scat found. Then after a predetermined time interval (several days or a week), return to make your count of new scat.

To make your estimate of the number of animals using your study site you need to assume a defecation rate for the species. For deer this has been determined to be between twelve and fifteen pellet groups a day. For most carnivores it will be about one deposit a day unless a lot of fruit is being eaten, in which case two or three deposits a day may be made. For small mammals little data is readily available but the rate could be determined by observing the defecation rate for captive animals of the same or related species.

Armed with an assumed defecation rate, a time period over which the scat has been deposited, and reasonable assurance that you have counted all the available scat in your study area, you are now ready to make your local population estimate.

The figures you will need are the area of your study plot and the number of scat or pellet groups you found in the plot. Thus, if

$$t = \text{scat per unit area}$$

$$a = \text{area of the sample}$$

$$y = \text{sum of all the scat}$$

Then

$$t = \tfrac{1}{a}\, y$$

We then divide t by the assumed defecation rate to determine how many animal droppings are represented for the time period. Finally, we

divide by the number of days in the study period to get an approxima-
tion of the population on the study plot.

This may seem an elaborate procedure to go through to find out
what your common sense indicates about whether there are a few or
many of the animals in the area. It is, but it helps confirm common sense
and often reveals its unreliability.

Going over a study area carefully, reading as much as possible of
the available sign, will frequently pay off in later direct observations of
animals. You will learn where it will be most profitable to set up blinds
or where to begin a stalk. You will be able to anticipate the moves an
animal will make once you have a familiarity with its territory. Bil Gilbert, in writing about his study of the coati-mundi or chulo, sums up the
usefulness of such spadework.

> It would be impressive to report that we quickly began to apply logic
> and woodcraft, developed a high probability plan for locating
> chulos, confidently closed in on the animals. However, this would
> be untrue. As in most natural history searches, we used our backs
> more than our brains during the first stages. We continued to walk
> and look, gradually increased our knowledge of the area, kept hop-
> ing to come across some major clue bearing on the question of where
> chulos might be found, how we could observe them.

FURTHER READING

Brainerd, G.W. "An illustrated field key to the identification of mammal bones,"
Ohio State Archeological Historical Quarterly, 48 (1939), 324–28.

Brown, Tom, Jr., and William Jon Watkins. *The Tracker*. New York: Prentice-
Hall, 1978.

Brown, Vinson. *Knowing the Outdoors in the Dark*. New York: Grollier Books/
Macmillan, 1972.

Driver, E.C. "Mammal remains in owl pellets," *American Midland Naturalist*, 41
(1949), 139–42.

Einarsen, Arthur S. *Determination of Some Predator Species by Field Signs*. Corval-
lis, Oregon: Oregon State College, 1956.

Falkus, Hugh. *Wildtrack*. New York: Holt, Rinehart & Winston, 1978.

Glass, Bryan P. *A Key to the Skulls of North American Mammals*. Minneapolis,
Minn.: Burgess Publishing Co., 1951.

Hausman, Leon A. "Structural characteristics of the hair of mammals," *American
Midland Naturalist*, 54 (1920), 496–523.

Jaeger, Ellsworth. *Tracks and Trailcraft*. New York: Macmillan, 1948.

Martin, A.C. and W.D. Barkeley. *Seed Identification Manual*. Berkeley: Univ. of
California Press, 1961.

Martin, A.C., H.S. Zim, and A.L. Nelson. *American Wildlife and Plants: A Guide
to Wildlife Food Habits*. New York: McGraw-Hill, 1951.

MURIE, OLAUS J. *A Field Guide to Animal Tracks*. Boston: Houghton Mifflin, 1954.

STAINS, HOWARD J. "Field key to guard hairs of Middle Western furbearers," *Journal of Wildlife Management*, 22, no. 1 (1958), 95–97.

————. "Use of the calcarium in the study of taxonomy and food habits," *Journal of Mammalogy*, 40 (1959), 392–401.

STEBLER, A.M. "The tracking technique in the study of larger predatory animals," *Transactions of the North American Wildlife Conference*, 1939.

Note: Popular material on animal clues is scarce; even the technical literature is thin. To obtain the journals listed above you will likely need to visit a university with a strong zoology or wildlife management program. Often the journals are in department libraries rather than the main library.

CHAPTER 5

STALKING
AND HIDING

FOR A GREAT MANY SPECIES, staying alive means avoiding detection by potential predators. On the other hand, for many predators, securing a meal involves remaining undetected by their potential prey until they are close enough to make a kill. Wildlife watchers, if they are to be successful, must learn to perceive those animals that are concealed and themselves learn how to move or remain undetected by those creatures they wish to observe. To the wildlife watcher all species are "prey." Since most animals perceive people as dangerous, they take every precaution to avoid close approach by humans or at least try to remain undetected if close approach is inevitable. Let's examine some strategies animals use to avoid or evade us and other animals who present a threat.

CONCEALING COLORATION

Because of our own color vision we tend to assume, quite incorrectly, that other creatures see the world much as we do. Birds and a few other mammals do see color. So do some insects, although they may be sensitive to some of the color spectrum to which we are not, and vice versa. A far greater number of animals see only in monochrome—shades of gray, if you will.

Also, the stereoscopic perception that we take so much for granted is very limited in most species since more eyes are located to the sides of heads than to the front, which greatly restricts the amount of visual field overlapped by both eyes. These two facts about the visual ability of most animals are at the root of understanding the effectiveness of the common strategies for avoiding visual detection.

The most common strategy is not to look like yourself when motionless. Double-talk? Not really. A creature is recognizable for what it is when its entire body pattern is visible. In motion it stands out from the background almost as much as it does when silhouetted against the sky. However, if its body hues are similar in tone to its general background, and if prominent stripes, bars, patches, or altered body position disrupt the characteristic body outline, letting it blend with the variable patterns of the background, the animal becomes far less detectable. Move that animal to a background for which it is not adapted and it becomes highly visible. A tiger with its tawny color and prominent vertical stripes seems to disappear among tall grass, yet the same tiger seen against the plain background of a zoo cage seems almost flamboyantly marked.

For us with color vision, it is difficult to picture how even bright colors meld into the background when perceived in monochrome. Those familiar with the challenge of black-and-white photography have a better understanding. A scene may be beautiful in color, but without careful use of lighting to provide shadows and contrast, the black-and-white photo of that same scene is muddy with all the objects more or less blending together. Even a male scarlet tanager filmed in black-and-white against bright green leaves is relatively inconspicuous because the two hues have the same relative value in monochrome. Of course the birds themselves have color vision and the sexual dimorphism is useful in sexual recognition. In addition the male's bright color may help draw the attention of avian predators, leaving the greenish-colored female undetected. Other non-avian predators with monochromatic vision would be more likely to miss both members of the pair.

Another strategy for concealing coloration is the phenomenon of countershading. Most organisms are darker above and lighter below. Since the lighter-colored regions tend to be under the body, they are generally shaded and thus appear darker. The darker upper regions of the body get more direct sunlight and thus tend to appear lighter. The net result is to even out the contrast and make the total organism appear much flatter and less distinctly shaped. Since relatively few animals have our stereoscopic vision to help provide three dimensionality to an object, counter-shaded animals, particularly if perceived monochromatically, become part of the flat background pattern when motionless. Combine this with disruptive patterning and the creature is visually almost undetectable. Even with the advantage of our color vision it may not be easy; more than one person has almost, or even actually, stepped on a motionless ruffed grouse before detecting it from the heart-stopping wing-whirr as it erupts skyward at the last possible moment.

"FREEZING"

Freezing is the art of remaining motionless in almost any position. Many animals need some slight motion to change the light intensity on some of the eye's retinal cells and thus trigger an awareness response to separate an object from the general background. This is particularly true of animals with monochromatic vision. With such species, if a moving individual suddenly freezes, it essentially becomes part of the undifferentiated background; this is particularly true if its body contours are broken by cryptic patterns. Even with color vision it is easier to spot something if it moves than if it remains motionless—even if that movement is only the slight flicking of an ear.

STEALTHY BUT RAPID FLIGHT

Most animals, whose senses are more sharply honed than ours, become aware of our presence before we are aware of theirs. Always alert for danger, the animal, upon detection, must evaluate that danger in terms of the degree of hazard it represents. Most species exhibit what animal behavior specialists refer to as "flight distance," that is, the distance to which the animal will allow approach before easing slowly away or fleeing. The actual flight distance will vary with the degree of perceived danger. A herd of antelope spotting a lion approaching them across the plain can tell from its body movements whether it is hungry and hunting or recently fed and out for a stroll. In either case they will eventually flee, but under the latter perception they will permit a closer approach before fleeing, that is, the flight distance will be smaller.

Some species will momentarily freeze to assess the danger and then ease slowly toward more secure cover or—as with whitetail deer— they will move stealthily away hugging the ground as closely as possible and once out of reasonable range of swift pursuit will rise up fully and bound safely away.

SOCIAL WARNING SYSTEMS

In addition to fleeing when their flight distance is exceeded, when danger is spotted some species use visual and auditory alarm signals. Undoubtedly some give off olfactory alarms as well, but such are more difficult for us to detect. Although the alarms are meant only for the species involved, other associated species have learned their meaning and often take evasive action themselves even when they are not sure precisely what the danger is.

Blue jays and red squirrels are noted for spotting predators and sounding the alarm. Many a deer hunter, owl, bobcat, or other prospective predator has had to move on because all animals in the area had taken cover at the alarm. Furthermore, some of these woodland tattlers will follow the predator and harass it for some time until in desperation it moves quite some distance away. Woodchucks and ground squirrels give a shrill alarm whistle. Many species have a distinctive bark, grunt, yap, chatter, growl, or other such warning signal. Small birds may gather in numbers at some other species' alarm note and "mob" the predator with bold attacks made possible by their greater maneuverability. A few species, such as pronghorns and whitetail deer, raise white hairs on rump or tail to flash a visual alert to others of their kind in an area; this may or may not be accompanied by an audible alarm note.

Silence is often of equal warning value. In any habitat there is always a general background noise from the normal activity of birds, insects, and other creatures. If disturbed, many animals will freeze and remain silent. Such silence may sweep like a wave before an approaching animal, such as man, who is perceived as a danger by the community at large.

I have often sat at a favorite gathering place for foraging black bears—a wilderness dump. It is usually possible to detect an approaching bear by this wave of silence in the area. Small creatures—from jays, raccoons, and even smaller bears—that have been feeding in the dump will suddenly abandon their feeding and disappear into the brush. Within a few minutes one of the more dominant bears will move on to the dump site and feed. Once finished, it moves off and soon the regular noise and bustle resumes and the smaller creatures return until the next wave of silence approaches.

DISTRACTIVE BEHAVIOR

Some species use distractive behavior, particularly when they are rearing young. One of the parents will call attention to itself by feigning injury, luring the potential predator toward it. The feigning parent manages to keep itself just out of reach as it moves away from its group. Meanwhile the rest have moved stealthily away. Once it is fairly sure the rest are safe, the distractor miraculously gains its full capacities and dashes away. Sometimes the ruse is only to move the potential predator away from discovery of a nest or den.

This past summer, while I was out walking, a beautiful male yellow warbler practically flew in my face; then fluttering feebly, it lit in a bush hardly an arm's length away. I almost succumbed to the urge to pursue him but I knew this trick too well. I froze and let my eyes do the walking through the vegetation. Sure enough, not three feet away, the female was huddled motionless on the nest. Only then, having spotted the nest, did I let the male lead me on as I left the nest undisturbed—but recorded in my notes.

SPECIAL DEFENSE
AND THREATENING BEHAVIOR

Some creatures try bluff instead of freezing or fleeing. They hold their ground and use threatening gestures to suggest that you find business elsewhere. With some, such as the skunk, it's not a bad idea to heed this warning. Bears have been known to make a bluffing charge, which is also well heeded, because if it isn't it can lead to a full-scale attack. Generally there is little to be gained by calling a bluff except a false inflation of ego. You have been spotted and you will see little "normal" behavior there for a while. Your recognized presence has severely altered behavior. You will, of course, have data on one type of agonistic display.

Some of the insects need to be approached with a degree of caution. As with other creatures they, too, have a flight distance. The problem is that when that distance is exceeded near the nest, the flight is likely to be toward rather than away from the intruder and the end results painful to the observer. Other insects, such as blister beetles, may eject chemical sprays that cause a painful rash.

And of course, in areas of the country where poisonous snakes are common the wildlife observer must be ever alert. The various pit vipers tend to remain motionless for long periods of time, particularly in relatively cool weather; and if you inadvertently move into their intimacy zone it could provoke a defensive strike resulting in a painful and potentially dangerous situation. This is particularly apt to happen if you are stalking something else and thus moving stealthily. The usual noisy, clumsy approach of humans normally alerts the snakes in time for them to glide away to safety unnoticed.

Whereas these last remarks are made for your protection while observing wildlife, the earlier strategies of how wildlife avoids detection are very helpful for the wildlife observer to adopt in order to effectively conceal himself from wildlife he wishes to observe or to engage in successful stalking of wildlife.

Clothing

The precise nature of your outdoor clothing will have to be geared to the climate where your observations will take place but some general principles relative to clothing hold for a wide range of locations.

1. Earth tones are a sound choice of colors. The exact hues depend upon the nature of the habitats in which you will work. The background colors of the desert are quite different from those of the deciduous forest.

Where hunters pose a danger to observers, consider wearing blaze orange. Generally this does not make a person conspicuous to animals that see in monochrome, but it makes you quite visible to hunters. You may want to use patches or stripes of blaze orange to break up your body shape rather than wearing garments composed completely of this color. Blaze orange was created for its high visibility and because it is a color that does not normally occur in nature even amid fall foliage. Some hunters are trigger-happy; they will shoot first and look closely later. If hunting is popular where you regularly observe, wear at least some blaze orange or don't be afield observing during hunting season.

Camouflage patterns are useful in certain terrain and not in others. I have seen people afield in camouflage gear that were far more conspicuous than those without. To get a feel of your visual impact while in your field-observing clothes, have a friend take panchromatic black-and-white photos of you in a variety of habitats. Manufacturers make much of their special camouflage patterns but none is perfect for all places. You will have to choose the pattern most suitable for your most visited habitats. You may do as well or better with your own designs. Use fabric paints to put grass and brush-like verticals on tan trousers and tie-dye shirts with various greens and some blue for spring and summer woodlands; tie-dye another shirt with yellows and some blue for autumn, for example.

2. Think about the texture of the fabric of your clothing. Hard-surface materials, such as nylon shells, are good for repelling moisture but they tend to produce glare and thus give you away. They also tend to rustle when you move or brush against shrubbery and thereby cause an auditory alert.

Wool both repels water and breathes well. It doesn't shine and is soft-surfaced so that it is relatively silent as you move. Many outdoorsmen consider it to be the ideal all-around material. Although flannels possess at least two of wool's favorable properties, they are not water repellent. For many, however, they are less irritating than wool.

3. Wear clothes that are relatively form-fitting without being binding. Loose clothing tends to snag on objects and to blow in the breeze, providing telltale movement even when you are trying to freeze.

4. Exposed hands and face are often the things that give away an otherwise well-concealed observer. Light gloves help conceal the hands and there are two basic ways to deal with the face. Mesh headnets are available in plain colors or camouflage pattern. You can see reasonably well through them but the animals cannot see in. They have at least two advantages: They hide the give-away shine of your eyes and they protect the face from the ravages of mosquitoes and other biting insect pests, which reduces the motion of slapping or brushing them away. Such nets are awkward to use with binoculars, however.

The other approach for facial camouflage is to use charcoal or grease paint to smear your face and break up its pattern. Although liberal use of the grease paint may create a coating that reduces insect annoyance, eye-shine can't be hidden this way. Just as for football players who use it under their eyes to reduce sun glare, black grease may serve the same purpose for the wildlife observer.

5. A hat with a broad brim or a long peaked cap is very useful not only to shed sun and rain but also to keep hair from blowing in the breeze and creating unwanted attracting movement. And in deer fly country a hat all but eliminates the nuisance of these pests since they are attracted to the oil and perspiration of hair. A good brim also keeps excess light from leaking in around your binocular eyepiece, which can create haze that reduces visual clarity.

6. Shoes are critical equipment and provoke more idiosyncratic argument than almost any other piece of apparel. Shoes are tools, and as with any tools, there are different designs for different jobs. Varying terrain and varying purposes demand different styles. For general walking a good sturdy hiking shoe or hunting shoepack is desirable, but their necessarily sturdy soles generally make them awkward for stalking.

I find it useful to carry with me a separate pair of shoes specifically for use while stalking. I prefer Indian-style moccasins with soft soles for this purpose. Sailing sneakers are also suitable. The key is that the soles must be flexible so that you can feel the ground surface through them. As you slowly place your foot you should be able to get an early warning of a stick or twig that might snap if you transfer full weight to the foot. You should also be able to feel loose stones that might rattle and give you away. Sturdier footwear simply won't permit such subtlety.

Coping with Your Scent

To most mammals, man is a real stinker, and, to most, human scent is the scent of danger. The best, most cautious stalker may find his presence revealed by a shift in wind unless precautions have been taken.

In reality there is no way to eliminate human scent and the stalker needs always to be alert to wind direction. However, scent can be reduced or masked. Formerly, field clothes were regularly buried in the ground or in rotted manure piles to kill the human scent and impart an earthy one. Few today are ready to go that far. Instead, you can make sachets of some of the more pleasant pungent materials of the habitats you regularly wander—red cedar, pinyon pine, or bayberry, for example. Keep these sachets wrapped with your field clothes. Wash your clothes after each field trip, and yourself just before each trip. Instead of using sachets, some people like to put their clothes over a smoky wood-fire. (Sources of commercial cover scents are listed at the end of Chapter 6.) Use scentless deodorants. Most scented kinds are quite foreign to the wild and call almost as much attention to the stalker as natural human scent would. Of course, if your quarry is such creatures as birds or reptiles that have a poor sense of smell, such elaborate precautions are superfluous.

BASIC STALKING

Stalking is basically the skill of moving toward animals undetected. It differs from using blinds in that it is active whereas hiding is passive and depends upon the animals coming to you. There is a time and place for both approaches. In stalking one must attempt to overcome the various devices animals have for avoiding detection, as well as using similar devices of our own. The art of stalking reaches deep to stimulate hidden ancestral feelings at the root of our being.

The first rule is always to check the wind before closing in. Keep the wind in your face as much as possible, so that the wind is blowing from the animal to you. If your check reveals that the wind is not in your favor, try to circle round so that it is before your approach. Before you make that wind check, think about the nature of your quarry. How high is its nose from the ground? Your normal tendency is to check the wind at your height, but local microconditions often reveal countercurrents at different heights. A former professor of mine who had specialized in microclimates had set up a series of very sensitive feather vanes to measure wind direction. These were set at different heights along a pole. One such pole station was along a railroad track. One evening he was sitting on the track making observations when he saw both a deer and a woodchuck approaching him. He sat motionless but the general direction of the wind was from him to the animals. He watched his feather vanes. Before long the deer stopped and tested the air. The upper feather vanes were moving. The deer quickly decided to bound away into the woods. But the lower feather vanes were still and the woodchuck kept coming. It was only about fifteen feet away before it finally caught the human scent and went scrambling for the ditch. Eddies and countercurrents must be considered for successful stalking.

Once the stalk has begun, one must study the terrain ahead and determine what concealment lies between you and your quarry. Every attempt should be made to keep some objects between you. Always avoid exposure that would show your silhouette to your quarry. Look around, not over, objects when possible.

As you move into a position where the quarry is essentially in continuous view, study its actions very carefully. If it is feeding, or preening, or some similar activity, observe it for subtle body movement clues, intention movements, which may indicate that it is going to stop its involvement. It may be a flick of tail or ears, a shift of body weight, or similar body movement. Once you determine a pattern you can start your movement forward. Move only when the animal is occupied and preferably looking away from you. When you spot an intention movement—freeze. Don't move again until the animal is occupied again and reasonably relaxed. Repeat over and over until you get as close as you wish or until the animal spots you and moves off. Stalking demands great patience and self-control and a successful stalk may take hours.

Humans aren't used to freezing in awkward positions the way animals do for many minutes at a time. To be successful at it requires practice and conditioning. You may recall a children's game called Red Light. Its essence is that whoever is "it" turns his or her back to the others and says "One, two, three—red light." The others may move forward while "it" is counting but must freeze when "it" says "Red Light." Immediately upon saying the two words, "it" wheels about to try and spot anybody in motion. Those spotted must return to the starting line. The chant is repeated over and over until someone gets close enough to rush in and tag "it" and hopefully dash back to the starting line before "it" can tag him. Thus the game encapsulates the very essence of stalking—move while the prey is occupied; freeze on the intention movement. Play this game with others to build your skill at freezing and stalking.

At home, in spare time, try freezing in various walking, crawling, or crouched positions. Try it with only one foot on the ground. Test yourself to see how long you can hold each pose without moving. You may feel foolish at first but the practice will pay off in the field.

Freezing takes good muscle tone and conditioning. Regular exercise and body tone routines will make serious stalking much more fun and rewarding. Work on push-ups and deep knee bends. Practice crawling on hands, knees, and elbows.

Some people like to combine aspects of hiding with stalking. They may use a bush or large clump of grass to push in front of them to provide some cover as they ease closer. With herd animals a light frame in the general shape of the animal may be constructed and covered with a hide of the species. The observer gets under it and uses it as a moving blind as he stalks the herd. Some of the best motion pictures taken of bison were taken using this technique. Some creatures, such as the pronghorn, some deer, occasionally coyotes, and some ground squirrels are very curious. For these animals the successful stalk may end by having the quarry come to you rather than your moving closer. Carefully raise a white bit of cloth or a piece of aluminum foil into view for a few minutes and then lower it again. Repeat this several times. The very curious will just have to come and investigate. Of course they approach not only curious but also very cautious. You will have to be well positioned in regard to the wind and you will have to be extra careful to avoid all warning motion.

In wetland habitats you can make your stalk from the water. Land animals are less prone to expect danger to come from the water. You can approach using a floating log as cover or you can make a floating blind by tying cattails and reeds to a large inner tube and placing yourself in the center. Some people find this more comfortable if they wear chest-high waders, particularly if the water is cold or leeches plentiful. You can also use camouflaged boats and canoes as floating blinds; these will be discussed more fully in the next section.

THE ART OF HIDING

Hiding is the antithesis of stalking. It is passive and depends upon the wildlife coming to the observer rather than the reverse. It involves a great deal of scouting of an area and skill in reading signs in order to locate sites with a high potential of visitation by wildlife. Nests and dens of specific animals are among such high-potential sites. They offer good opportunities to observe care-giving and care-soliciting behaviors, play behavior, and the development of a number of basic behaviors in the growing young. Springs and salt licks make profitable sites as do trail intersections. Sites with a broad overview of wetlands, clearings, valleys, and the like should not be overlooked.

The most important part of hiding is some form of concealment. The simplest is some natural object such as uprooted tree roots, a downed log, a boulder clump, or similar item that provides as much cover as possible. The observer then gets as comfortable as possible, remains motionless, and awaits the possible appearance of wildlife. As we shall see, this is a bit easier said than done.

Today most people use some form of artificial blind; designs run from extremely simple to elaborate. What follows are some examples of each.

Behavioral Blind

Outwardly the "behavioral blind" is the simplest for it requires no special equipment. It is in reality the most difficult to execute because it takes great patience and self-knowledge. As a technique it seems to be most effective in open terrain, although in a few cases it has been used in wooded or thicketed habitats.

The behavior blind is based on the lack of physical concealment rather than concealment. It involves the hopeful observer's moving about where all can see and busying himself in nonaggressive ways. The observer conceals himself in innocuous behavior. The act of stalking is the act of a hunter. The body is tense, the movements are stealthy. This all implies danger to the animals even when your intent is peaceful.

Using a behavioral blind means moving about slowly and randomly. Direct rapid motion in body language is aggressive or in reverse implies retreat from a potential enemy; both situations cause other animals to be wary. One needs to sit quietly, apparently grooming or digging or engaging in some other "normal" occupation. This may involve some real acting. Intermittent attention must be used and prolonged staring at any point must be avoided. You have to be seen frequently and regularly by the animals until you are accepted as a natural, nonthreatening part of the surroundings. With some alpine creatures, such as marmots in a national park, this process may only take a few hours. Even then you must avoid prolonged direct eye contact or staring. Observe out of the side of your eyes and regularly look elsewhere. Keep your entire body as relaxed as possible.

This technique is best where animals are generally undisturbed by mankind, such as in national parks. Diane Fossey has used it effectively in her long-term studies of gorillas, as has Jane Goodall with chimpanzees. However, the photographer Tom McGuire used it successfully on a heavily hunted population of bighorn sheep. Within two weeks the animals were feeding all around him, which permitted photos with low-power telephoto and even wide-angle lenses to be taken. Some of the animals even approached and nudged him.

This behavioral blind or habituation technique will not work for everyone or for all species. It is most successful with larger species that are used to modifying their flight distance based on their perception of the intention movements of possible predators. It also works best for people reasonably at peace with themselves and capable of whiling away time doing nothing without becoming tense and frustrated.

Brush Lean-To

The brush lean-to is a relatively simple device. A horizontal bar is lashed between two trees. Long poles are leaned against the bar and lashed to it. Poles are then lashed at right angles to these and parallel to the horizontal bar. This makes a framework to hold a covering of leaves and brush. Brush is then cut and stuck vertically in the ground in front of the lean-to opening. It should be dense enough to break up the pattern of your body shape but sparse enough that you can see out reasonably well. Sitting in the dark interior of your mini-cave you will be difficult to spot if you remain reasonably still. However, in such a casual blind, movement is relatively easily detected and one must be careful not to let light reflect from binoculars, glasses, or shiny metal ornaments such as belt buckles, or even shoelace eyelets.

Pop Tents

Pop tents, that is small tents with external fiberglass supporting rods and a sewn-in floor, make excellent blinds. They can be assembled easily and moved about once erected. The colors of some tents today are designed for visibility rather than concealment so you may want to use spray paints to change the color or break up their peculiar pattern. Viewing is done through the screen mesh ventilation material. As with brush lean-tos it is difficult to see in from the outside but motion is relatively easily spotted.

A similar device is the canvas ice-fishing tent which can also be easily converted to a blind. These are relatively small and rectangular and designed for a person to sit in on a stool. Many models have a clear plastic viewing window. However, the frame of these tents is generally clumsier to assemble than the pop tents and they lack a sewn-in floor which makes them difficult to move once set up.

A Homemade Blind—Tent Style

A homemade blind can be devised using light aluminum bars with holes drilled (see Figure 5.1) and using aluminum extension tent poles as uprights. Of course, a similar frame can be constructed of wooden boards and poles but it will be heavier and clumsier. The cloth covering, which may be burlap, canvas, or even old sheets, should be cut as diagrammed and all seams sewn except for one vertical corner. The finished cover should fit snugly over the frame when erected and closure of the entry corner should be tight, using snaps, zippers, or Velcro. Loose covering will flap in the breeze and frighten wildlife away. Noth-

Figure 5.1. Homemade blind. Left, aluminum angle bar and telescoping-pole frame; center, attachment of angle bar to poles; right, pattern for cover of blind (sew seams indicated by arrows). The remaining side is used for the entrance.

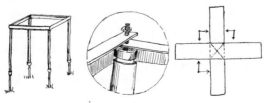

ing is more frustrating than to sit patiently for hours only to discover later that flapping material kept everything away.

With your homemade blind you can put in a number of viewing ports so that you can shift your point of view if necessary. These must be able to be opened from the inside. Simple ties are the easiest and quietest closures but may permit the material to flap in the breeze. Velcro makes the tightest closure but may give a revealing tearing sound if a new viewport is opened during an observation period.

As for the fishing tent, this design is difficult to move about when erected unless you want to modify it with a sewn-in floor and a bottom frame.

Even though they are heavier, many observers have used packing boxes for refrigerators and other large appliances as temporary blinds. They are often bulky, difficult to move, and not very weather-proof; however, the price is right.

Automobiles

With many animals, particularly the larger ones, an automobile makes a very suitable blind. These animals tend to accept the car in the environment as another large animal and don't associate it with the human danger. They permit much closer approach before fleeing than stalking normally does. Much of the study of large carnivores and hooved animals in Africa has been done from within the classic Land Rovers. In the United States, Hope Ryden did much of her observations of coyote dens from a van. She parked the vehicle in the animals' territory and stocked it with food. She stalked in and out of it as with any blind and spent many days and nights observing from inside the vehicle.

Cars are useful because they provide good rests for spotting scopes and binoculars and access to electricity to run red-filtered spotlights for night-time observations or to power tape recorders.

Of course, the use of autos is restricted to normal roadways unless you use a four-wheel-drive vehicle with oversize tires. They are most valuable on open plains or in areas with numbers of gravel-surfaced roads. Such roads also prove convenient for animals to use as travel lanes, so if you find the correct location much can be observed.

Hammocks

For those of us with a touch of the lazy, light hammocks make a useful blind of sorts. I always carry a fist-sized hammock and tie lines in my day pack. If I find a good observation point I tie the hammock between two trees using a simple timber hitch, stretch out, and wait. I usually tie the head end a foot or so higher than the foot end to improve visibility with the binocular. The hammock gets both me and my scent off the ground and gives me a nonhuman shape. A bit of rocking motion doesn't seem to disturb many creatures. I have observed a number of birds and small mammals this way and been quite comfortable doing so. A clear plastic sheet hung over a line above the hammock and staked at the corners makes a rain shelter.

Elevated Blinds

The hammock only gets you a bit above the ground, really not enough for getting out of visual or olfactory range of larger animals such as deer, moose, or bear. Nor would one be suitable for a tree blind opposite a large bird nest.

There are a number of devices on the market for deer hunters that are also suitable for general wildlife observation. The simplest is a collapsible ladder with a seat on the top that is leaned against a tree and then secured at the top with a strap (see Figure 5.2). There are seats with a band that go around the tree and are hitched up the tree to the desired height. The platform is large enough to sit on or stand upon if you wish, as an archer would. There are also some that are sectional, free-standing towers with a platform or seat on top. The fancy models have a swivel seat and a tent-like canopy to shield the observer from the elements and from easy view.

Blinds for observing tree nests are usually built into adjacent or nearby trees at about eye level with the nest. They are fabricated in the manner of children's tree houses in combination with adaptations of the homemade blind discussed earlier. Such blinds take a good deal of preplanning because they usually must be built in stages. If the parents are not to be overly disturbed and driven from the area, one should not work on the construction for more than fifteen minutes at a time and not more than two widely separated time blocks a day.

Figure 5.2.
Sectional ladder tree stand.

Floating Blinds

You can make amazingly close approaches to many animals using a canoe once you have mastered the sneak stroke; essentially that involves a power stroke and a feathering of the blade of the paddle, all done without removing the blade from the water and using tightly controlled motion. A piece of foam rubber glued to the gunwhales on the side you normally paddle will help reduce noise of the paddle accidentally banging the side of the canoe. If you are stuck with an aluminum canoe, put a foam mattress in the bottom to absorb sound (and take the chill off your knees) and pad the gunwhales. Paint the canoe dull brown or olive drab to eliminate the giveaway glare of the silver metal. You may wish to carry a "blanket" of camouflage netting to drape over you and the canoe if you want to anchor in one place and be hidden.

For generations, duckhunters have used one- or two-man craft modified into blinds and their boats are very suitable for general wildlife watchers who want to operate in aquatic habitats. The 1880 Barnegat Sneak Box and the Southbay Duckboat are custom-built boats of merit and the pirogue of the southern bayou is easily adapted for a floating blind. Canada's Windswept Gunning Skiffs of Ontario are commercially available. None of these boats is inexpensive but all are well-crafted, shallow draft boats that permit getting around in very shallow waters without getting stuck. Some are rowed but the pirogues at least have been outfitted with small electric motors. The boats have railings on which to tie bunches of marsh vegetation to provide the adequate cover.

The wildlife photographer Jack Swedberg designed a very useful floating blind. At first it was essentially an inner tube covered by a dome of chicken wire interlaced with vegetation. It was a good beginning, but it had drawbacks. His final model was more elaborate (see Figure 5.3). He made a frame of styrofoam pontoons sheathed with plywood which made a very stable base for mounting his camera. Again he made a wire dome, but this time he added a canvas covering before the vegetation. This kept dust and dirt out of his hair and equipment. The vegetation

Figure 5.3.
Floating blind (cutaway view).

was dried cattails and the end result was a mound that looked just like a muskrat house. He wears an extra-long pair of waders over long johns and pants to keep warm, dry, and free of leeches. Further refinements included easy removal of the dome and moving the rear piece of the frame forward so the frame was a boxy A-shape to allow easier entrance and exit to the blind.

PERMANENT BLINDS

Another way to go is to build a good solid observation blind in a reasonably convenient place and equip it with all the accessories you would like such as electricity for running nocturnal red lights, microphones hidden throughout the area, and other amenities. Then you set about putting out water, food, salt, and even scent to lure the wildlife to your observation site. An outstanding example of such a set-up is the Desert Water Hole Observation Blind at the Arizona-Sonora Desert Museum. Perhaps the most elaborate one is the observation room at the Laboratory of Ornithology at Cornell University. It overlooks a man-made pond and has the natural sound piped in from microphones hidden in the woods and marsh.

A number of wildlife refuges have observation towers and blinds to help visitors view the wildlife in places where there generally are good concentrations of wildlife.

Actually your own house may be used as a convenient blind by attracting wildlife to feeding stations outside windows. A great deal of wildlife behavior watching can be accomplished from such locations.

A most fascinating permanent blind was built by Ernest C. Bay, a professor of entomology at the University of Maryland, and described in detail in the October 1972 issue of *Scientific American*. It involved building a waterproof building with aquarium-type windows on an artificial pond site. Once the five-by-seven-by-five foot building with its 18" by 24" windows on either side was completed, the pond was filled, creating an underwater observatory. The observatory was entered by a hatch in the roof. This observatory was constructed at relatively low cost and is replicable by interested amateurs who would like to study the organisms of small ponds.

Another interesting observatory/blind is the "brushpile" that Edwin Way Teale constructed to serve as a writing studio in summer and as an observatory for studying insects in particular, as well as other wildlife. It consisted of a wooden frame with a writing shelf built in that was then covered with brush. Teale could see out through the interstices but much of the insect life took over the brushpile as living space, providing many opportunities for prolonged observation and even photography.

USING A BLIND

Using a blind usually involves much more preparation than plopping a blind at a site, climbing inside, and waiting for some action. Most birds and mammals have a good mental image of the territory they are most active in and treat with great suspicion any new object that suddenly appears in that territory. They will avoid the area near such an object until they have habituated to its presence—that is, come to a feeling that the object is harmless and now a new part of the normal appearance of their territory or home range.

Of course some creatures are inordinately curious and may come around the object warily to read it out and even to challenge its presence—vocally, at least. Such was the case where a friend of mine set up a tent on his back hill for the children to sleep out in. He inadvertently put it right on the trail a local gray fox regularly used. Its challenging barks gave the youngsters a chilling experience. I was called in to resolve the mystery of what was causing such harassment to innocent children. A night in the tent and a morning reconnaissance of the area for tracks and scat quickly solved the mystery.

The proper procedure for setting up most blinds involves putting out the blind at least a week to ten days prior to actually occupying it in order to give the animals of the area time to accept it as a harmless part of their surroundings. You must take extreme caution if you set up a blind near a nest or den where human presence could drive the parents away. And if severe stress is at all apparent the blind should be quickly removed. No reputable wildlife observer will knowingly put stress on an animal that will hinder its reproductive activity. As suggested earlier, blinds may be constructed little by little over time or they may be erected in an area at a distance from the den or nest and slowly moved a little closer each day until a proper distance has been achieved.

I spent hours observing a fox den from behind a blind made of hay bales left in the field at the edge of which the den was located. Each day we moved the bales a few feet closer. We began about 75 yards from the den and ended up within 30 yards so that we could not only see the pups at play but also often hear their vocalizations. The adults almost always approached from the brushy field rather than get into the open hayfield so we were seldom detected unless the breezes were from the wrong quarter.

Getting to a blind without disturbing the wildlife for long periods can be a problem. It is often resolved by getting help from a friend. Few birds or mammals can count. If two people approach a blind but one drops off while the other continues on and out of sight, the wildlife generally perceives only that human danger has come and gone and after a reasonable period of caution will return to normal activity. Otherwise, the successful observer will probably have to be up and into the blind before first light and remain until after dark, or if he is making nocturnal observations, enter before sundown and remain until after sunup.

Nocturnal observations of prolonged behavior normally have to be carried out using illumination enhancement that doesn't disturb the creatures. For many species this means using red filtered light. Red is a color that many monochromatic-perceiving animals don't register well but which humans do. Battery-powered floodlights with red filters can be used, or under ideal conditions, an area can be wired to an electrical system to light up a large area. In England a whole experimental woodland was so illuminated to allow extensive nocturnal observations.

Conditioning Yourself
for Time in a Blind

Spending prolonged periods in a blind can be both physically and mentally trying. Space is cramped to begin with and the observer has to be as quiet and unrestive as possible in order not to raise suspicions of the animals to be watched. Intense periods of animal activity that make the waiting all worthwhile tend to be alternated with extensive periods during which little is happening; yet the observer must remain alert and ready for the next period of activity. Time in a blind is time when you find out as much about yourself as about the creatures you came to watch.

There is of course usually note taking to be done and elaborated on. This will take up some time and some people take along reading material. There is always the hazard that when concentrating on notes or reading you may miss the beginning of the next period of activity. To avoid this you have to develop the skill of intermittent attention; that is, concentrating on the near at hand for a short block of time, then quickly scanning the field of observation to note any changes, then back to the near at hand, and so forth, until something new demands attention.

There is a great tendency to fall asleep and this can mean considerable losses of observation. Like the big fish that got away, the most amazing activity happens if you doze off. In order to rest both mind and body yet remain alert, it helps to learn to induce the Relaxation Response—a group of physiological responses that produces most of the advantages of sleep but not the lack of alertness. It is the type of result received from meditation. However, as Dr. Herbert Benson explains in his book *The Relaxation Response,* one does not have to be an Eastern mystic or a believer in any particular religious sect to achieve the response. To satisfy your curiosity you may want to read the book, but the essence of the procedure follows. It takes a little practice but it works and is very useful for keeping relaxed and alert over the long hours.

Your blind is already the quiet place that is recommended for inducing the response, so adjust your sitting position so that you are as comfortable as possible. Close your eyes or focus a fixed stare on a distant object. Now relax all your muscles beginning with your toes and working up the body to your face, then maintain the total muscle relaxation. Now concentrate on your breathing. Breathe through the nose and become aware of your breathing, saying silently to yourself: In... Out... In... Out or One... Two... One... Two... Continue breathing easily and naturally while focusing on the two words. Distracting thoughts will keep invading. Don't worry about them—just put them aside by refocusing on the breathing words.

Continue in this fashion for ten to twenty minutes. When you have finished, continue to sit quietly for several minutes more. Don't stand up for a few minutes, because if you have maintained the passive relaxed attitude, keeping distracting thoughts at a bare minimum or excluding them entirely, the changes characteristic of the relaxation response will have occurred—oxygen consumption will have gone down, alpha brain waves will have increased, and blood lactate (a waste product of metabolism in skeletal muscles) will have decreased. These are all symptoms of the restful state. You must let your body processes return to normal before launching into activity again.

The Relaxation Response reduces anxiety and tension induced by the cramped quarters and incipient boredom. This in turn increases alertness, making for better observation. With practice, the Relaxation Response comes on more rapidly. Try it; you'll like it! Muscles that are cramped from being in one position are another matter and they will not be automatically relaxed by the Relaxation Response; indeed, they will have to be uncramped before you can achieve it. The muscles need regular working and the blood needs to circulate through and around them to bring in oxygen and remove lactic acids and other wastes. Of course in the blind you can't do active exercises to achieve circulation and muscular activity. The answer lies in isometric activities, that is, the working of muscles against each other with little motion. For example, if you curl the fingers of each hand, hook them together in front of you, and then pull each hand against the other, you are exercising the muscles of the hands and arms with little motion—an isometric exercise. This is not the place for an extensive listing of isometric exercises but there are a number of relatively inexpensive volumes available in most bookstores or at your local library. It pays to invest in one and select a regimen of activities that can be accomplished under the conditions of your blind.

If you are armed with the Relaxation Response and some good

isometric exercises, your time in the blind will be much more tolerable and rewarding. Of course, other bodily functions can also be demanding and it is not inappropriate to include an empty bleach bottle or plastic milk container as a temporary holding tank.

FURTHER READING

BAUFLE, J.M., and J.P. VARIN. *Photographing Wildlife*. New York: Oxford University Press, 1972.

BENSON, DR. HERBERT. *The Relaxation Response*. New York: William Morrow Co./Avon Books, 1975.

HANENKRAT, FRANK T. *Wildlife Watchers Handbook*. New York: Winchester Press, 1977.

LESLIE, CLARE WALKER. *Nature Drawing: A Tool for Learning*. Englewood Cliffs, N.J.: Prentice-Hall, Inc., 1980.

OSOLINSKI, STAN. *Nature Photography: A Guide to Better Outdoor Pictures*. Englewood Cliffs, N.J.: Prentice-Hall, Inc., 1981.

ROSSMAN, ISADORE, and VICTOR OBECK. *Isometrics: The Static Way to Physical Fitness*. New York: Stravon Educational Press, 1966.

STONE, C.L. "Amateur Scientist," *Scientific American*, 277, no. 4 (October 1972), 114–18.

SWEDBERG, JACK. "The Blind Approach," *Massachusetts Wildlife*, 31, no. 4 (September-October 1980), 10–14.

SOURCES

BLINDS AND TREE STANDS
- Baker Mfg. Company
  Box 1003
  Valdosta, Georgia 31601
  (*seat climbing stands*)
- Braden Wire and Metal Products, Inc.
  1310 West Laurel Street
  P.O. Box 5067
  San Antonio, Texas 76201
  (*box blinds with or without towers*)
- Hunters Equipment Mfg. Company
  P.O. Box 5254
  1220 South Chadbourne
  San Angelo, Texas 76901
  (*portable hunting stands*)
- East Enterprises, Inc.
  2208 Mallory Place
  Monroe, Louisiana 71201
  (*portable hunting stands*)

CAMOUFLAGE CLOTHING
- Gander Mountain, Inc.
  P.O. Box 248
  Wilmot, Wisconsin 53192
- Martin Archery
  Rt. 5, Box 27
  Walla Walla, Washington 99362
- Ranger Mfg. Company
  P.O. Box 3676
  Augusta, Georgia 30904

CHAPTER 6

LURES AND
LIVE TRAPS

IN ORDER TO GET OBSERVATIONS, you may want to attract wildlife to your observation post—be it a wilderness blind or your home viewing window. In order to catch animals for temporary observation or individual marking, baits and lures are also valuable. Baits and lures basically appeal to the most fundamental drives of animals—food, water, sex, and curiosity. Consequently they must be used thoughtfully and judiciously, not indiscriminately.

BAITING

The most widely used attractant is food. Everyone who puts up a bird feeder in winter is using this strategy. In fact, backyard feeders point up the joys and problems of baiting in wildlife. Once bait stations are put out they must either be very temporary or maintained continuously, at least through periods of food scarcity. Most species are opportunistic and when they find a good thing in the form of a bait station they may become heavily dependent upon it, losing some familiarity with the realities of food gathering in their normal territory.

The impact of this can be serious for some species. Baiting geese to observation areas with grain has kept whole flocks from migrating properly and subsequent freeze-ups have brought about abnormal mortality. Evening grosbeaks will move into a neighborhood feeder and confine their activity to flying from a nearby roost tree to the feeder and back. Widespread backyard feeding has also contributed to the northward extension of southern species such as cardinals and titmice. Without the supplemental food these birds would not survive a harsh winter in any numbers.

Feeding stations also tend to bring about abnormal concentrations of various species. Depending upon the nature of the species, concentration may spark greater amounts of aggressive behavior resulting in a greater amount of stress, scars, and occasional mutilations. Concentrations of some species also may create a feeding station for predators. One winter, a local nature center feeding station regularly attracted eighteen gray squirrels. A red-tailed hawk moved in and by spring only one pair of squirrels remained.

Such potential consequences must be considered before getting involved in any baiting program, whether it is a backyard planting for wildlife, a bird feeder, or a bait station for a permanent or temporary blind. Some fascinating behavioral studies have been done using regular baiting to bring the desired species close enough for observation and get them somewhat habituated to the human presence. Jane Goodall was able to observe much chimpanzee behavior by baiting with bananas near her base camp and Japanese scientists studied several generations of freeranging macaque monkeys baited to observation blinds by potatoes and grain. In each of these cases the scientists also learned that the baiting altered the normal behavior of the population!

Having explored some of the concerns associated with baiting, let's explore some of the materials that can be used primarily as short-term attractants. For most of the studies the amateur will make, it is best to bait for relatively short periods of time and then change the site or temporarily stop baiting.

Foods

Some foods are attractive to a number of species; others appeal only to specific animals. Thus choice of a food bait will depend upon your objectives.

If you wish to attract a specific species you may have to do some testing on your own. After checking the literature, or your own prior observations, you will want to check the attractiveness of certain seasonally preferred foods or even some completely foreign foods that might have some appeal. To do this, put out bait in small stations and clear the area around the bait so that the taker will have to leave tracks. You will, then, by reading the tracks, be able to determine if the species you seek is strongly attracted to any of the bait. In fact, that may open up some exciting new avenues of wildlife watching.

Some baits have become quite standard because of their proven attractiveness to certain species or groups of species. Rolled oats and peanut butter is a standard for many small mammals such as mice, shrews, and ground squirrels. The odor of the peanut butter seems to be the major attractant. Some people add melted suet and raisins to the mix but this is not essential. Indeed, peanut butter alone is often sufficient. If you are putting out a number of bait stations, the rolled oats/peanut butter mix can be blended with salad oil to a looser consistency such as that of toothpaste and dispensed from a plastic squeeze bottle such as is frequently used for catsup and mustard. In hot weather oily baits can become rancid rather easily; keep unused bait refrigerated.

Commercial canned dog and cat foods will often lure in predators and omnivores like raccoons, skunks, foxes, and mink. Cat foods with a strong fishy odor often are the most successful, for the fish oil acts as a long-distance advertisement. You may also be surprised at the array of insects brought to your bait station.

Road kills can be collected and put out for some predators and scavengers. Crows, vultures, opossum, and others come for such offerings.

Alcohol is not a human exclusive. A number of birds and mammals, as well as a host of insects, are attracted to fermented fruit. Visit your grocer's produce area and ask for over-ripe fruit. Mush it together and put it out. Pears and bananas are prime fruits for this, but cherries, plums, strawberries, and other members of the rose family are also good; citrus fruits are less useful. And it is amazing how many animals that have never had an opportunity to see or taste a wild banana are attracted to this fruit. Many finicky newly captive creatures that have refused all other foods have started feeding when offered bananas.

Moths can be attracted with a fermented mix of stale beer, molasses, and over-ripe fruit painted on tree bark. Set up a route through the local wood-lot, painting with this mix; then visit at night with a flashlight and observe the local noctuid moths that have been attracted. Different species will show up at different hours throughout the night.

Suet is a regular attractant for insect-eating birds such as woodpeckers, nuthatches, chickadees, starlings, and others and it is also an attractant to small mammals and dogs if placed where they can get to it. Suet can be used throughout the year. However, in summer it should be checked regularly and if it becomes rancid it should be immediately removed.

Some birds and insects (such as butterflies and moths) are attracted to sugar-water feeders. These are available commercially primarily as hummingbird feeders and are most commonly seen in the western United States where these birds are plentiful. However, orioles, grosbeaks, tanagers, and some warblers are also attracted to the solution, as are some sphinx moths and several butterflies.

The solution is generally one part sugar to four parts water. In this dilution the refined sugar doesn't seem to be too harmful although a prolonged diet of this mix seems questionable. Some people substitute honey for the sugar because it contains a simpler sugar. Others suggest that possible impurities in some strains of honey may be just as potentially harmful as the refined cane sugar. The key is not to use this bait so continuously that the wildlife becomes overly dependent on it as a primary food source.

For some species a live bait is used. This becomes a mix between a food, scent, and curiosity bait, since the animal's motion, calls, scent, and food potential all attract. The live animal is placed in an enclosure where it can be seen but not caught. In some cases the living lure is just tied out where the animal to be baited in sees it but is not put off by an enclosure. This has been a centuries-old standard way of luring in birds of prey using pigeons or starlings. For years, waterfowlers used captive, wing-clipped birds to lure in wild migrants. In fact, in the Northeast, many of the year-round resident mallards and Canada geese are the offspring of such living decoys.

Use of living decoys raises some ethical problems. What kind of psychological stress is the live bait under? What are the chances the bait will actually be killed? What are the chances of learning something significant about the animal baited in? Can this knowledge possibly justify the stress or sacrifice of the bait animal?

Aquatic animals can be baited into an area as easily as land creatures. Fishermen for millenia have used the technique of chumming, that is, tossing cut up pieces of fish overboard to attract in schools of other fish. Actually, in addition to fish, worms, insects, ground liver, and other entrails can be used for chumming as can commercial trout pellets. Fish will learn to come to chumming sites on a regular basis if it is done on a regular schedule.

Joining the fish in their own habitat using a snorkel or SCUBA system gives the greatest opportunity for watching fish behavior. Many species will learn to take bits of food from your hand. There are relatively few hazards from baiting fish in fresh water but things are different in the sea. Barracudas, sharks, moray eels, and other potentially dangerous species will come for the bait as well as the smaller, safer species. If they do, make no attempt to withhold the bait. Hand it over gracefully and move calmly out of the area.

Scent Lures

Scent lures are most effective with mammals and some insects. Mammals gain a great deal of their information about the world from odors and thus can be influenced by special scents. The same is true of many insect species. By contrast, birds have an extremely limited sense of smell. Snakes, turtles, amphibians, and fish may make good use of odors but we know relatively little at this point about how to use this sense to lure them to observation points except by chumming (see the discussion of food baits). Actually with chumming it is probably the scent that is the greatest lure with the fish following towards increasing concentration of the chemical scent to the actual food.

Many species of mammals have scent glands which they use to mark vegetation, earth mounds, rocks, or other prominent features in their territories. A number also use their urine and feces to create scent markers. All these bodily excretions are rich in chemicals that reveal the general physical and sexual condition of the maker to the educated nose. Such scent posts are readily investigated by other members of the species and often by other species as well. Wildlife watchers can take advantage of this curiosity about scents to create artificial scent posts to attract wildlife and guide them to blinds and other viewing areas.

Animal scents can be gathered by cutting the urine-filled bladder and/or scent glands from road kills. Some people find such collecting messy and distasteful, and they can turn to scent lures available from trapping supply houses. Scents should be used very sparingly; a little goes a long way.

In addition to animal-generated scents there are some plant scents that have a powerful attraction to some groups of mammals. Catnip, for instance, is not only an exciting scent to house cats but to most members of the cat family, large and small. Cougars can get the same devil-may-care, spaced-out look, and kittenish behavior in its presence as any alley cat. Valerian has a similar attraction to members of the dog family. Anise is reportedly a favorite of bears. And, while not a plant, fish oils will attract many of the mustelids, that is, the weasel family.

Many insects communicate by means of pheromones. These are chemical signals produced by the animals. Ants lay them down wherever they go, producing a trail they can follow to get back to their home. Other insects use pheromones to announce their presence to distant members of the opposite sex. Place a ripe female silk moth (cecropia, luna, polyphemus, or related species) in a screened enclosure and before long males will appear and cluster about the cage. Increasingly, scientists are using knowledge of such sexual pheromones to attract certain pest species to traps, species such as Japanese beetles and gypsy moths. There is still room for much more work on the use of pheromones to attract specific species.

Butterflies are beautiful but many species are attracted to odors that are to us less than beautiful, such as manure, carrion, and rotten and fermenting fruit. Bait stations of such material will attract them in. Many species like to gather around mud puddles. Creating and maintaining artificial puddles can pull these in. A number of these species are wary and won't allow close approach and observation, but if you use these lures and a blind you can watch them for extended periods.

Luring animals basically involves catering to one or more of their basic needs. Whereas food and scents are the most frequently used, there are others that can be quite effective. Water is a potent one, particularly in areas or seasons where it is scarce. Bird baths have been garden fixtures for years, attracting local birds to drink and bathe, and these can be elaborated on in various ways. Prefabricated or home-built pools with a recycling pump to provide running water and the sound of dripping water will increase the attractiveness of water not only to birds but also to local mammals and amphibians.

During winter when water is frozen, a heated water supply that uses a standard poultry water heater can be a powerful attractant. In dry climates any water supply becomes a wildlife magnet. Indeed, in desert regions the wildlife is normally widely dispersed but during the hot, dry season it becomes much more concentrated in the area around water holes. In desert areas evaporation of surface water is a problem. To counter this a device known as the gallinaceous guzzler was developed to provide water for game birds, but it is used by many small species. It consists of a broad concrete apron to catch any rain and drain it into a covered water storage tank with access ramps leading down to water level so the wildlife can get down to drink but the sun cannot penetrate to evaporate the supply.

Nesting materials will lure in some birds and mammals during the breeding season. Yarn, horsehair, cotton, and similar materials hung out on bushes will interest certain species. Careful observation of those that come to use your offerings will lead you to their nesting or denning sites where perhaps you can make further observations from a blind.

Den boxes and bird houses are also attractants for some species. With a little modification, they can be useful in observation. Insert glass or a one-way mirror in one side and hinge the normal wooden side so that it can just close over the glass and be opened for viewing. If you use one-way glass you will need interior illumination in order to see. A flashlight bulb and batteries mounted inside the roof with an external switch will do nicely. Such modified bird boxes are often used by other than birds—flying squirrels, wasps, tree frogs, and others may end up as observable tenants.

Additional modifications keep out unwanted users such as gray squirrels which enlarge the openings and starlings and house sparrows which, though interesting in themselves, drive away other possible tenants. A metal flashing around the entrance hole, spray painted to a dull finish, will help discourage the squirrels, while a pivoted "paddle" (see Figure 6.1) can be used to close the entrance early in the season when starlings and house sparrows are starting their nesting. It is opened when the preferred species migrate back a few weeks later. By then the unwanted guests are usually well established in their domestic chores elsewhere. The paddle can also be manipulated to make the nest box a trap to catch and mark the occupants for individual identification.

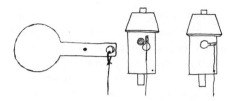

Figure 6.1. Left, door-closing "paddle"; center, entry hole open; right, closed.

The following list gives some basic nest box dimensions and entrance hole sizes for specific wildlife:

1. *4" × 4" × 8" basic box set 4 ft. to 6 ft. above the ground*
   1" hole centered 6" from the floor (house wren)
   1-⅛" hole centered 6" from the floor (chickadee)
   1-½" hole centered 6" from the floor (tree swallow; Carolina wren; bluebird; violet-green swallow; flying squirrel; deer mice)
   1-¼" hole centered 6" from the floor (nuthatch; downy woodpecker; Bewick's wren; tufted titmouse)
2. *6" × 6" × 15" basic box set 12 ft. to 25 feet above the ground*
   1-½" hole centered 8" from the floor (hairy woodpecker; flying squirrel; deer mice)
   2" hole centered 8" from the floor (crested flycatcher; red-headed woodpecker)
3. *7" × 7" × 18" basic box set 8 ft. to 20 feet above the ground*
   2-½" hole centered 14" from the floor (flicker; saw-whet owl)
4. *10" × 10" × 24" basic box with elliptical hole 4" wide × 3" high set 20" from the floor and 8 ft. to 20 feet above the ground*
   (wood duck; sparrow hawk [kestrel]; screech owl; gray squirrel)

Old nail kegs with the opening partly boarded over and set horizontally in a tree crotch often attract raccoons, opossums, gray squirrels, and in some locales, even fishers.

An interesting artificial den and observation box uses the tendency of a number of species to utilize woodchuck burrows and drainage pipes. Build into a slope, as Figure 6.2 shows; the cover of the den box can be removed to reveal a glass roof, thus providing the opportunity to observe the occupant. A plunger can be used to block the pipe and confine the animal to the den box. The occupant can also be reached by lifting out the glass and can then be individually marked and released if

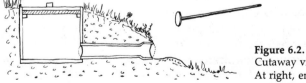

Figure 6.2.
Cutaway view of artificial den box.
At right, entry closer.

desired. This den device has proved useful in observing cottontail rabbits, woodchucks, weasels, skunks, opossums, and raccoons. Sometimes the den is used only by transients. If you are lucky an animal will use the den to rear a family and this can provide many hours of interesting and valuable observation. Beware of the temptation to observe the den box too frequently if there is a family using it because the activity may induce the mother to move or abandon the young. Use the den in conjunction with a temporary or permanent blind for maximum results.

CALLS

Animal calls are another potent lure. These may be the territorial songs of a species, mating calls, mobbing calls, or the calls of an injured or restrained animal. These calls stimulate aggressive, sexual, or curiosity behavior in other animals and tend to be effective lures only at certain times of the year. At other times these calls may be totally ignored.

Bird watchers have long used a sibilant pish . . . pish . . . pish call to lure small birds out of thick brush for observation. Another effective call is a distressed squeaking sound made by kissing the back of the hand or the side of the index finger. The pishing call seems to have a stimulation to the bird's curiosity but both calls will induce "mobbing" behavior in birds, that is, a number of birds of the same species or even of different species will come together to vocally protest and even to physically harass a potential large predator such as an owl or crow. Pish and squeak calls work best during the rearing season and are less effective at other times. A little device known as an Audubon Bird Call makes the squeak call mechanically with rosin and wood, but it is generally effective. It was developed from a device used by hunters in Italy where songbirds are hunted.

The P.S. Olt Company manufactures a line of mechanical devices that simulate the sound of a rabbit or rodent in distress to lure in predators such as foxes, weasels, and the like. These devices are quite useful but they take some practice and skill to create a realistic sound. Squeals lasting about ten seconds with thirty- to sixty-second intervals between them usually work best. The sound appeals strongly to a predator's curiosity. Once the sound has been perceived the animal will move toward the source of the sound, often circling, to see what is happening. You may not even be aware of its presence unless you are a very alert observer, therefore, remain as still as possible in order not to alarm it too soon. To bring the predator in very close your sound must be very realistic; there is considerable difference between gun range and good observation range. April, May, and August are the best months for calling and the best time is the three hours before dark. If you don't get results from your calling at a given site within ten to fifteen minutes, move on.

Actually all sorts of devices have been constructed by hunters over the millenia to call in game. Indians used birch bark megaphones to simulate the mating call of the moose and a wide variety of ingenious contraptions have been invented to imitate the various calls of the wild turkey. It is fun to create your own devices for other animals' calls but it is a real art to make the sounds seem real; and now again modern technology has stepped into the breach. Some companies are now marketing tapes and records that can be played on portable machines in the field and which produce sounds that are much more convincing than those made by people using other forms of mechanical calling devices. Similarly, bird watchers often take tape recordings of bird song afield and play it. Males, and sometimes females, on the territory where the song is played will be attracted to discover the intruder. Thus the birder gets a good look at the bird and can make some notes about territorial behavior and aggressive displays.

At first glance the technique seems harmless enough and it is effective. However, where birders are plentiful and bird-watching sites limited, the breeding behavior of the birds may be disrupted by overly frequent responses to the taped calls. It is the aggregate effect of using the tapes that is harmful rather than the technique itself. The responsible wildlife observer will be alert to this and refrain from using tapes where wildlife watchers are abundant.

Taped calls can be useful in frog watching also. Frogs are very sensitive to vibration and as one moves about the marsh or pond edge the frogs nearest by stop calling until they feel sure all is well. Once you reach a point you feel is good for observing, let silence reign for a short while, then imitate the frog calls either vocally or play your tape. This will lull the nearby animals into thinking all is safe again and they will take up the chorus. Once they are calling again, switch off the tape and locate the singers by ear. It should then be relatively easy to put your light on them.

TRAPPING

In order to individually mark animals or to check their weight, sex, or external parasites it is necessary to capture them. Trapping and handling animals undoubtedly stresses many of them, although some become trap junkies and are recaptured over and over again. We must be sure that all efforts are made to confine the animals for as short a period as possible and to be sure that the trap provides reasonable comfort and protection from exposure to the elements.

Live traps for birds and mammals are available commercially from several firms and come in a range of sizes suitable for different species. (Addresses of some of the more widely known companies are provided at the end of the chapter.) However, the amateur wildlife observer may prefer to build his/her own live traps and thus this section is devoted to some of the simpler, relatively inexpensive models.

Simpler peoples who live by hunting have developed some ingenious traps that can easily be modified for our uses. Bag nets and constriction traps are useful for animals that use runways (see Figure 6.3). The trap is set in a runway and the animal driven along its pathway system until it runs into the trap. The animal is quickly removed, processed, and released. A constriction trap is essentially an open wicker cone used in a travel-way or placed in the entrance of a burrow. The animal must be caught before it backs out. The bag net is made such that its rim has a projection that can be stuck in the ground to keep the rim erect. A long net bag is attached. As the animal goes through the rim it becomes entangled in the bag. It, too, demands quick follow-up to prevent the animal from freeing itself, but it gives more leeway than the constriction trap. Rim size and net mesh must be proportional to the animal you seek to trap.

Funnel Traps

Funnel traps have been useful for catching a number of creatures from fish to birds and mammals. Basically funnel traps are simply an enclosure with a funnel entrance that allows easy admittance but requires either sheer luck or high intelligence to find the exit (Figure 6.4). To most people, commercial minnow traps are the most familiar example of this type. These are simply a wire cylinder with a wire cone projecting into each end. The fish enter for bait placed in the cylinder but don't readily find their way out. Such minnow traps can easily be constructed at home. The advantage of funnel traps is that they are multiple capture units.

Rectangular funnel traps have been useful for capturing ground feeding birds and a circular funnel trap has been successful with usually wily birds such as magpies, jays, and crows.

Figure 6.3.
Left, constriction trap; right, bag net trap.

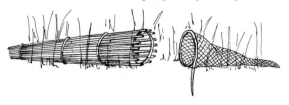

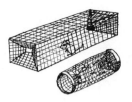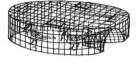

Figure 6.4.
Representative funnel traps.

A funnel trap originally designed for starlings has proved very effective in capturing weasels, animals known to be notoriously difficult to live trap. It is baited with live starlings. Researchers Marsh and Clark caught twenty-seven weasels in one month using this trap (see Figure 6.5).

Traps such as the funnel traps that are left set without attendance for many hours or even a day or so are very apt to become bait for larger predators as was the case with the starling trap that catches weasels effectively. It often becomes necessary to put live traps inside larger mesh wire enclosures or other protecting devices to assure that the animal you want alive doesn't become a meal for another species that robs your trap.

Pit Traps

Perhaps the simplest trap for small mammals, amphibians, reptiles, and beetles that the amateur can make is the pit trap (Figure 6.6). For this a can, jar, or plastic juice container that is at least three times taller than wide is buried so that the rim is at ground level. Non-glass containers are preferred because holes can be punched in the bottom so that any rainwater that might enter can drain away. Cover the trap with shingles or floor tiles that are raised off the ground on two-inch blocks. Small mammals, amphibians, reptiles, and insects seeking shelter will go under the covers and fall into the pits. They will be unable to leap out or climb out if the pit traps are of proper dimensions.

Such pit traps can be set permanently in place on a study area and used intermittently. This means they must have some type of easily removable cover. If you use cans of the proper dimensions they can be covered with the plastic covers used to recover open catfood cans or coffee cans. Otherwise you can cut wooden disks the size of the inside diameter of your trap and glue these to masonite squares a little larger

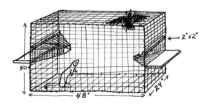

Figure 6.5.
Multi-capture weasel trap.

81

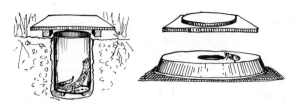

Figure 6.6. Left, standard pit trap with shelter cover. Right top, upside-down cover for closing pit traps when they are not being tended. Right bottom, cake pan modified as pit trap for beetles (screening makes bottom).

than the diameter of the disks. The disks are inserted into the top of the traps when they are not in use. Small animals in the study area become accustomed to using the shelters for grooming, eating, and other functions. Indeed, they should be inspected from time to time for scat to see who is using the area. When you next decide to trap you need only go around and remove the pit covers. Trapping success will usually be even higher than when the traps are freshly put out.

If you want to get fancy, you create what is in essence a double pit; that is, you get a can that is just enough larger in diameter than your trap so that the trap will slip inside it. This can has both ends removed and is put in the hole first. The trap is then slipped inside. The advantage to this is that when you remove the trap to get at your animal the earth does not fall back into the hole, making it difficult to put the trap back properly flush with the ground. It is a bit more work initially, but if you use a pit trap quadrat with any frequency it is worth the saved aggravation.

The pit trap has been elaborated on in several ways to make it more efficient (and more costly). One of the better adaptations uses a gallon jar and a wooden box (see Figure 6.7). The animals enter, slip on the trap door, and drop into the jar which should be provided with some nesting material. The jar lid is cut to provide an opening for the trap doors.

Figure 6.7.
Deluxe pit trap.

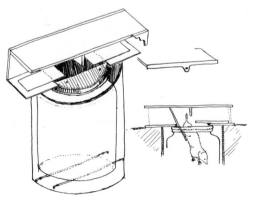

Notice that the jar is set inside a stovepipe sleeve that functions in the same way as the second can mentioned previously.

Pit traps are often used in combination with a drift fence. When animals encounter a barrier such as the fence, they tend to turn and move along it in search of an opening. In this case the opening they find is directly over a pit trap. For amphibians and reptiles the drift fence is usually made of ½" or ¼" mesh hardware cloth set in a shallow trench and heeled in. Straight stretches of fence are usually set at angles to one another and an opening and pit trap are located at the angle. With small mammals the fence may include funnel-shaped aprons that end up at the pit trap or some other type of live trap. A snake trap can be made that combines the drift fence with a form of constriction trap. Drift fences with traps are particularly useful during the times when a species' young of the year are dispersing. In general they tend to capture far more juveniles than resident adults.

Mechanical Traps

An old favorite live trap for small mammals utilizes a mousetrap, a can, and some hardware cloth (Figure 6.8). The trap is fastened to the can with a stovebolt and the hardware cloth is wired to the top of the trap fall. The trap is baited and set just as it would be normally. However, when sprung, the fall carries the hardware cloth up to close the opening of the can rather than hit and kill the animal. Tall juice cans or two-pound coffee cans are best to use because the added length reduces the chances of the animal's being catapulted forcefully against the back of the can by the closing mesh. I like to use cans that take the plastic covers that come with catfood and coffee. I cut out both ends and use the plastic cover for one end. This creates a resilient back wall and an easy entrance to remove the trapped animal. It also means visiting the trap regularly for given adequate time many animals can chew their way through the plastic.

A new trap design that is inexpensive and quick to build and that can also produce multiple captures, uses polyvinyl chloride water pipe as its base (Figure 6.9). It can be modified for various sizes, but for our description we use a nine-inch piece with a 1.5-inch inside diameter. A piece of aluminum tube with an outside diameter of 1.5-inches and a length of 1.5-inches is cut and two stainless steel fins are attached to it.

Figure 6.8.
Modified snap trap live trap.

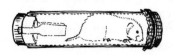

Figure 6.9.
Squeeze-entry live trap.

These are cut from .003 shim stock and are 1″ × 3″ and are bent so they will just touch lightly against each other when riveted in place on the aluminum. Two inch-long cuts are made opposite each other in one end of the piping to provide a little ease when the aluminum with its fins are fitted into that end. The other end of the pipe is covered with wire mesh and held in place with a plastic rim cut from a piece of larger size pipe. With some organization it is possible to produce ten to fifteen of these traps in an hour.

Several good designs for catching animals at burrows have come into being in recent years. One of the simplest involves making a long rectangle of hardware cloth bound with poultry clips (Figure 6.10). The trap door is long and slanting and bent at the end so that it lies flat on the floor when closed. The trap is set into the burrow opening by digging some earth away. When the animal emerges from the burrow it squeezes under the door to get out. Once it is past the door, the door settles down to the floor of the trap and it is very difficult to get a nose under it to raise it and slip away. Indeed, the animal is usually standing on the door holding it down.

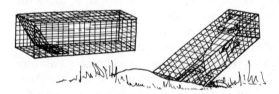

Figure 6.10.
Burrow-entrance live trap.

The so-called Gens trap (Figure 6.11) uses a metal cylinder and a concave door that lies almost flat on the floor of the trap when it is open. A 14-gauge wire soldered around the opening acts as a door stop and a hinge pin for the door. The other end of the trap is modified to take a screw top canning jar lid with a hardware cloth insert. The trap is

Figure 6.11.
Gens live trap. Right, detail of doorway.

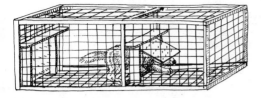

Figure 6.12. Multi-capture trap for mid-sized mammals. Note bar that prevents doors from swinging both ways and rough surface on door to discourage scratching and gnawing.

shoved in the burrow. As the animal tries to exit and skids around on the smooth metal, it kicks the door shut behind it. As it rests, its own weight holds the door shut. This trap is most effective when set at angles of 20° to 60° but it will also work from vertical to horizontal, although with somewhat less success. The advantage of the trap is that it has no locking or tripping mechanisms to jam.

To mark a litter for individual recognition it is desirable to catch the entire litter at once. The trap illustrated in Figure 6.12 has been effective in catching coyote litters and with appropriate modifications could prove useful with other animals as well. One caution: Parents won't approach the den while the trap is in place and this may result in the youngsters' going hungry for excessive periods of time. There is also a high likelihood that the parents will move the young to a new den shortly after you mark the young and remove the trap. This may do more to disrupt your observations than enhance them. Using a trap such as this should not be undertaken without full consideration of the consequences and alternatives.

Drop-door box traps of various patterns have been made and used for generations. Several designs and triggering devices are illustrated in Figure 6.13 for those who wish to avoid the costs involved with commercially made box traps.

A number of turtle species are fairly easy to trap for marking by using a floating trap (Figure 6.14). This may either be baited or used baitless as a sunning spot. A wood or styrofoam frame is made that will float readily. A cage of hardware cloth or fish netting is attached to this frame. A fringe of finishing nails is then driven in around the inside of the frame. Turtles climb onto the float and enter the inner pool either for the bait or by accident. Once they are inside, the nails prevent them

Figure 6.13. Three box trap triggering strategies. Circle details "figure four" triggering device of right-hand setup.

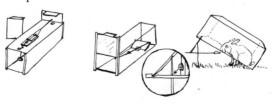

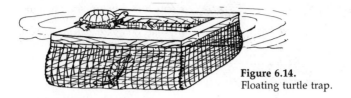

Figure 6.14.
Floating turtle trap.

from climbing out until you remove them. Don't forget that it takes energy to swim about, even for a turtle, and that they too get tired. If they are not removed from the trap in a day or so they will drown.

Nets

Some animals can be captured directly with nets. Many are blinded by bright lights and will remain immobile to be netted. Netting also works for hole-nesting species. Most will flush from the nest if the tree is pounded. However, if they see obstructions they stay where they are. This can be remedied by using a clear plastic net. This can be made by putting plastic bags in the equivalent of an embroidery hoop. Indeed, embroidery hoops can be modified for this use or else metal rings are constructed. The rings with plastic bag are pivot-mounted to a U-shaped brace attached to a handle. A telescoping aluminum handle is most convenient. A string is rigged just behind the mouth of the bag as shown in Figure 6.15. The net is placed over the hole, the occupant flushed, and the string pulled to constrict the bag until the animal can be removed.

Birds and bats are frequently caught with "mist nets" that are made of very fine but tough threads. These have netting that is loose and they are long-pouched. Flying animals do not detect the mesh until they fly into it and find themselves entangled in the mesh pocket. The more they struggle, the more entangled they become. Removing animals from mist nets takes skill and dexterity; the longer the animal is held during the process the greater the stress on it. Mist nets are very useful but because of the skills needed to use them properly, a permit is required. Anyone wishing to use mist nets should apprentice under an experienced bird bander.

Professional wildlife biologists use nets in a variety of other ways, all of which demand special training and experience that is not easily acquired by amateur wildlife watchers.

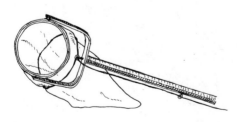

Figure 6.15.
Clear plastic bag net and drawstring.

RESTRAINING DEVICES
AND TECHNIQUES

Catching the animal is only the beginning. The animal will need to be handled for marking, which can be traumatic for both the animal and the handler—but always more so for the animal.

Gloves

Using gloves may protect you from being bitten or clawed but the gloves will also lower your sensitivity to the pressure you are exerting and cause you to handle the animal much more roughly than you may intend. This must be carefully guarded against. I generally prefer to work bare-handed and risk the biting and clawing. This gives me an extra agility that usually compensates for the limited protection of the glove.

Constriction Devices

A constriction cone is a useful device for restraining many species. As can be seen from Figure 6.16, the animal moves away from the trap or holding cage and down into the cone. Drop bars are put in place to prevent the animal from backing out. It can then be closely observed and marked through the mesh. When you are finished the drop bar is removed and the animal encouraged to back out and run off. Blowing gently into the face of a reluctant creature will usually get action.

Be careful, gentle, and patient in any such maneuvering because handling puts a great deal of stress on any wild creature. Stress is not good for the animal's health and it may cause its behavior to be substantially altered for some time. Some species are far more accepting of such handling than are others.

For work that requires anesthesia you will need special equipment and materials, and you will have to get training and prescriptions from a veterinarian or professional biologist. All use of anesthetics or im-

Figure 6.16. Two constriction devices. Left, to be used with varying-sized animals, depending on where divider is placed. Right, cloth is placed over trap mouth before door is opened; once animal is in cone, stuff cloth in to hold animal in place.

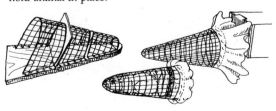

mobilizing drugs involve considerable risk to the animal. These risks should never be taken lightly or without a clear-cut, defensible purpose.

Choke Poles

For handling larger mammals such as raccoons, foxes, and the like, a useful device is the choke pole used extensively by dog-control officers. This consists of a short tubular metal pole with a braided steel wire noose that can be tightened to a given position and locked in place. This gives the handler a considerable amount of control over the animal without choking it to death. Choke poles do obviously create a considerable amount of stress for the animal. However, when used properly, the choke pole enables the handler to do the marking or other procedures more quickly and thus minimize the total overall stress.

FURTHER READING

BALSER, D.S. "Tranquilizer tab for capturing wild carnivores," *Journal of Wildlife Management*, 29 (1965), 438–42.

GLINSKI, R.L. "Birdwatching etiquette: the need for a developing philosophy," *American Birds*, 30 (1976), 655–57.

HARTHOORN, A.M. *The Chemical Capture of Animals*. London: Bailliere-Tindall, 1975.

MANVILLE, RICHARD H. "Techniques for the capture and marking of mammals," *Journal of Mammalogy*, 30 (1949), 27–33.

TWIGG, G.I. "Catching mammals," *Mammal Review*, 5 (1975), 83–100.

SOURCES

SCENT LURES
• National Scent Company
  Garden Grove, California 92640

SCENT COVERS
• Cedar Scent
  P.O. Box 7081
  Rochester, Minnesota 55901

• Pete Rickard, Inc.
  Box 25
  Cobbleskill, New York 12043

CALLING DEVICES
• Burnaham Brothers
  P.O. Box A-120-C
  Marble Falls, Texas 78654
  (*recordings*)

- P.S. Olt Company
  Pekin, Illinois 61554
  (*mechanical devices*)

  LIVE TRAPS
- Havahart, Allcock Mfg. Company
  118 South Water Street
  Ossining, New York 10562
- Mustang Mfg. Company
  Box 10880
  Houston, Texas 77018
- National Live Trap Corp.
  P.O. Box 302
  Tomahawk, Wisconsin 54487
- Sherman Live Trap Company
  P.O. Box 683
  DeLand, Florida 32720

  MIST NETS
- W.B. Davis
  712 Mary Lake Drive
  Bryan, Texas 77801

CHAPTER 7

INDIVIDUAL RECOGNITION

IT IS GREAT FUN JUST TO WATCH ANIMALS, but it seems to be even more fun when one can clearly recognize individuals of a species and get to know more and more about the behavior of each individual. Humans are both emotional and potentially rational. The rational part of our make-up may recognize that in the natural scheme of things it is survival of populations and their gene pools that means evolutionary survival but our emotional part is attracted to the individual and its struggles. In the long run, the two fuse because it is the accumulation of individuals that comprise populations and species. The field biologist George Schaller commented:

> As I began to recognize many of the animals individually, the study moved from an abstract plane with an emphasis on collecting quantitative data to a more emotional and hence more satisfying one. Knowing the history of many of the animals, I had empathy with their problems, I anticipated their future.

Each individual is a mix of behaviors gained from inheritance and experience. Most of the so-called "lower" animals have a maximum of inherited behavior while the "higher" animals have a much greater potential for learned behavior. For example, humans seem to be genetically programmed to acquire language, but there is an enormous range of individual option regarding the specifics of what that language will be. Similarly, humpback whales appear to be genetically programmed for "songs" but the specific patterns vary with the particular population of humpbacks and even within a population the song patterns appear to vary from year to year.

Part of the fun of wildlife watching is determining which of an individual's behaviors it shares with other members of its species and which are its own individual actions. And it is not even that simple; among the higher creatures, where learning from one another is a factor, certain behaviors may be common to a given social group or even geographical population but not to the species as a whole.

In England some enterprising great tits, relatives of our chickadees, learned to pull the top off milkbottles left by milkmen on people's doorsteps and steal the cream. This may at first seem strange but apparently the tits enjoyed milk fats just as our chickadees enjoy suet. In any case, the behavior of opening milkcaps and stealing cream spread widely in some areas of England. On the other hand, there were many other areas of England where this social behavior was not learned and no great tits indulged.

Japanese researchers studying macaque monkeys over several generations identified a number of learned behaviors ranging from washing potatoes to dropping handfuls of mixed wheat and sand in water so they could skim off the edible wheat which floats while the inedible sand sinks. This study in itself deserves an entire book, but the point to be made here is that certain kinship lines learned and passed on these behaviors over several generations while others did not.

Behavior patterns may also vary as ecological adaptation to different locales and habitats, as Hans Kruuk observed among the spotted hyena populations of Ngorongoro Crater and the Serengeti Plains of Africa. Obviously the only way to discover such things is to be able to recognize individuals of a species so that we can study and compare their behaviors and note the consequences of these behaviors in dealing with the environment. By studying large numbers of individuals, we can determine which behaviors are common to all members of a species and which are characteristic of only certain populations or individuals. Techniques for recognizing individuals are the focus of this chapter.

Discriminating Looking

At first glance all individuals you study may look alike. It's the same kind of perception that has caused some people to look at those of other races and comment that "they all look alike to me." An open mind and closer observation begins to reveal the individually unique details that set one apart from the other. Once you have spotted these characteristics and seen them over and over again, the individual's markings and aspects of its behavior pattern set it apart and make it familiar. Other observers will initially have trouble in recognizing individuals that are obvious to you until they have also had some similar experience and observation time with your study population.

Individual recognition of animals that have not been artificially marked takes careful observation over time, along with the keeping of detailed notes and photographs or sketches (Figure 7.1). Look for abnormal color patterns, nicks, scratches, unusual movements, and the like. Photographic records are extremely helpful, particularly so that the observations of others can be correlated. The process is that each observer photographs the animal he or she is watching, then matches the photos to a master "mug book" of the known individuals of the study area.

For example, it has been determined that the amount and distribution of white on the underside of the flukes of humpback whales, along with the shape and scar patterns of the dorsal fin are individually distinctive. Scientists, with the aid of amateur photographers and whale watchers, have been regularly and systematically photographing the flukes and dorsal fins of these whales and have assembled mug books from them. Now a humpback whale that has been observed can have behavior recorded against that particular individual. Already the technique has allowed researchers to determine that several whales spotted on the Caribbean breeding grounds are the same individuals as had been spotted that summer on Stellwagen Bank off the Massachusetts coast.

The same process of close observation and comparison of photos has been used to identify giraffes by the patterns on their necks; lions by scars and other features; gorillas by nose patterns; rhinoceroses by nose wrinkle patterns; and chimpanzees by various facial features. Anyone who has followed the articles and books about Jane Goodall's long-term studies of chimpanzees soon learns to recognize a number of the chimps in the photos without referring to the captions.

In order for this technique to work well you must see the individuals quite frequently to fix their uniqueness in your mind or have a good collection of photographs that you can study closely and compare and contrast one photo with another. If you maintain a bird feeding station, study your visitors carefully—both the birds and the virtually inevitable squirrels. Focus particularly on the most regular visitors. See if you can't spot one or more that have characteristics that give them an individual

Figure 7.1. Pronghorns may be individually recognized by the pattern of chest and face markings. It takes close observation. Two of these drawings represent the same animal. Can you tell which ones?

identity among their species. Carefully record precisely what those identifying features are. Then see if you can teach another member of your family or a close friend to pick out that (or those) individuals from among the others. If you begin with one you will be surprised that before long you will be able to identify more and more of the same species individually. There are some species that never quite seem to lend themselves to this technique, either because of their characteristics or the observer's lack of perception. I have tried over and over to individualize my chickadees but unless they have some gross feature, such as a missing leg, they remain more alike than peas in a pod.

Whenever possible, direct observation is the preferred method of establishing individual identity within a study group of animals. For one thing, there is no trauma to the animals, as is inevitable with the capturing and handling necessary in most artificial marking techniques. Also, with artificial marking techniques, there is always the likelihood that the marker will interfere in some way with the normal activity or even the safety of the creature marked.

ARTIFICIAL MARKING

Unfortunately there are many cases in which the individual variation is too infrequent or too subtle to be of use in identifying more than a very occasional individual. For example, a colony of little brown bats scurrying about is impossible to sort out into readily identifiable individuals. The bats themselves can do it but their clues are auditory, not visual, and even their auditory clues are generally beyond the range of human hearing. By chance, Leonard Dubkin was able to make some interesting observations about one species of bat when he spotted an albino baby in a small colony he was watching. The White Lady, as this amateur naturalist called both the bat and the book he wrote about her, let him follow the relationships of at least one recognizable individual to other bats and to its environment.

As mentioned earlier, chickadees are among those creatures difficult to individualize. They come in to a feeder so quickly, leave so quickly, and look so much alike that one can't tell whether the group is made up of three or four individuals or a dozen. Do the same birds come every day? all winter? Do certain of the chickadees stay together and move as a group? Are the birds you meet in the woods down the street the same birds that visit your feeder? Are the birds at your feeder the same ones that also are free-loading at your neighbor's?

Only some method of artificially marking the birds will permit us to rapidly recognize the individual birds and begin to get information to answer such questions. John James Audubon was one of the first Americans to use some form of artificial marking on a bird. He wrapped silver wire around the legs of a pair of phoebes that nested near his Virginia home to help him determine if the same birds would return to the same site the following year.

In later years a procedure was developed for using aluminum bands with serial numbers. These have been used on both the legs of birds and the forearms of bats. Since these creatures roam widely, often over two hemispheres, some central record-keeping system had to be established to eliminate the confusion that uncoordinated banding by individuals would have produced. Thus, to centralize the record keeping and assure a consistency of data, in addition to providing a single place for records of sightings or recovered bands to be sent, in the United States the provision of bands was made the responsibility of the U.S. Fish and Wildlife Service. They set the standards by which an individual will be permitted to have and apply these bands and insure that no two individual animals will carry the same number.

Much has been learned from the banding of birds and a significant amount of this banding work has been accomplished by dedicated amateurs. Recovery of bands has helped determine major migration routes, wintering grounds, and longevity of some species. Also of value has been data on moult patterns, size variabilities, and other physical data gathered about the birds at the time they were captured for banding, or ringing, as the British call it.

There are problems, however. The birds are caught in traps or mist nets and then measured and weighed before banding and release. This is a temporary trauma for the animal, but a trauma nonetheless. Furthermore, in order for the bird or bat to be identified, it must be killed or recaptured so that its number can be read.

The odds of recovering a banded individual away from its original banding site are very small and large numbers of individuals must be banded for each one that is later recovered. Meanwhile the data on the rest has been accumulating in astronomical amounts. This has provided real problems for the Fish and Wildlife Service, even aided by computers as they have been in recent years. It should be noted at this point that the Service is eager to have more people use this information stored in its data banks for research studies.

Today to get a bird-banding permit you must be at least eighteen years old and be able to demonstrate skill in identifying all of our common birds in their various seasonal plumages. This usually is accomplished by apprenticing to another licensed bander for a year or more. The applicant must also have the endorsement of three well-known ornithologists or outstanding naturalists and have a valid research project underway in order to qualify. (For additional information and/or application, contact Migratory Bird Research Laboratory, U.S. Fish and Wildlife Service, Laurel, Maryland 20810.)

Actually, for the average wildlife watcher, regular numbered bird bands are of little value in quick recognition of individuals in the field. Of more value are the color bands used to supplement the numbered band. These are made of colored plastic, are available in a range of sizes, and are applied in various coded sequences. For example, using a sequence of a maximum of three bands and a range of five colors and placing all the bands on one leg, you could use the band closest to the body to represent hundreds, the middle band to represent tens, and the lower band to indicate digits. Each color would represent a different number, that is white = 1, blue = 2, red = 3, yellow = 4, and green = 5. Thus a bird carrying a sequence from body to foot of blue, red, and white would be bird number 231. This coding would allow you to mark fifty eight different individuals in your immediate area. This generally is as many or more individuals that you can easily keep track of. Such color banding is usually done on permanent residents rather than on migratory species. A special permit for color banding is needed from the U.S. Fish and Wildlife Service. It is usually issued only in conjunction with a defined research project.

Some people have accomplished color banding by using Scotch brand pressure-sensitive tape wrapped around the bird's tarsus twice but not tightly enough to exert pressure. These tapes are available in white, yellow, red, green, blue, brown, light gray, and black. Thus you have far more coding combinations available to you than you are ever likely to need, particularly if you color band both legs. Be sure to record your code so you, or others, can decipher it later. Actually, the more individuals you mark the more difficult the observing/decoding task becomes and you may miss noting some good behavior because you are concentrating on reading the color sequence on the leg. Note that even with homemade color bands you must have a special color banding permit from the Fish and Wildlife Service.

Banding bats, which is coordinated by the same office, provides some other problems. In addition to being able to identify the various species and learning to handle them safely so that you don't get bitten and risk rabies, one has to ask the value of the data. Much that can be learned about North American bats from banding has already been learned; but that is not to say that more cannot or will not be learned. However, one thing learned is that taking, waking, and releasing hibernating bats for banding causes the bats to use up needed fat reserves. A number of banders working a given cave a number of times a winter may cause too great a dimunution of these reserves and cause high spring mortality, a time when the bats' normal food supplies are low and they have no bodily reserves. In recent years pesticides have directly or indirectly taken their toll on bat populations, as has the disturbance from a growing number of spelunkers, and yes, bat banders. After banding bats for over a decade I could come to no other conclusion than that I was probably doing more harm than good by continuing this effort. I recommend that others have a very specific project in mind or work mostly with breeding colonies if they intend to band bats.

Hewitt and Smith were looking for a more prominent marker to put on a bird that would stand out visibly but not mutilate or injure the bird or affect its mobility. Their solution was a wing tag of fluorescent, plastic-coated fabric. The material used—"Sea Flag"—is available in aurora pink, blaze orange, and signal green from Safety Flag Company, P.O. Box 1005, Pawtucket, RI 02800. The tag was shaped as shown in Figure 7.2, and the tag end is cut a bit wider if an identification pattern, design, or number is to be added.

The strip is passed around the humerus, the wingbone closest to the body, right next to the innermost tertial feather. The little tab goes on the underside, the large one is uppermost, and the two are joined with a metal staple, paper rivet, or round eyelet. If you use an eyelet the tag material will need to be punched beforehand. Indeed, it is also the easiest method to use for the paper rivet. A completed tag of this size, with its fasteners, weighs less than a gram.

For some short-haired mammal species, such as rabbits, collars have been used. Patent leather has proven a fairly fade-resistant material for this and it comes in a variety of colors such as red, green, yellow, blue, and white. This can be further individualized with quick-drying enamel and/or reflective paint for night spotting with a light. For rabbit-sized animals a collar ⅝" to ¾" wide is appropriate; a collar up to an inch wide is useful for somewhat larger creatures. The collar bands can be made of various lengths. Punch a ³⁄₁₆-inch hole ½ inch from one end, then at 6-¼ inches from that point start punching similar holes every ⅜ of an inch.

The collar goes round the neck with enough looseness for the worker to easily be able to insert one finger between neck and collar. Fasten through appropriate holes with leather workers' eyelets and trim off excess. It is useful to use different base-color collars for the different sexes and then further individualize the base with the paints.

The use of such eye-catching markers on birds or other animals raises some ethical issues that must be considered on a species by species basis. Will the marker put the wearer at greater risk by making it more visible to predators and/or will the marker disrupt species identity clues that interfere with courtship and mate selection or generate ostracism from its peer social group? If the chances are high of a "yes" answer to either question, don't use the marker. If the answers are not readily

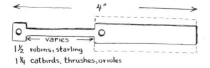

Figure 7.2.
Wing tag marker.

apparent, mark only one or two individuals and study them carefully until you are sure of the answer. Do not mark numbers of individuals until you are quite certain that the markers do no harm.

In choosing a marking technique one needs to study the structure of the organism to see if there are features that will help in the marking. Bil Gilbert and his boys in studying chulos (coati-mundis) noted that the animals usually carry their tails straight up. Thus they marked these animals by wrapping colored waterproof tape around their tails, thus turning these appendages into individual marker flags. Each color band was two inches wide and several colors were used for the code. These bands stayed in place for three to six months.

Fragile though they look, butterfly wings can withstand small pressure-sensitive tags (Figure 7.3). The site for the tag is first rubbed clean of its normal scales and then the tag is applied. The tag site should be down close to the body so that the tag's weight has the least impact on the work of flying. Monarch butterflies have flown thousands of miles carrying such tags as they migrated from Canada and the northern United States to California, Florida, and Mexico. There are other butterflies that make lesser migrations to be studied and tags could also keep track of individual butterflies that are essentially homebodies and make no such herculean journeys. But just how far afield do they roam? Does the same individual visit your garden every day? Does it have a daily routine of visiting flower clumps? Tags will have to have an address or phone number if other observers are to get information back to you.

Dragonflies can be similarly marked so that you can map the territories that each defends around a shoreline or trace the migration routes that some of them take. They can also be individually marked with spots of model airplane dope. This material comes in a wide variety of colors, is easy to apply, and dries very rapidly. This technique works also for beetles, wasps, and other fairly large insects that you may want to keep track of individually.

Some researchers have used a variety of dyes to paint identification numbers on the sides of animals. There is some merit to this when studying a close group of colonial animals such as ground squirrels, but effective dyes are limited and difficult to prepare, and the result lasts only to the next molt. Thus the time the marking is useful varies from a

Figure 7.3.
Monarch butterfly with wing tag.

couple of weeks to about nine months. Picric acid, Nyazol A, and Nyazol D are among the most effective of such dyes and each is tricky to use or prepare. [See Melchior and Iwen (1965) for details.]

Mutilation Techniques

Most of the other marking techniques involve some degree of mutilation and thus demand considerable reflection upon the propriety of their use. Some require little more than poking a hole through skin or shell that many consider no more distressing than a person's having his or her ears pierced. Of course the human does this of free will; when you do it to the animal it has no choice in the matter. How frivolous is your intention in marking the animal? Do you intend to take full advantage of being able to identify the individuals, to gather all the data you can, and share it widely with others? If no, do not use mutilation marking. If yes, do everything in your power to reduce any pain that might be inflicted and any risk of infection that might occur.

Even banding can have its mutilating effect. I have seen many bats whose bands had been misapplied (which is easy to do under the pressure of banding several hundred individuals in a given day) and where the edges of the metal band have irritated the wing membrane and caused scar tissue to form and even to partially engulf the band. The irritation also may cause the bat to chew at the band and eventually the tooth marks obscure the numbers, making the band useless to the observer as well as an annoyance to the animal.

Turtles are among the easiest to mark using a mutilation method. This method also appears to be free of pain and essentially free of risk from infection. As Figure 7.4 shows, the top part of the turtle's shell (the carapace) overhangs the hind legs and tail from the point where the upper and lower (plastron) parts of the shell are joined. The area is divided into equal segments by the scales that wrap around the edge—usually five to each side of the midline.

A turtle is marked by taking a hand drill and drilling a hole through one or a combination of these scales or scutes all the way through the bone. Care must be taken not to nick the leg in the process; for this reason, an electric drill should not be used. The following code is gener-

Figure 7.4.
Turtle marking using marginal shields.

ally used: With the turtle facing away from you, note the scutes as either to the right or left of the middle and numbered one to five away from the midline. You will drill and note such as R1 or L2 on the first ten animals you mark, and then move to combinations such as R1-L2, R1-L3, R1-L4, and so forth. Using this technique you can individualize most of the turtles in a local pond. Some people have filed a notch in the shell rather than used a drill, but raccoon teeth and other natural encounters can mar the edge of the carapace in a similar way, thus confusing your scheme of things. Nothing else but man is likely to drill a neat hole through the shell.

It is difficult, though not always impossible, to spot the holes and count the scutes with a binocular. Usually the turtle has to be recaptured to confirm its identity. Thus such marking is usually more useful in population studies than behavioral ones. However, colored, plastic-coated electrical wire can be twisted through the holes to make a flag that makes identification from a distance somewhat more feasible.

To mark salamanders, frogs, and lizards, researchers often clip off toes in a variety of combinations. The toes are snipped off quickly with very sharp scissors such as manicure scissors. Given the level of complexity of the nervous system of these creatures, there apparently is little, if any, pain and the animals seem to be little affected by the amputation. In fact, salamanders will regenerate the missing digits in time and they will have to be reclipped if the individual is to retain its identification mark.

In clipping toes, only one toe from any one foot is clipped. Counting toes is done from the one closest to the body outward. Thus the lizard in Figure 7.5 would be noted as RF1-RR3-LR2, that is, right front toe 1, right rear toe 3, and left rear toe 2. Lizards are often marked with acrylic paint for greater visibility of identification but this is less durable than toe clipping. However, with the permanence of toe clipping an individual whose paint has worn off can be recaptured and accurately repainted by referring to the original notes.

Toe clipping has also been used for marking mammals but, at least for the larger species, because of their more highly ordered nervous system the process creates greater and more prolonged pain. However, distribution of pain receptors in small mammals suggests that for them there is less pain. Nonetheless, it is not an activity to be undertaken

Figure 7.5.
Toe-clipped lizard.

lightly and without clear-cut justifiable purpose. The fact that we survive digital amputation does not mean that it is all right for researchers to go about chopping off combinations of our fingers and toes to better identify us.

One of the rationales for toe clipping mammals, particularly small species, is that often they cannot readily be observed directly. However, they can be tracked and the missing toes result in distinctive tracks that identify the individual track maker.

French (1964) used a clipping code that permitted use of 899 numbers while removing no more than one toe per foot. Figure 7.6 illustrates that code.

Snakes are marked by clipping out wedges of skin on the belly scales. The cuts must be made to the quick in order to stimulate formation of permanent scar tissue. These belly scales, or ventral scutes, are counted forward from the scale over the anus. By using marks to the right and left of the midline a number of combinations is available that permit individualizing a number of specimens of a given species. Unfortunately the snakes must be captured and examined each time you want to establish an identity.

Although fin clipping has been used to mark fish for capture-recapture population studies, the technique seems to have little value for general observations. Even the variety of tags used to clip onto gill covers, through the back muscles or onto the jaw, are of little use unless the fish can be recaptured for close examination. These types of markings have been most useful for establishing migration routes and age records with game fishes or food fishes that are destined to be sought after for sport or commerce. Marking fish for recurrent observation in the wild is an area in need of much creative invention.

Tags of various sorts have been used on mammals also. Most of these tags are made of relatively noncorrosive monel metal and are generally inserted in the ears. Such tags are prone to catch on brush and be torn out and, even in place, they are difficult to read unless the observer is very close. With large animals such as bear and deer, scientists have cut notches in the ears in code fashion. Ears are prone to natural cuts and scars from accidents and aggressive encounters so the pain of inserting tags or cutting notches is not excessive, but the natural events mentioned can confuse things by making new marks that alter your code. An advantage to ear marking is that alert animals usually

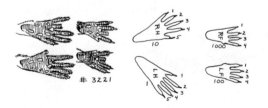

Figure 7.6. Mammal toe clipping. Right, marking code; left, marked animal (read: 3221).

look at you with ears elevated, which gives a good view for reading the marking code.

Some mammals have been tagged with the plastic or nylon tapes mentioned earlier. Usually these are 1cm × 3.5cm flags of vinyl-coated fabric often with cross striping of different colors attached for coding purposes. These flags are attached by lifting the scruff of skin between the shoulder blades, the most difficult point to reach when the animal scratches. The scruff is pierced by a sharp, sterile needle threaded with a piece of fine anodized wire. The wire is then twisted through the tag material to make it all secure. The tag will usually remain in place for four to six weeks before the skin sluffs off the wire. There are also kits available for attaching buttons with I-shaped pieces of plastic. These kits can be used to attach such tags or you can even use colored buttons as identification markers.

There have been a number of special techniques adapted to the uniqueness of individual species including branding the horns of wild sheep, tattooing, and so forth. You may well invent some new ones of your own. Guidelines for such techniques as follows:

1. Any device should be applied with minimal contact with the animal. Catching the animal should not be an overly traumatic experience.
2. The device should not interfere with the animal's movement or make it unduly outstanding to predators or aggressive members of its social group.
3. The device should not be painful or prone to induce infection.
4. The device should not cause the animal to alter its normal behavior.
5. The device should be easily spotted by an observer and its number or code readily apparent and clear.

Tattooing has been used for a number of species but it does usually involve recapture in order to read the marks as well as considerable handling to do the marking. It is thus not of significant value to the field observer. Bats are a possible exception. With these animals the tattoo punch is applied to the wing membrane between the fourth and fifth fingers or between the fifth digit and the body. The holes heal within ten days and leave a white scar tissue. Under good conditions this can be seen when the animal is in flight. Normally, however, these animals too will have to be rehandled to read the number since it can't be seen when the wing is folded. The technique is simple and a worker can mark a bat a minute. It causes no lasting injury and there is no loss of readability over time.

A temporary but useful and generally unharmful marking technique for some mammals is hair clipping. This involves cutting out patches of guard hair to reveal the underlying fur or to change the perceived color. Many guard hairs are composed of bands of color so that if you cut off the ends that one normally sees, a different color is revealed.

Viewed from above, the back of the animal can be divided into three main sectors—the shoulder area, the midback or saddle, and the rump. There is also a right and left division from midline. This permits you fifteen different combinations of areas from which to clip patches of hair. The technique is useful for marking the animals in a single family or small colony that you may be studying. The patterns will be lost with the next molt.

For those who have a very valid reason to make a long-lasting mark, the relatively new technique of freeze branding is an option. With this technique the pigment-producing melanocytes in the hair follicles are permanently destroyed by surface freezing. When the hair grows back in a few weeks it comes in white. After each molt it still comes back white.

The technique requires some skill because too short an application of the freezing agent will not do the job and too long an application destroys the tissue. Two basic approaches to freeze branding are used. One approach uses a branding iron of copper or brass. These can be purchased from some veterinarian supply houses in sets of numbers 0 to 9. Usually the smallest available is $2'' \times \frac{3}{8}''$ but you can make smaller ones with copper rods threaded into dowel handles. The branding iron is cooled in liquid nitrogen or dry ice and alcohol. The cooled iron is applied to a shaved area of skin. For small mammals the usual time is 25 to 35 seconds. If you are freeze branding infants, 10 to 25 seconds is usually the range of time required.

The other approach uses a spray freezing agent and a template rather than a branding iron. This approach is easier but, using commercially available coolants, is less reliable. Researchers use dichlorodifluoromethane (CCl_2F_2) sprayed from aerosol cans equipped with push button valves. Unfortunately this material is not commercially available. A number of the commercially available products have been tried with poor results. Only one, *Quick Freeze* (Miller Stephenson Chemical Co., Danbury, CT 06810), gave generally suitable results. The animals were clipped in distinctive patterns of lines and dots. A template of plastic or cardboard was placed over each area and the area sprayed for eight to ten seconds. Spray time was critical—five seconds gave variable results while more than ten seconds caused extensive tissue damage.

To do the freeze branding, the animals must be lightly anesthetized with ether or metophane—a tricky task in itself which should never be undertaken without some training and assistance from a veterinarian. In some states neither of these anesthetics can be purchased on the open market.

After the freezing, scabs develop on the tissue. White hair is usually visible at the brand site in about three weeks. The hair will normally be fully regrown in five to six weeks. However, the white marks will last indefinitely and they are visible at a considerable distance. The technique has merit where the likelihood of continued observations of the individuals for several years is good.

Freeze branding is not limited to mammals. Recently herpetologists have found it feasible on snakes, salamanders, and frogs. It requires some modification of equipment for the smaller size of the animals but contact time with the brand is somewhat less critical than with mammals (see Chapter 12).

Nocturnal Markers

My first experience with nocturnal markers was purely serendipitous. It was a June evening and spring peepers were being discovered in numbers in the scrub willows near a small pond at the edge of a meadow. The sun was just dipping below the horizon yet I wanted to follow the movement of several of these diminutive frogs to discover something of their hunting techniques. I kept watching until it was almost impossible to follow the action in the dimmed light. Then I noticed that fireflies were flashing in the meadow and it gave me an idea. I caught several of the insects and some of the peepers. I smeared the abdomen of a firefly on the back of a peeper and then released it. The same was done to several others. The material continued to glow for over half an hour and let me follow the peepers' movements as they moved about through the shrubbery.

Today modern chemistry has come up with a product that is a lot easier on the fireflies. It is called Cyalume Chemical Light and is manufactured by American Cyanamid Company, Organic Chemicals Division, Bound Brook, NJ 08805. It is sometimes found as light sticks in sporting goods or hardware stores or in science supply houses such as Edmund Scientific Company, 642 Edscorp Bldg., Barrington, NJ 08007. It comes in two parts—a yellow-green liquid and a clear activator solution. Mix the two together and cold light is emitted for several hours with a gradual diminishing of brightness. Brightness varies with both temperature and the proportion of liquid to activator. The warmer the temperature, the brighter. The more activator used per unit of the cyalume, the brighter the light but over a shorter duration.

Cyalume has been used to mark a variety of creatures in order to follow their movements for several hours. One method involves blowing 3mm diameter glass spheres from O.D. soft glass. (Most high-school chemistry teachers can help with this.) The cyalume and activator are added and the opening sealed with plasticene (children's modeling clay). The spheres are glued to the bat, or flying squirrel, or snapping turtle, or whatever with branding cement (Control Data Corp., Box 80638, South Industrial Park, Lincoln, NB 68501). With frogs a soft iron wire was placed around the pelvic region and the sphere glued to the wire on the dorsal area.

As shown in Figure 7.7, the cyalume can also be applied as a collar. (With mammals you may have to anesthetize lightly in order to put the collar on properly.) Cut clear plastic tubing of a length appropriate to collar your animal. Plug one end with a wooden plug that extends enough to eventually plug the other end of the tubing securely as well. Add the chemicals to the tube, encircle the neck, and join the two ends with the wooden plug. Release the animal and observe.

For most purposes a 1:1 ratio of cyalume to activator is appropriate but you may want to vary it to 3:1. With these collars you should be able to spot the marked animals for several hours from up to 125 yards.

Unfortunately the chemical cold light marker is very temporary. For continued observations over two weeks to a year, an electronic collar with LEDs (light-emitting diodes) is much more appropriate. Making such collars is more complex and demands some basic skills in electronics, although none beyond the capabilities of most hobbyists. The collar was originally designed for use with beavers but can be adapted for other creatures. Three LEDs are used on each collar in different combinations of red and yellow—the two most visible colors available. These color combinations can be distinguished from about one hundred yards. The light itself can be spotted over a greater distance but the color code is not distinguishable. The diagram in Figure 7.8 gives the basic wiring of this night identification collar.

Parts needed to make the device are as follows:

1. LM 3909 oscillator, available from National Semiconductor Corp., Santa Clara, California 95057 (a low current, high efficiency, integrated circuit for flashing LEDs)
2. 500 f electrolytic capacitor
3. 3.3–9.1 K ohm pulse resistor
4. LED models XC-526 and XC-22Y, available from Xciton, Latham, NY 12110. These have 80° viewing angle, low forward voltage, low current demand, and a diffuse lens (1.7 v typical)
5. Two 1.35 v batteries (mercury) or one 2.8 v lithium battery

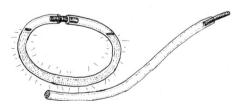

Figure 7.7. Cyalume collar. Right, tube and plug. Left, filled with cyalume mixture and joined to form collar.

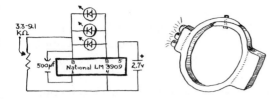

Figure 7.8. Right, LED collar completed; left, wiring diagram LED collar.

6. Printed circuit board for structural integrity or solder point to point
7. Neoprene webbing
8. Silicone- or urethane-based waterproofing material

Assemble the parts according to the wiring diagram. Mount the LEDs opposite the remainder of the circuit so that the batteries serve as a counterbalance to keep the lights at the nape of the neck. Waterproof thoroughly with the silicone or urethane. The collar is fastened on with pop rivets to an anesthetized animal. The finished package should not exceed 6 percent of the animal's body weight. The key to the life of the collar and weight reduction lies with the batteries chosen. The following table will help you in your choice. Note that lithium batteries are lighter than those containing mercury.

Type	Model number	WT	Rated capacity (mah)	Operating duration (days)	
				1 LED/.34 mah	3 LEDs 1.02 mah
Mercury	RM-312	1.1	45	5	2
(P.R. Mallory	RM-675	5.1	180	22	7
& Co., Inc.	RM-625	8.5	350	43	14
Tarrytown, NY 10591)	RM-1	24.4	1,000	122	41
2 × 1.35 = 2.7 v	RM-12	79.2	3,600	441	147
Lithium (2.8 v)	440	11.3	1,000	122	41
(Power Conversion, Inc.	660-3	48.0	3,800	466	155
Mt. Vernon, NY 10550)	550	83.0	8,000	980	327

The last type of individual marking we will discuss is radio tagging. This is a complex technological technique whose details are changing very rapidly. New techniques of electronic miniaturization are permitting ever smaller transmitters and new work with batteries means smaller, more powerful, longer-lasting power sources. Nonetheless, radio telemetry is still more in the realm of the professional researcher than the amateur. However, the radio or electronics buff may be intrigued to meld these hobby interests or even professional skills with wildlife watching.

Essentially the process involves designing and constructing miniature transmitters and power packs that can be covered with water resistant epoxy resins and attached to the animal by collar or harness. The

105

animal is then released to go about its daily routine. Using a portable loop antennae receiver or equivalent, the wildlife watcher monitors the signals from the animal's collar and, through triangulation techniques, the animal's general location can be plotted on a map. The radios can be used merely to plot the animal's movements on paper or to reduce the general searching of an area to locate the animal for closer direct observation. Radio telemetry has been particularly useful in studying large free-ranging predators such as grizzly bears and leopards. Joy Adamson indicates both the usefulness and the frustrations of the technique in her book *Queen of Shaba,* which narrates her experiences in studying a tame leopard reacclimated to the wild.

Radio telemetry is expensive and time-consuming in its own way because it may generate such a volume of data that you will need a computer to process it. However, because of the rise in availability of home computers and the romance of the technology to some people, it may be an activity more widely explored by amateurs in the near future.

Radio telemetry is not limited to radio tracking. Some creatures have been wired so that their temperatures, heart beat, and other functions were automatically monitored, converted to electrical signals, and transmitted. As was noted in the Introduction to this book, Frank Craighead even used a communications satellite to relay signals from a wild-ranging grizzly bear back to his field laboratory.

Those interested in pursuing this technique will have to investigate the most current literature and/or contact a local university researcher for the most up-to-date designs for both transmitters and receivers. Any designs given here would be out-of-date almost immediately.

As with the other marking methods, there are some ethical considerations for the use of radio collars. Under the adverse conditions of the field, batteries seldom hold out for more than a month or two. Actually a few weeks is a more likely estimate given the present state of the art. The collars themselves are far more durable, so the animal is usually obliged to carry the collar or harness for months or years after the device is useless for gathering information. One must question the justice of burdening the animal with the device for that length of time. Do the ends justify the means? There is also the question of sensitivity to the rights of others to experience wild animals unfettered by collars that clearly diminish the aura of wildness. Indeed, this question is to be considered with any artificial marker.

Despite the fact that a considerable part of this chapter has been devoted to various marking devices, including those that involve some form of permanent mutilation, I want to conclude the discussion with strong encouragement to devote as much energy as possible to direct observation techniques for recognizing individuals of a species before any other marking device is used. Many a person who used artificial markers found that after a while the markers were largely superfluous;

he could tell the individuals apart by observation without the marker.
More careful observation earlier might have obviated the need for artificial markers in the first place. Where markers are needed, nonmutilating
techniques are to be preferred; the mutilation techniques should be used
only as a last resort when the information gathered may in some real
way justify their use.

FURTHER READING

AMLANER, C.J., and D.W. MacDONALD, *A Handbook on Biotelemetry and Radio
Tracking.* Oxford and New York: Pergamon Press, 1979.
FRANTZ, STEPHEN C. "Fluorescent pigments for studying movements and home
ranges of small mammals," *Journal of Mammalogy,* 53 no. 1 (February 1972).
STONEHOUSE, B., ed. *Animal Marking: Recognition Marking of Animals in Research.*
Baltimore: University Park Press, 1978.
Symposium. Uses of Marking Animals in Ecological Studies, *Ecology,* 37 no. 4
(1956).
TWIGG, G.I. "Marking mammals," *Mammal Review,* 5 (1975), 101–16.

SOURCES

FREEZE-BRANDING EQUIPMENT
• Omaha Vaccine Company, Inc.
  3030 L Street, P.O. Box 7228
  Omaha, Nebraska 68107

MARKING MATERIALS INCLUDING RADIO-TRACKING TRANSMITTERS
• Robert E. Hawkins
  Wildlife Materials, Inc.
  Rt. 3
  Carbondale, Illinois 62901

TATTOO EQUIPMENT
• Weston Manufacturing and Supply Company
  1942 Speer Blvd.
  Denver, Colorado 80204

• Omaha Vaccine Company, Inc. (*see address above*)

CHAPTER 8

PATTERNS
OF BEHAVIOR

BIRD WATCHING IS THE MOST POPULAR AND WELL-KNOWN TYPE of wildlife watching. It owes its popularity in large measure to the life work of Roger Tory Peterson, who not only developed the first easily used popular guide to bird identification but also helped promote the hobby of bird listing, that is, keeping a list of the species one has seen in the wild. Bird listing has escalated to the point of competition where individuals or clubs vie to see who can spot the greatest number of species in a given twenty-four hour period or a given year.

The ready availability of good field guides to most common wildlife species for many parts of the world has made listing a very acceptable activity not only for birds but also for a wide range of wildlife (see the Bibliography). But listing tends to be a very superficial wildlife-watching activity that appeals primarily to the collecting urge. A top-notch lister may actually know very little about the birds she or he has ticked off on the list. Once the check mark has been made, it's off to spot a different species. If one lacks the money or time to travel widely, it doesn't take long to spot most of the regular inhabitants of a region. Without a next step, wildlife listing quickly wears thin.

A second step for many is to keep count of how many of each species are spotted during each outing and in what habitats. This broadens understandings of basic relationships of species to habitats and the ebb and flow of populations. But ultimately the most fascinating thing about an animal is what it does. How does it respond to its environment? To find out we must determine just what its physical and social environments are and record its actions in relation to that world.

Behavior watching is the addictive phase of wildlife watching and it can be pursued on two levels. The first, which is in itself a sophisti-

108

cated form of listing, involves becoming familiar with what is known about a species' behavior from books and then setting out to observe all these behaviors for yourself. This means both armchair natural history and field study. From your reading you can begin creating an ethogram or chart of behavior, then set out to confirm the details of each behavior pattern through your own observation.

The process of science hinges on confirmation of data by sources other than those of the initial published observer or researcher. Each time you see a behavior you have only read about, you add to its stature as fact. You will also want to note how many times you observe the same behavior pattern and under what conditions. If you carefully record all this information you will be contributing to science as well as to your own enjoyment. Often you will find variants of the behavior pattern or the conditions under which it occurs. These set the stage for a new contribution by you to the species' ethogram. If you gather enough information, you may well wish to publish your observations so that they can be confirmed or refuted by others.

The second approach to behavior watching involves deliberately setting out to observe behavior that will fill the gaps in the ethogram for any particular species. For a few species we can already create a fairly complete ethogram but, for most, there are great gaping holes in our knowledge. Until only a very few years ago there were species of birds on the North American continent for which a nest had never been found and birds are generally better known than most other animal groups. The naturalist Don Stokes recently published a very useful book titled *A Guide to the Behavior of Some Common Birds*. Some birds that you would expect to find covered in such a book are missing. The reason for this is that in spite of the fact that they are common, the information was not available.

If gathering such information seems like too great a challenge for amateurs, consider these words from Niko Tinbergen, a Nobel Laureate and one of the founders of the modern study of animal behavior.

> Many amateurs feel they can no longer keep pace with it [the field of animal behavior] let alone produce new and original contributions. I don't think such pessimism is justified. It is not only possible, it is very desirable that non-professionals go on to contribute, for lack of specialized training has advantages as well as disadvantages. Of course training gives knowledge and discipline of thought, but it often tends to smother originality of outlook. The amateur may approach the subject with a certain freshness of mind which may have profound influence.

There are many aspects of animal life histories to which the wildlife watcher can contribute, but building behavioral inventories, or ethograms, is probably the one within the grasp of most amateurs.

First we must recognize two broad categories of behavior—genetically determined, fixed action patterns or instincts, and learned behavior. All living things act in response to their environment and it is these actions that make up behavior and behavior patterns. Many behaviors are determined by the genetic make-up of the species and each individual responds in essentially the same way to specific environmental stimuli. These we consider to be instinctive or innate behaviors. For other behaviors there is a genetically built-in capacity for response, but a wide range of specific responses is possible. Depending upon the species, the range of possible response may be narrow or wide. The actual response is usually a learned behavior.

Much of the learning is simple trial-and-error learning. A response is made if it satisfies the animal's need. The response is likely to be repeated under the same conditions next time. If it is unsatisfactory, the animal tends to avoid that response. Habituation is one of the simpler forms of learning; it involves not reacting to stimuli that should normally evoke an avoidance response. The animal must be able to discriminate between various stimuli in order to habituate.

At slightly more advanced levels of learning, animals are able to store information from their perceptual environment and act on that information in limited ways. They learn where in their environment food, shelter, water, or other basic needs can be met. If their environment is altered, they learn its new patterns and adapt their activity accordingly.

The capacity for complex learning is generally reflected in the development of certain brain structures, particularly the cerebral cortex. The details are beyond the scope of this volume. Suffice it to say that among mammals, which have the most advanced cerebral complexity, the primates, including humans, and the cetaceans have the most complex brain structures for learning and show the most complex learned behavior.

Each species has some fixed action patterns. For some, virtually all of their behavior is of this type. This is particularly true of most invertebrates. However some invertebrates, such as the octopuses, some insects, and a few others can and do modify their behavior through learning although the range of choices is quite limited. Among vertebrate animals learning plays a greater role, and among some mammals, such as the primates and perhaps whales and dolphins, it is more important than fixed action patterns.

Fixed action patterns are very successful in habitats that change very slowly over time. They can only respond quite slowly to change since they require natural selections of genetic variations over a number of generations. This means a species, to adapt, must produce many generations over a short time or the changes must occur more slowly over long periods of time. Learned behavior is much more adaptive to short-term change, particularly for species that reproduce slowly.

One thing that behavior watchers have to be alert for is that under normal conditions an individual or even many individuals of a species may habitually show the same responses to given stimuli. It may appear that what is being seen is a fixed action pattern. However, under stress or other altered conditions the animal may demonstrate that it can readily learn to behave differently. There is clearly the habitual remnant of a fixed action pattern that is no longer strongly genetically determined but more open to variation through learning.

PATTERNS OF BEHAVIOR
SYSTEMS

Each species has its own unique behavior patterns that adapt it to the environment. When the behavior patterns of a number of different species are compared, we can see that they tend to be classifiable into several systems from which we are able to build the working outline for a behavioral inventory or ethogram.

Ethology is the study of animal behavior, particularly instinctive behavior, and it is from this root word that the *etho* segment of ethogram derives. The *gram* part comes from the root word *grammar*. Grammar involves the form and structure of words and their arrangement in phrases and sentences. Behavior deals with the movements of an animal—what it does. Each movement is the equivalent of a word and the sequence of movements is a behavioral phrase or sentence. In short, an ethogram is a recording of the actions of a species in relation to their sequence and adaptive function. The anthropologists Tiger and Fox use the term *biogrammar* for the same purpose. This term is easier to grasp at first but more ethologists seem to use *ethogram*, and for this reason we will use it here.

The ethologist John Paul Scott identifies ten key systems of adaptive behavior and these, along with a few others, are the basis for our ethogram outline (see Appendix A). They are:

Ingestive behavior	Maintenance behavior
Eliminative behavior	Care-giving behavior
Agonistic behavior	Care-soliciting behavior
Sexual behavior	Shelter-seeking behavior
Investigative behavior	Allelomimetic behavior

In the following pages we will discuss each of these systems in detail.

Ingestive

Eliminative

Care Soliciting (left); Care Giving (above)

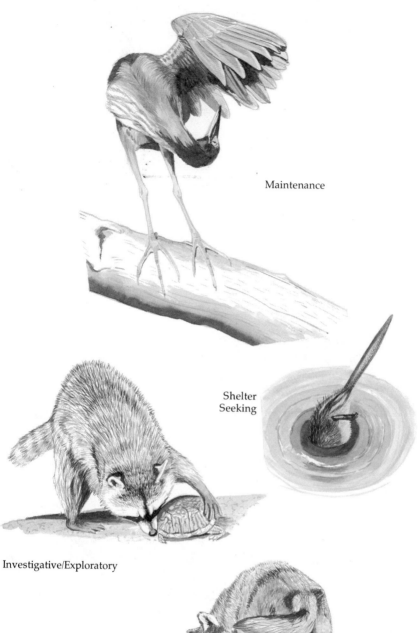

Maintenance

Shelter
Seeking

Investigative/Exploratory

Agonistic

Sexual (Courtship)

Allelomimetic

Reproductive (left);
Interspecies Maintenance (above)

INGESTION

Ingestion is a fancy term for behaviors related to eating and drinking. Ingestion is a very fundamental type of behavior. All animals are selective in their food, either because of limitations of anatomy or by preferred selection of certain items over others. Detailed studies of food preferences have been done for a few species but are very general for others. Where food preferences have been determined by studying remains in a dead animal's stomach, or a live animal's scat, the information can be very biased. What is most recorded is the remains of foods with very resistant parts; more completely digested materials go unrecognized or their importance in the diet is underestimated.

There is a need for much more information on the foods selected by many species and this needs to be done in significantly greater detail than is often done. We need to know what species are selected and from what range of choices. In other words, we also need to know more of what was not eaten even though available. Identification of the foods must be increasingly refined as well. Crowcroft, in his study of shrews, found that it was not sufficient to say that the common shrew ate woodlice. Faced with a choice of several woodlice species, the shrews showed a decided order of preference for the different species. Grazing animals are not just eating grass; they are selecting some species over others and many of the chosen plants are not even grasses. Selection of different foods at different times and in different amounts can have profound effects on the composition of species in a given habitat, and indeed, may contribute to significant shifts and changes in that habitat. However, what a creature eats is only a part of the recording of its ingestive behavior.

Very often the nature of such behavior will be hinted at by structural adaptations of the species. The shape and construction of mouthparts and the structure of the limbs will give clues regarding how the animal goes about its food gathering. The range of alternatives is immense. There are structures for nipping, crushing, tearing, sucking, engulfing, grasping, rasping, drilling, and many more. And with each alternative go associated behaviors for the full accomplishment of such activities.

Insects show a wide variety of food-gathering behaviors and their mouthparts usually provide some basic clues. But even similar structures may result in different behaviors. Tent caterpillars and gypsy moth caterpillars have very similar chewing mouthparts yet the tent caterpillars very neatly eat up all their food leaves, leaving only occasional tough mid-veins. Gypsy moth caterpillars, on the other hand, tend to be sloppy in their feeding behavior and the observer will find under their feeding tree irregular chunks of uneaten leaves.

Some species of ants associate with aphids and herd them about on plants where the aphids can use their piercing-sucking mouthparts to get food from the plant juices. The aphids concentrate the sugar in the plant sap and excrete excess fluid and some sugar. The ants have learned to tap the aphids with their antennae to induce them to excrete a sweet liquid drop which the ant then eats. The ants herd the aphids to underground chambers at dusk and back up to the leafy pastures the next day.

Ingestion behavior of fish is partially telegraphed by the location of their mouths. Top feeders, such as minnows, have mouths that open upward; bottom feeders have mouths that open downward; and those that have forward opening mouths tend to take their food in the open water. Some fish lay in currents and wait for the food to drift to them; some have elaborate body lures that attract unsuspecting prey; and others actually seek out their prey.

Deer, cattle, and other ruminants, with their multiple stomach compartments, gather food quickly, keeping their heads down only for short, relatively safe periods of time. Later, they seek a safe spot where, while they keep watch for potential predators, they can chew their cud. That is, they regurgitate the partially digested food from the storage area of their stomach back to the mouth where it can be more properly ground up and reswallowed for efficient digestion.

The stalking, hunting behavior of predators is part of ingestive behavior as is the pattern of the kill. Wolves may attempt to disembowel their prey; a weasel tends to bite the base of its victim's skull; a cougar will try to break the victim's neck. Such kill patterns vary not only between species but a given species may also vary its pattern depending upon the nature of its prey.

There are a great many interesting ingestion techniques to observe: Snakes that with their elastic skin and unhingeable jaws swallow their prey whole; horseshoe crabs that can grind up their food only by walking on and crushing it with their leg joints; spiders that trap their victims, inject the digestive juices, and then suck out the digested material; herons that stalk and confuse fish with crazy dance steps; and gulls that drop shells on rocks to open them. These are just a few of many examples that could be mentioned.

Beyond the initial thrill of observing such behaviors comes the chance to watch closely time and again to note which behaviors are repeated, which seem to be unique to that individual, and which seem to be common to that species. Try to observe how similar or different are the ingestive behaviors of closely related species.

Ways of ingesting water also vary among species. Most birds have to tip their heads back to let the scooped up water run down the throat. Many mammals suck up water, others lap it, and still others drink it in the manner of the birds. Bats often drink by skimming over the water and dropping the lower jaw just below the surface to scoop up a drink. Some creatures, such as frogs, don't drink with the mouth but absorb water through their skin. Many desert creatures never really drink at all; they utilize water that is the by-product of the food they digest. Even the simple act of drinking provides a wondrous diversity of behavior.

In recording ingestive behavior be sure to note time of day and surrounding weather conditions which often have a great influence on such behavior. Much feeding behavior is very stereotyped, particularly among the invertebrate species, but among the more advanced vertebrates a fair amount of individual variation and innovation may be observed. The range of behavioral variability is generally limited by body structure and habitat constraints. We still have relatively little data on the spectrum of such variability in many higher species, particularly in view of diverse habitats and geographical locations.

Considerable information is needed on exactly what the food preferences are of a species in a given locality along with the relative importance of each food by seasons. This is a challenge to the amateur naturalist. It requires becoming intimately familiar with the use of keys to identify the plants and animals of the region and the building of reference collections of identified parts of various species as an aid to identification of observed foods.

ELIMINATIVE BEHAVIOR

No creature is anywhere near 100 percent efficient in processing the food it takes in; therefore, waste products must be eliminated from the body. Elimination of bodily wastes is one of the most basic activities, yet there is relatively little information about these activities for many species since, even today, discussion of behavior centering around elimination is not very socially acceptable and is often considered to be the province of low lifes and smut peddlers. This is unfortunate because, basic process that it is, aspects of eliminative behavior have often been ritually incorporated into an animal's other behavior patterns such as greeting gestures and courtship rituals. Elimination is also often part of territorial marking and communication in some species.

For a great many species elimination of solid and liquid wastes is a virtually automatic process that occurs whenever and wherever the pressures of accumulating wastes trigger the muscular contractions that will force its evacuation. The animal itself takes little or no notice of its wastes nor do many other species, although some, such as dung beetles, will find in the wastes a resource to be utilized. But for a considerable number of species there are clear-cut patterns of behavior associated with elimination. Sometimes these are related to elementary sanitation, sometimes to concealing the waste that would be a clue to predators or, in the case of predators, clues to prey. For still others the body wastes are deposited to serve as olfactory signal posts to others of their species.

Most tree dwellers have no special eliminative behaviors since their wastes drop away out of their normal perceptual world. Indeed it has seriously been suggested that the almost universal littering habits of humans, particularly children, are an evolutionary carry-over from our arboreal family tree. Many tree-nesting birds demonstrate complex eliminative behavior during the nesting season when the adults will pick up the youngsters' fecal material, which emerges from the body in a tough mucous sac, and take the sac away from the nest and drop it. Later the young will develop the instinctual motions that will back them up over the nest rim before they release their wastes.

Some small mammals, such as meadow mice, create short spur runways off their main transportation system which they use solely for defecation. Others, such as the woodchuck, carefully bury and cover their body wastes, as do many members of the cat family.

There are characteristic body postures associated with elimination that are essentially seen at no other time. Anyone who has watched dogs for any length of time is aware of the cocked leg of the males and three-legged squat of the females as they urinate, and the peculiar humped-back posture associated with defecation. Cats assume a squat, accompanied by a distinctive far-away look in the eyes, during the elimination process. However, beyond what we know about such things for barnyard creatures and pets, there is little in the literature about such postures.

The liquid and solid wastes of the body, since they are the result of food processing and cleansing of the bloodstream, contain many chemical clues to the health and sexual state of the animal. Also, since the digestive tract has its own distinctive mix of microflora and fauna, each animal's waste probably has its own characteristic individual odor to those equipped to detect it. Since many mammals are equipped with discriminating olfactory equipment it is not surprising that they have developed behaviors that not only deal with the removal of the wastes but also ritualize the process and use it for communication. Many of those that utilize a rather fixed territory have very specific latrine areas around the territory where they deposit waste. These areas will be visited by any strangers who will likewise leave their mark there. Most hooved animals regularly check each other's urine for clues to sexual receptivity. Much information about such behaviors remains to be recorded.

Another behavior related to both elimination and ingestion is known as *coprophagy*—the eating of feces. Most humans consider this to be thoroughly disgusting behavior but it is routine and necessary for some species. Most rabbits indulge in this behavior and actually produce two distinct types of feces. One is the usual tan to brownish cellulose pellet we see, and the other is only semi-solid and is quickly reingested. Since rabbits lack the four-stomach efficiency of cattle and deer, yet eat the same difficult-to-digest plant foods, passing the material through the digestive system twice is a way of getting maximum food value. A number of female mammals, including dogs, regularly consume the fecal droppings of their very young offspring, and other species, such as shrews and some mice, indulge in some form of reingestion, the purpose of which remains imperfectly understood.

CARE-GIVING BEHAVIOR

Most care-giving behavior is elicited as the result of rearing young but is not limited to that purpose. Care giving shows up in mutual grooming within social groups or between mated pairs and may also occur with other species under a variety of extraordinary conditions.

Observers need to be disciplined while taking notes on care giving. Carefully note what the behavior was, toward what individual or object it was directed, and how frequently it occurred. Refrain from judging motivation. It is very easy to fall into anthropomorphic traps. For example, throughout history there have been observations of dolphins holding a drowning swimmer to the surface. Such behavior has been widely touted as showing that dolphins have an affection for the human species. Dolphins have also been observed keeping an injured dolphin to the surface which permits it to breathe and resist drowning. Mother dolphins regularly assist their newborn infants to the surface so that they can breathe. The overall pattern is to keep a weakened animal at the surface until it can fend for itself. It will do for injured humans what it does for other dolphins. How much more is it legitimate to say about such behavior? On what evidence do we base the motivational speculation?

Care-giving behavior in many species appears to be controlled by hormonal cycles and is basically related to stages in the cyclic process of rearing young. Birds show a low intensity of care giving when eggs are first laid and may easily abandon the nest at that time. However, as the period of incubation proceeds and the young hatch and grow, the commitment to care giving increases. Mammals respond similarly in that they are more likely to abandon newborn young than older ones. Among fishes, amphibians, and reptiles the degree of care-giving behavior varies widely from species to species. Some show no care-giving behavior beyond fertilizing the eggs, while others have developed rather elaborate behaviors ranging from simple nest building to remaining with the young and providing simple care even after emergence from the egg.

Alligators guard their nests for many weeks and even carry the young delicately in their mouths to nearby water. Many male fish guard their nests and eggs fiercely. Some species of fish carry the eggs in their mouths until they hatch and even afterward will take the young into their mouths if danger threatens. Some salamanders lay their eggs and walk away. While others curl around the egg mass and tend it until the young emerge.

Even invertebrates are not without care-giving behaviors although such are less widespread than among vertebrates. Female wolf spiders carry their egg sac beneath the body until the eggs hatch and then the young will ride about on the mother's back. They will explore around the mother but at the least hint of danger, scramble back to the security of her body. Ants and bees carefully tend the eggs, larvae, and pupae of their kind, seeing that they are properly fed and moved about in the hives to places of optimum temperature and humidity.

Lack of care-giving behavior is as noteworthy as its presence. In building an ethogram of a species this should be recorded. One should also note, where possible, the age and sex of the recipient of care and the conditions under which it is proffered.

Grooming is an important behavior for most species and it is usually listed under the category of maintenance behavior. It is generally a solitary pursuit but, in some more social species, individuals groom each other and such activity becomes a form of care-giving behavior. It is linked to the formation of social bonds. Hooved animals may stand parallel to one another, head to tail, and keep insects at bay by tail swishing. Monkeys and apes may go over each other's fur to remove dandruff scales and occasional parasites. Humans scratch each other's backs.

CARE-SOLICITING BEHAVIOR

A variety of behavioral signals may be used to stimulate care-giving behavior. Many species have distinctive call notes used by the young to get parental attention. These are very potent signals that may even trigger care-giving behavior in closely related species that happen to be in the vicinity. Mammals also have care-soliciting vocalizations. A human baby's cry is as potent an example as any and few sounds are more difficult to ignore—as any parent of a teething baby can testify. Some animals will respond only to the care-soliciting vocalizations and related behavior of their own offspring, while others respond far less selectively and will end up adopting the offspring of others. Dogs often respond well beyond canine signals and have been known to adopt such diverse animals as raccoons and pigs. The human tendency to keep pets is linked to strong responses to diverse care-soliciting signals.

In addition to vocalizations, care is often solicited by postural signals. Birds often adopt a crouching stance and flutter the wings "helplessly." This set of actions is particularly used by fledglings when they are trying to get the parents to continue to feed them. In some cases there is clear-cut interactive signaling at the nest. For example, herring gulls have a red spot on their beaks and when youngsters pick at the spot, the parent responds by opening the mouth and regurgitating food for the young. Similarly, members of the dog family's pups may smell and lick the parent's muzzle to induce feeding behavior. Many birds are induced to feed a gaping mouth of a particular color even when this is only a model and not a live nestling.

Care-soliciting behaviors are interesting because they often reappear later in life as part of courtship and mating rituals. Familiarity with the care-giving and care-soliciting postures and actions utilized between parents and young can be quite useful in analyzing the components of courtship and pair-bonding behaviors.

MAINTENANCE BEHAVIOR

One frustrating fact of wildlife watching is that animals spend a great deal of time apparently "doing nothing." Actually, that "do nothing" time is usually devoted to grooming and sleeping. Its body covering is a very important feature of an animal's structure. It retains or loses body heat; it reduces friction of the body as it passes through air and/or water; it may even provide concealment or avoidance signals. To function effectively it must be kept in top shape. Thus feathers are preened to pull all the "zippers" together so that flight is efficient. Waterfowl feathers are preened using an oil gland to keep them waterproof. Mammals clean their fur to maintain its insulation value, water repellent features, and general comfort. Insects keep their antennae cleaned so that they can receive chemical signals well.

All animals will work to remove external parasites that not only drain energy but may impede movement. Some birds and mammals take elaborate dust baths that seem to discourage insect parasites by clogging their breathing pores. Some birds go through an elaborate procedure of rubbing their feathers with ants. This process of anting is not well understood but apparently the formic acid in the ants discourages parasites. Some species have a symbiotic relationship with another species for parasite removal; thus tick birds hop about on rhinoceroses and others and many reef fishes go to regular cleaning stations where several species of smaller fishes may go over their bodies to remove parasites.

Species vary in the grooming rituals they use and within a species there may be a wide range of individual variation on a general pattern.

One would think that, since animals spend so much time at this, maintenance behavior patterns would long ago have been carefully documented. Such is not the case. Such activity is usually written off with the simple note that the animal groomed itself. Does a bird scratch over or under its wing? Does the animal have a fixed sequence of grooming certain areas? Under what conditions is dust bathing used versus water bathing?

It is useful to know such actions in detail because they often show up as displacement behavior, that is, when an animal is frustrated from completing a normal, appropriate behavioral sequence, it may suddenly undertake some action totally inappropriate to the situation. Maintenance activities are frequently displacement activities.

Resting and sleeping behaviors have also not generally been carefully recorded. What conditions prevail when the animal chooses to rest or sleep? What postures are chosen? Are postures related to apparent depth of sleep? Are there any ritualized movements of the eyes or limbs that take place while the animal is asleep? What senses seem to be most "on alert" while the rest of the body is "off duty"? Is sleep an individual or group behavior? Does this change with age or position in the social structure? Clearly, even at rest, the animal is not "doing nothing"; the alert wildlife watcher can add considerable knowledge to his or her collection.

EXPLORATORY BEHAVIOR

Exploratory behavior is a very powerful and basic pattern. Through it, creatures learn the features of their environment that will help them meet their needs for food, water, shelter, and sexual or social companionship. For some species, particularly the simpler ones, exploratory activity appears to be essentially random and governed by positive or negative response to chance encounters with objects or forces in the environment. For some other species, however, exploratory behavior is quite structured and may result in habitual actions.

Among humans, exploratory behavior is very strong and usually takes precedence over all others (except eliminative) when the person is confronted with a new environment. When a person visits a motel, the first or second thing he or she does is check the closets, drawers, and any side rooms. And when one visits a new neighbor or friend, one checks out the house and grounds as thoroughly as cultural propriety allows. In human populations we tend to call exploratory behavior "curiosity."

Exploratory behavior is so powerful because for so many creatures it may mean survival. Knowing just how many jumps it is to the nearest cover can mean life or death to many prey species. Survival advantage goes to the individual controlling a space that it has thoroughly explored. Thus territoriality is a widespread phenomenon. When the young of territorial species disperse, they are continuously moving into new terrain and kept moving by territory holders. They seldom get a chance to know an area well through exploration, which keeps them highly vulnerable to predators familiar with the area. It is small wonder that juveniles are the age class with the highest mortality rate.

More observations are needed on the behavior patterns that are specifically related to exploratory efforts. What changes occur in this behavior once an animal has secured a territory of its own? How do the individuals react to new objects or other changes in their territory? Such information is difficult to gather but it is not beyond the realm of the creative, resourceful observer exercising his or her own form of exploratory behavior.

AGGRESSIVE/SUBMISSIVE
(AGONISTIC) BEHAVIOR

The professional student of animal behavior lumps these two aspects of behavior together under the term *agonistic behavior*. To observe such behavior there must be two individuals (or one mirror image) involved within a reasonably close unit of space or time. That is, an individual may respond aggressively or submissively to the scent or other symbolic presence of a rival as well as to that rival's physical presence.

Each species has its own array of weapons with which to threaten a rival—beaks, talons, claws, teeth, larger size, vocal threats. These it will use to drive a rival away from desired food, choice territory, or desirable mate. Generally the object of the threat is a member of the same species, but not uncommonly it may be a member of another species, particularly when the aggression is correlated with care giving—such as when a Canada goose attempts to drive a raccoon from its nest.

Aggressive actions between members of the same species are generally in the sabre-rattling class and seldom result in fatalities. The more potent the weapons the species possesses, the greater the likelihood that an encounter will result in bluff and retreat. For this to happen there must be a mechanism to reduce the intensity of the aggressive act. This mechanism is *submissive behavior*. Submissive postures act as a kind of behavioral code of ethics and as with all such codes it is not one-hundred-percent effective in preventing fatalities. As a rule of thumb, submissive postures are the exact opposite of aggressive behaviors. If the aggressive posture is to puff up the fur or feathers to increase the appearance of size, the submissive posture will usually be a flattening down of the body covering to appear smaller. If aggression involves standing tall, the submissive posture will be squatting low or rolling over. If aggression is direct forward motion with a fixed stare, submission will be retreat with eyes averted.

A classic example of submission is when a wolf in battle tucks its tail between its legs and rolls over with its throat and belly exposed. The normal response is then for the victor to cease attacking and go off a few steps to signal success by cocking its leg and scent marking with urine. While the victor is so occupied the vanquished will attempt to slink off before his motion invites a new attack. Such submissive postures are learned early and can be seen in the response of domestic puppies when a threatening adult appears.

The species-specific postures of aggression and submission usually appear fairly early in an animal's growth and will be seen in play encounters. Continued observations will reveal that certain individuals in a group show more aggressive postures to certain individuals and submission postures more frequently to others. For many species a hierarchy of dominance will become apparent. In species that normally associate in groups, these dominance hierarchies may be important features of the groups and the changes in ranking within a group may alter the group's stability. Determining rankings means being able to readily identify individual members of a group.

Knowledge of a species' agonistic postures is important not only in reading the social interactions of groups but also in analyzing components of sexual behavior.

COURTSHIP AND MATING (SEXUAL) BEHAVIOR

Sexual behavior incorporates both courtship and mating. With nonsocial species in particular, sexual displays will often involve many aspects of agonistic behavior. The goal of courtship behavior is to induce the hormonal cycles that will synchronize the readiness for fertilization of egg and sperm and to reduce the aggressive instincts of both members of a pair long enough for them to physically mate and bring about reproduction. Thus courtship displays are often complex behavioral patterns assembled from components of exploratory, care-giving, care-soliciting, and agonistic postures. Patterns of courtship are very diverse, often complicated, and generally fascinating (see Figures 8.1 and 8.2).

Figure 8.1. Behavioral sequences. This illustration involves two behavioral sequences among Jewel Cichlids. The top four pairs are in an agonistic encounter. Note carefully the degree of erection of each fin. In (A), the two strangers size each other up with fins partially extended. In (B) they pull parallel for a lateral display with fins fully erect and extended (the fish on the left shows the greatest extension). In (C) they close for mouth fighting. In (D), the male on the right shows submission with lowered fins and color change. Dominant male (left) pursues with partially erect fins; this indicates a subsidence of aggressive intensity.

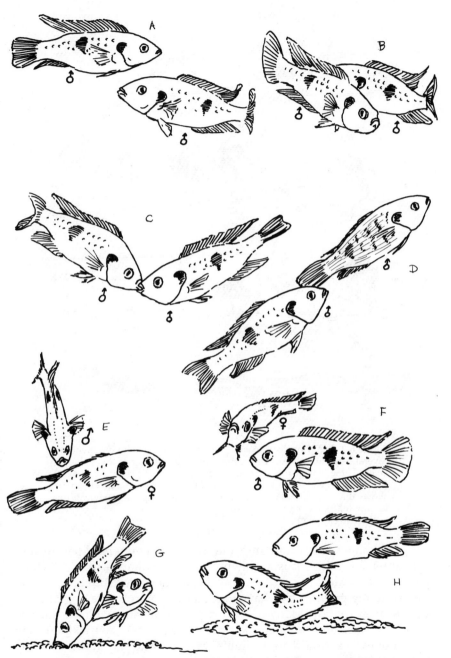

The second sequence involves a courting pair of Jewel Cichlids and represents displays over a much longer time period than above. In (E), male shows frontal display with gills flared, fins erect, and superior position; the female responds with nonaggressive display of folded fins and inferior position. (F) represents a very similar lateral display that is to establish the male's dominance in the territory. (G) Male nips at substrate, perhaps to indicate nest site. (H) Female skims the bottom and lays eggs; male soon follows and deposits fertilizing milt.

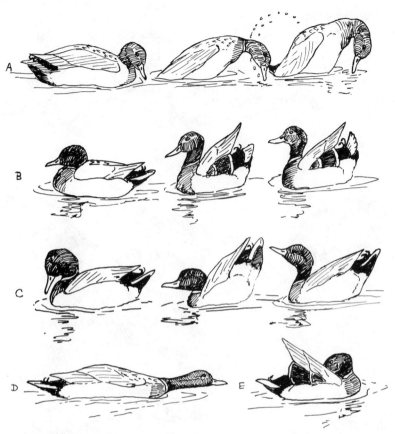

Figure 8.2. Behavior displays and sequences. This illustration involves several behavioral sequences in the courtship behavior of the Mallard Duck. Three movements, from left to right, in the display are known as: (A) the grunt whistle, (B) the head-up–tail-up, and (C) the down-up. (D) shows the nod swimming display that often accompanies the head-up–tail-up. In (E), mock preening display exposes the blue speculum feathers of the wing to the partner.

For some species courtship and mating is a very brief perfunctory encounter; for others it is a drawn-out process that results in lifelong pair bonding. Most of our waterfowl begin their courtship behavior on the wintering grounds and have formed their pairs before migration to the nesting grounds. Many of our temperate climate mammals such as foxes, skunks, and woodchucks, go through their courtship in late winter or early spring. Those wildlife watchers who stay at home during these colder times will miss the courtship rituals. Weasels, however, court in late summer; many bats do so in the fall. Those species that have late-season courtship and mating habits often have mechanisms for delaying fertilization or implantation of embryos until nearer the season for most beneficial delivery of young.

Courtship may involve "gift giving" in the form of twigs or food or bright shiny objects. It may involve chasing, mock fighting, flirting or complete indifference on the part of the female. Males may pursue individual females or defend territories, mating with any female who chooses to live in that territory. The range of options is vast and the specifics for many species remains unrecorded.

Also unrecorded for many species are the details of nest building, den construction, and the behavior surrounding birth itself. Most species are very secretive about such behavior for very adaptive reasons and a large measure of pure luck in being at the right place at the right time is involved in unraveling these secrets.

SHELTER-SEEKING BEHAVIOR

Each species is adapted to a range of environmental conditions. When conditions exceed that range the animal usually seeks some form of respite. This is shelter-seeking behavior. If the sun becomes too hot, the animal may seek shelter under a rock or tree. To avoid rain the animal may seek a rock den or hollow tree, or if the animal is an insect it may merely move to the underside of a leaf.

For some animals, such as horses and cattle of the plains, shelter seeking may be as simple as heading into or away from the wind, depending upon the way their hair lies on their body. By contrast young tree hoppers, or spittle bugs, whip up excess plant sap from their food plants with their feet to create a foam that hides them from enemies and keeps them from drying out.

A number of species are distressed by rain. Where do they go when the rains come? Which species remain active in the rain? What do butterflies do? birds? mosquitoes? Which species build shelters? Which find shelter? Don't forget aquatic species which often have elaborate shelters to protect against predators. What environmental stimuli induce the animals to seek their shelter?

Although discussed in detail in a later section, hibernation and migration can actually be considered as specialized aspects of shelter-seeking behavior. In using these responses the animals are really seeking shelter from the cold and a lack of food. Animals may also use different parts of their home range during different times of the year as a part of shelter seeking. For example, deer may seek a windswept slope that will blow irritating insects away in summer and an evergreen swamp in winter as shelter from icy winds and snow. Shelter-seeking behavior is often subtle and takes keen perceptions on the part of the wildlife observer.

ALLELOMIMETIC BEHAVIOR

The technical term *allelomimetic behavior* really does not have a simple equivalent, although it might be thought of as mob behavior. It derives from the words *allelon*, of one another, and *mimetic*, to mimic, and refers to behavior in which all members of a group appear simultaneously to mimic the actions of the other members of the group. Examples of such behavior are the wheeling and turning of a flock of blackbirds or shorebirds, the synchronized movements of the vast school of fish, the apparently simultaneous flight of a swarm of locusts, or the dashing off together of a herd of zebras. Such behavior is often awesome for it is difficult to see how all the individuals can function almost as a single organism without someone calling the signals. There is much we do not yet know about how such synchronized action is possible. Its adaptive significance is easy to see for the activity tends to confuse predators and protect the majority of the individuals.

Allelomimetic behavior is difficult to study because so much action is going on simultaneously. One has to observe the group almost as a single organism to determine the environmental stimuli for the various behaviors and then examine the individuals of the group for clues to the triggers for the apparently simultaneous action. This usually demands motion pictures of the activity that can be studied over and over, frame by frame. It may also mean follow-up experiments to prove or disprove various hypotheses. For example, watching the behavior of locusts suggested that air currents over the antennae of these insects could stimulate them to fly and that air from flapping wings of one would stimulate the one behind starting a chain reaction that would quickly have the entire swarm in flight. Experiments in the laboratory backed up the hypothesis. Very often what appears to be simultaneous action is due to the fact that the reaction time of our senses is slower than that of the species studied. The behavior of the creatures to a stimulus is based on a much faster reaction time than ours, thus giving the appearance to us of simultaneous action.

COMMUNICATION

Communication is a widespread phenomenon in living things. It is an outgrowth of a basic property, irritability, of the basic stuff of life—*protoplasm*. Protoplasm responds to stimuli from the environment. Even the simplest microbes are attracted by some things in their world and repelled by others. In animals that exhibit sexuality, signals between the sexes are essential for bringing about union and permitting reproduction. This is communication at its most primitive levels. Perhaps at the other end of the scale is communication exhibited through the various linguistic and symbolic representation abilities of humans. A broad spectrum of communication styles lies in between.

The basic media for communication are light, sound, and chemistry. Animals use one or more of these to gain information about each other and the remaining parts of their perceived environment. We are also learning that some creatures are able to interpret electromagnetic pulses and perhaps can even produce them.

Anatomists have been able to demonstrate that, in general, those areas of the nervous system are enlarged that are most responsive to the primary stimuli that a particular species uses for communication, be it smell, sight, or sound.

Wildlife watchers have to be very careful in interpreting communication behaviors they observe. People are biased to sight and sound and even then to signals within certain wavelengths of energy. We may see an animal do something for no apparent reason because we are unstimulated by the wavelength of light or sound or by the scent that triggered a response in the animal we are studying.

The various components of the total environment are constantly emitting signals of great diversity—light waves, sound waves, electromagnetic waves, chemicals, and others. No species is able to respond to more than a narrow spectrum of these signals with its sensory equipment. The German ethologists refer to the total realm of environmental signals as the *umwelt* and that segment of signals to which a species responds as its *merkwelt*. In English we might call it the animal's perceptual world.

For animals which use sight as a major means of communication we are able to make the best observations of their signals and responses. Perhaps one reason so many people enjoy birds is that they, like us, rely heavily on visual cues to communicate. So too do many fish, particularly the tropical reef fishes that lure so many to the growing hobby of fish watching.

Visually oriented species use their whole bodies to communicate, with color, pattern, and movement all playing roles in sending signals. One has to build a collection of all the various signals possible and their combinations before being able to attach reasonable meaning to them. In addition one must always note the context in which a signal is given. For example, just before flying, many ground-feeding birds crouch slightly. If, as you approach, they are somewhat nervous that danger is near, you may spot this crouch. If you freeze your action, the bird may relax and return to its feeding. Move carefully forward again and the bird may crouch again. Freeze again. With care you may be able to approach quite closely before the bird actually completes the sequence and flies away. The little crouch before flight is called an "intention movement" and precedes another action. Learning to read intention movements is an important part of the stalker's skills.

Individual body parts are important components of visual communication and their relative positions at any time should be carefully noted. The position at which members of the dog family carry their tails, the elevation of various fins of a fish, the degree of fluffing of feathers and fur, along with general body carriage all have their communication value.

Observing communication between two or more creatures is tricky because the observer must be alert to both the signals being sent by animal A and the response to those signals by animal B. Don't be surprised by your poor comprehension at first. The situation is somewhat akin to having had a year of high-school French and then finding yourself plunked down in Paris without an interpreter. In both cases you may get the rough gist of the messages but completely miss the fine points. After hundreds of hours of observation and broad exposure to the variety of alternative poses and sequences available, one begins to understand what is happening. It is such communication by two or more animals that cries out to be recorded on movie film. You can view the film over and over, first concentrating on one individual and then on the other until the sequence of posturings begins to make some sense to you.

Once you think you have some understanding of the motions and their meanings you can begin to make predictions about what response to expect from a given signal. From continuous observation you can test the validity of your hypotheses.

With aural communication that is within our range of frequency we can make similar observations about sound signals sent and the behavior they elicit in others. Watch not only how members of the same species respond, but also how other species respond as well. Many species other than blue jays respond to the jay alarm call. The distress calls of rodents will get response from more than just other rodents. In Africa the baboon and the impala often share the same foraging areas and both respond to each other's alarm calls which, to our ears at least, are nearly identical.

Other forms of communication using high-frequency sound, such as with bats, shrews, and some others, along with olfactory clues, severely tax our normal sensory range and push us to the use of sensory extenders and amplifiers such as oscilloscopes and chemical analysis. Those with a mechanical bent will undoubtedly rise to the challenge of ferreting out ways of probing these areas of communication.

HOME RANGE
AND TERRITORY

There are several categories of behavior that are composites of aspects of the others, that is, if the basic categories of behavior mentioned earlier can be considered to compose basic words and simple phrases then these behaviors could be compared to sentences. Home range and territory fall into this category. Although closely related, the two terms are not synonymous. Both involve aspects of ingestive and eliminative behavior along with care-giving and care-soliciting behaviors, while territorial activity usually involves sexual and agonistic behaviors—home range need not. Confused? Let's see if we can clear it up.

Home range is the geographic area an individual regularly uses to meet its needs for food, shelter, water, and social interaction. The animal may use different parcels of its home range more intensively at different seasons of the year and under varying weather conditions. Different parts of the home range may be used for different purposes.

A territory is an area that an individual, pair, or social group defends from others of its kind and sometimes even other species that are perceived as a threat. A territory may be as big as the home range but usually it is not. It is generally only a much smaller area such as a nest, den, or foraging area. Territories are usually defended for only part of the year.

Studying territorial behavior involves being able to identify individuals and mapping where these individuals are sighted and their behavioral actions including scent marking, singing, aggressive activities, and locations where pursuit of a rival ceases.

Home range is more difficult to discern for most species, even when you can recognize individuals. Members of the different sexes may have quite different home ranges and these often change with the seasons and changing food sources. However, knowledge of home ranges is important in developing reasonable conservation plans for various species and in determining how large an area must be protected in order to assure a viable population of any particular species. Determining home range normally involves marking individuals and establishing live trapping or observation grids so that individuals can periodically be caught and/or observed and their location and implied, or actual, behavior mapped and noted. In some cases individuals have been fed dyed or radioactive materials which are passed in the scats. The scats are then located and mapped. All these techniques are used with rather complex statistical methods to approximate the home range. Radio tracking of individuals is increasingly being used to plot home range but battery life is usually too short to permit data gathering through a full annual cycle.

In plotting home range, an observer will want good maps of the local vegetational types, for within a given geographic bounds a species will usually show preferences for certain types of habitats and these preferences may vary with the seasons.

HIBERNATION, EMERGENCE, AND MIGRATION

Birds and their migrations have been extensively studied by both an army of amateur bird watchers and professional ornithologists, yet an amazing amount remains to be learned before most of the questions can be answered definitively. We have learned that there are many ways of navigating on the journeys, ranging from visual clues to response to electromagnetic fields, and that most species can use more than one mode but that none can use all of them. Much remains to be determined about who uses what navigational means under what conditions. The general routes used by different species are reasonably well known and the approximate dates of arrival and departure of local populations are known for a number of bird species. Much of this knowledge has been garnered through the extensive bird-banding activities conducted under the coordination of the U.S. Fish and Wildlife Service. Indeed, so much data has been accumulated that it can only be processed by computers. There is still much observation to be done correlating local movements of various bird species with weather and other environmental conditions. As backyard bird feeding continues to expand as a popular activity, some formerly migratory populations are becoming nonmigratory or migrate much shorter distances. For some species this puts the population at greater risk in the face of unusual weather conditions; for others it may reduce the risks inherent in long flights and increasingly hostile conditions on the wintering grounds. The opportunity exists for some good amateur studies.

Other migrants are even less well understood than the birds. With the help of many amateurs, monarch butterflies have been rather extensively banded and their migration routes are becoming better known, as are their very localized wintering grounds. But there are some other migratory butterflies whose migratory habits have hardly been studied at all. Dragonflies migrate and deserve more attention as well. Migration of our tree bats is poorly understood; flyways are inadequately defined, as are times and distances of flights and many other factors related to their migration and environmental conditions. Many cave bat species have migratory patterns as well. Some species' migrations are very local such as the vertical migrations through life zones in the mountain regions and the annual treks of frogs, toads, and salamanders to the breeding ponds and their subsequent dispersal once the breeding season is over. The field is wide open.

Hibernation is another phenomenon that deserves more exploration. Dates of disappearance and emergence for a variety of hibernators and "seasonal resters" need to be amassed over the breadth of a species' range. Physiologists have been working a long while on the mechanisms that trigger hibernation but their findings remain equivocal and controversial. There is much to learn. My observations indicate that adult woodchucks on territory gain weight faster and disappear earlier, whereas young of the year without their own territories are unable to gain adequate weight as rapidly and thus remain active much later into the fall. Do your observations confirm mine? If not, how do they differ? My observations are for southern New England. Do yours vary because of a different geographical location?

Earlier I referred to hibernation or "seasonal resting." That is because of technical arguments about what constitutes "true" hibernation. Many researchers argue that all of a series of conditions must be met for true hibernation to be occurring and these conditions tend to exclude all but a few rodents such as woodchucks, jumping mice, hamsters, and the like. Others, myself included, see hibernation as an adaptation to recurring cycles of adverse weather, particularly harsh winter weather. Several groups of organisms have evolved similar but technically different strategies for riding out these periods with minimal input and expenditure of energy. Thus, in addition to the rodents, some bats and carnivores are also hibernators among the mammals, along with some reptiles and amphibians and several insects including queen hornets and the beautiful mourning cloak butterfly. Others rest through periods of heat and drought—a process labeled aestivation by the scientists. Whatever the definition, various species exhibit seasonal retreat from normal activity, and the alert wildlife watcher will note the time and conditions under which the animals depart from and return to normal activity.

DENSITY-DEPENDENT
BEHAVIOR

This kind of observation depends upon previous study of the behavior of a species under relatively normal population levels. However, as populations of animals become abnormally high or low, patterns of normal behavior may change or "new" patterns emerge. Mass movements of mice and lemmings during population irruptions is an example. This appears to be an allelomimetic behavior that is suppressed in normal populations. It causes the animals to keep moving even against insurmountable barriers such as a broad waterway, giving the false impression that the creatures are committing mass suicide. That may be the result, but the motivation is quite different.

Under the stress of high population, aggression may increase, resulting in increased killing of the young and cannibalism. Normal reactions to a variety of stimuli may be considerably altered and all should be recorded where possible.

On the other hand, when numbers become abnormally low, behaviors have to change. Individuals may have to range farther to seek mates or they may be more ready to accept mates of a related species, increasing the rate of natural hybridization in the area. For example, red wolves in the South Central States have had to seek coyote mates frequently enough that there are almost no genetically pure red wolves left. Biologists have declared the red wolf extinct in the wild and have captured the few remaining purebred stock for attempts to increase their numbers through captive breeding. If successful, they may someday be returned to the wild.

Perhaps it should be noted here that known hybrids are often very interesting behaviorally. Those species that have genetically fixed behaviors, when hybridized, produce behavior patterns that are a mix of both patterns. For example, the group of waterfowl species generally called "puddle ducks" has courtship behavior that involves head bobbing or pumping and rearing up in the water. That group known as diving ducks has courtship that involves head tossing. Male hybrids between species of the two different groups may bob the head, then rear and throw the head back, which puts them completely off balance and results in a very indecorous aquatic summersault. Females of either parent species are confused and since the hybrid male is sending inappropriate signals, the females of neither species will breed with it.

Frogs and toads likewise occasionally hybridize in the wild, resulting in individuals whose mating calls fall somewhere between those of the parent species. These, too, seldom find a mate unless they encounter a similar hybrid.

SOCIAL BEHAVIOR

Some species are characterized by individuals that go about their day-to-day activity alone, associating with others of their kind only for mating, and sometimes, the rearing of the young. Other species are basically social in nature and individuals regularly associate together and interact as they go about their daily lives. Such social organization usually gives an adaptive advantage for all.

Patterns of social organization are quite varied, ranging from very loose association with minimal interaction and communication, as with giraffes, to very tightly structured and complex organization, as, for example, with baboon troops. There is a broad spectrum of organizational patterns in between.

Determining social structure in an animal species takes prolonged and detailed observation and, if it is to result in information of general application, the observations should be made of groups of the species over a large geographical unit. The observer must be familiar with as many individuals of the group as possible. It is generally felt that if social observations are to be valid, the observer should be able to individually identify at least ten percent of the population in the study area.

One needs to determine which animals associate with which others. How stable are the associations? Can outsiders mix in easily or are they driven off? Is there any pattern of hierarchy in the associations?

Gathering information about such questions involves many and regular observations. Photography is often helpful because the photos can later be compared with a mug file to identify the various group members. This is valuable in determining associations but it will take many detailed observations of individual interactions to get the hierarchial information. It is also important to be able to identify the different sexes and have a good idea of the age class to which an individual belongs.

One must be very careful in interpreting social interaction data. As time passes and the observer really gets to know a study population well, behavior that originally appeared simple may be found to have disturbing complexities. Following individual females and their offspring over several generations, one may find that associations that seemed random at first actually are related to kinship. Following the development of dominance patterns may also show that offspring of certain lineages are more likely to end up with hierarchial status much the same as their parents. In other cases, where very little overt aggression is seen in adults to maintain hierarchial status, it may be found that that status is actually set during adolescent play and seldom seriously challenged thereafter.

Studies of social organization require real dedication and may seem to be primarily the province of the professional. But it is not impossible for those who must stay close to home to make prolonged, detailed studies of backyard species (as Margaret Morse Nice did with the song sparrow).

ENVIRONMENTAL FACTORS
OF BEHAVIOR

Behavior is in essence always a response to the environment. That environment is not only other creatures but the physical world as well. To truly understand the behavior of a species, it is necessary to determine what factors of the environment affect it, in what ways, and to what degree. How does it respond to rain, snow, wind, light, darkness, warmth, cold, and so on? Environmental factors often stimulate internal chemical changes that induce breeding behaviors, migrations, moults, and other behavioral patterns.

Whenever possible, gather and record as much physical data about the environment as you can, being sure to recognize the existence and nature of microhabitats. Grasshoppers in a field go through a daily vertical migration during hot weather. As the sun beats down and heats the soil, the temperatures near the ground become too great and the hoppers move up to a relatively cooler site. As the sun goes down, the soil radiates heat but the air above is cooler, so the hoppers move down closer to the earth. Lacking internal temperature control mechanisms, they have to control their physical comfort by seeking better conditions.

Desert mammals seem to withstand a wide range of temperature extremes within a twenty-four-hour period. Unlike insects, they have internal temperature regulating mechanisms but even these can't handle the extreme temperatures for long. Actually many of these desert mammals have a quite narrow range of temperature tolerance. They survive through behavioral adaptations. They dig their dens in locations that hold to a narrow temperature range and choose to be active during those sectors of the daily temperature cycle that best correlate with their range of temperature tolerance.

In nature everything is ultimately linked to everything else. The wildlife watcher who wants to understand well what is happening must become alert to everything around him.

FURTHER READING

ALCOCK, JOHN. *Animal Behavior: An Evolutionary Approach.* Sunderland, Mass.: Sinauer Associates, 1975.

BASTOCK, M. *Courtship: An Ethological Study.* Chicago: Aldine, 1967.

BROWN, VINSON. *How to Understand Animal Talk.* Boston: Little, Brown, 1958.

EIBL-EIBESFELDT, I. *Ethology: The Biology of Behavior.* New York: Holt, Rinehart & Winston, 1970.

KENDEIGH, S. C. *Parental Care and Its Evolution in Birds.* Illinois Biological Monographs No. 22. Urbana: University of Illinois Press, 1952.

KLOPFER, PETER. *Habitats and Territories: A Study in the Use of Space.* New York: Basic Books, 1969.

KREBS, J. R., and N. B. DAVIES, eds. *Behavioral Ecology: An Evolutionary Approach.* Sunderland, Mass.: Sinauer Associates, 1978.

LORENZ, KONRAD. *King Solomon's Ring.* New York: Thomas Y. Crowell, 1952.

SCOTT, J. P. *Aggression.* Chicago: University of Chicago Press, 1958.

_____. *Animal Behavior,* 2nd ed. Chicago: University of Chicago Press, 1972.

SEBECK, T. A. *Animal Communication.* Bloomington: Indiana University Press, 1968.

SKUTCH, ALEXANDER F. *Parent Birds and Their Young.* Austin, Texas: University of Texas Press, 1976.

SOUTHWICK, C., ed. *Animal Aggression: Selected Readings.* New York: Van Nostrand-Reinhold, 1970.

TINBERGEN, NIKO. *Social Behavior in Animals.* London: Methuen, 1953.

_____. *Curious Naturalists.* London: Country Life, Ltd., 1958.

WILSON, EDWARD O. *Sociobiology.* Cambridge, Mass.: Harvard University Press/ Belknap Press, 1975.

CHAPTER 9

BEHAVIOR WATCHING

IN HIS CLASSIC BOOK *The Vertebrate Story*, Professor A. S. Romer wrote:

It is not enough to name an animal; we want to know everything about him: what sort of life he leads, his habits and instincts, how he gains his food and escapes enemies, his relations to other animals and his physical environment, his courtship and reproduction, care of his young, home life (if any). Some aspects of these inquiries are dignified by such names as *ecology* and *ethology*; for the most part they come broadly under the term *natural history*. Many workers who may study deeply—but narrowly—the physiological processes or anatomical structure of animals are liable to phrase this, somewhat scornfully, as "mere natural history." But on reflection, this attitude is the exact opposite of the proper one. No anatomical structure, however beautifully designed, no physiological or biochemical process, however interesting to the technical worker, is of importance except insofar as it contributes to the survival and welfare of the animal. The study of the functioning of an animal in nature—to put it crudely, how he goes about his business of being an animal— is in many regards the highest possible level of biological investigation.

The name of the game ultimately is survival—survival of the species. That is possible when a species' adaptations permit it to effectively meet its basic needs from the environment. Behavior is all the actions the species takes as it goes about its life, utilizing the environment effectively and reproducing its kind. The interactions of the species with its environment is the raw material of ecology.

Actually, ecology is studied on two general levels. The first level is quite abstract and involves studying the general interactions of a wide range of organisms and the physical environment—the biophysical community. It is concerned with energy flow in the whole system, the replacement of various species as the environment changes over time, and other broad concepts. This level of ecology is called *synecology* and derives from the root of synthesis since it deals with the synthesis of information about many species.

The second level is more concrete and is the study of the relationship of an individual species with other species in its surroundings and with the physical features of its habitat. This is called *autecology*. Whereas synecology is, and must necessarily be, a field for the professional, autecology is a promising realm for amateur studies.

The key to autecological investigations is behavior watching. We must know what an animal does and can do in order to determine how it relates to other species and the physical environment. Without extensive collections of autecological data as a base from which to synthesize, it would seem that synecological conclusions must remain quite questionable. Indeed many ecological concepts such as niche, succession, community, and stability are theory rich and information poor; that is, they are built from a very small base of concrete data.

The behavior watcher has two basic options to choose from. He can take random notes on whatever species are spotted on trips and rambles or he can choose one or two species and focus in on locating and observing them. The first option is usually the easier and provides diversity, but the information gathered tends to be fragmented, which can lead to a sense of frustration. The second approach takes more time, discipline, and skill and you may find that many field sessions come up empty of new material, but ultimately the rewards are greater as you get to know a species more intimately. In essence the two options are akin to the options of becoming acquainted with many people superficially at cocktail parties or selecting out a few people with whom to develop more extensive and intimate friendships. Of course these are not absolute choices; one can do a little of both.

CHOOSING A STUDY SITE

Wildlife watching can be done almost anywhere. The observer might watch house spiders in a corner of the room; house sparrow in the yard; sphinx moths in the garden; solitary wasps in the gravel pit; frogs in the marsh; raccoons in the woodlot; ground squirrels in the park; or waterfowl at the refuge. The list is endless. Wildlife watching at some level can be enjoyed by almost anyone who so desires.

Each species has a fairly specific area of home range used by each individual. For some, this encompasses only a few square yards in a life time. This is particularly true of some insects, snails, and other invertebrates. On the other hand, there are species such as our migratory birds that range over several hemispheres. In choosing a species and sites to study it, it is necessary to consider its range. How free are you to follow it in time and space? If a species ranges great distances you may have to content yourself with learning about only limited aspects of its behavior. We are just beginning to learn that some songbirds, whose behavior we thought we knew well, actually have a range of different behaviors on their tropical wintering grounds. Some of these behaviors are brought on by the fact that the populations are dispersed in the north during the breeding season but concentrated in the more limited habitats of the wintering grounds. It is only recently that trained observers have had the opportunity to study some of these birds in the tropics.

For those with limited time and money for travel and observation, it is best to discover the many mysteries of small wild neighbors near at hand. In so doing you find yourself in the company of such distinguished wildlife watchers as John Henri Fabre, Howard E. Evans, Margaret Morse Nice, and Edwin Way Teale. If your own home and grounds offer too limited opportunities for wildlife watching, explore your community carefully. Almost every community, even in big cities, has some wild corners where some wildlife lives—vacant lots, parks, golf courses, public gardens, waterfront areas.

Weekends may be your major opportunity for real wildlife watching. You will want to visit areas reasonably close by so that you can get in as much observation time as possible. At the end of this chapter is a list of some publications that can help you locate sites where there are generally concentrations of wildlife. One thing to understand is that concentrations of wildlife may also mean concentrations of wildlife watchers. If you are focusing on collecting general behavioral observations this may make little difference. On the other hand, if you are concentrating on a detailed exploration of a given species and want to follow specific individuals such a site will seldom do. A reasonable degree of privacy is needed.

To find areas that will afford some degree of privacy you will want to find out who the major land holders are in your area and seek permission from some of them to use part of their land for your studies. Similarly you might get permission to use study areas established by local universities, nature centers, science museums, national and state forests, wildlife or game refuges, or Nature Conservancy holdings. Some of these will have established guidelines for researchers on their land in order to protect the interests of the wildlife and other researchers. Be prepared to abide by them.

In order to locate sites where you might find less common species for study, don't hesitate to inquire about the animals from local outdoor-oriented people—hunters, forest rangers, boaters, loggers—who are afield much of the time and are likely to have made at least mental note of occasional sightings of the species that interests you. I have even advertised in newspapers with success. To locate summer colonies of bats, I placed an ad in the local weekly papers and soon had a number of good leads. Likewise, in trying to track down recolonization of porcupines in my home state I contacted all veterinarians for information about quilled dogs that had been brought to them for treatment. This tactic paid off, as did a newspaper ad in which I requested information about porcupine sightings or den locations. In a short time I was able to show that a species "officially" extirpated from the state decades before was actually quite widespread and growing more abundant. From the information received I was also able to establish several study sites where the animals could be observed.

If a site encompasses more than five or six acres you should have a topographic map of it. You can get such maps from the U.S. Geological Survey. Detailed addresses are given in Chapter 11. Such maps familiarize you with the basic features of the site, such as the hills, cliffs, waterways, wetlands, woodlands, and the like. If you are using a site frequently, it is useful to have blowups made photographically of the section of the topo map where your site is located. These can be a base for xerox duplicates, on which you can map habitat types and locations of observations, or plot the movements of your subjects.

Having chosen a site, be it backyard or piece of wilderness, you should first familiarize yourself as completely as possible with it. You should know its vegetation, wind patterns, water regime, outstanding microclimates and any other features that might affect a species' choice of activity sites. Animals do not use all of an area over which they range; some places get heavy use, others almost none. There will be travel routes, congregating areas, defended territories, and neutral common areas, which will tend to vary with the seasons. A good wildlife watcher will systematically cruise the study area, noting any signs of the target species' presence and activity and mark them on his or her map. As much as is possible, try to put yourself in the skin of your subject and try to intuit what factors it is responding to in this habitat.

Whenever you are afield, cruising or observing, it is wise to carry a day pack with some basic equipment for both your studies and your personal comfort. Water, casting plaster, plastic bags, camera, and notebook may prove useful to the wildlife work; and a snakebite kit, a first aid kit, crackers or tortillas, cheese, an apple, and some gorp, will contribute to the inner needs. If you are so equipped, you can spend a whole day afield without having to return to home or base camp for needed incidentals.

BACKGROUND DIGGING

It is surprising to some wildlife watchers that good field studies usually involve a good deal of armchair naturalist work. It is important to find out just what is already known about a species. This will involve considerable reading and searching into both the popular and technical literature. At first you may be content with the popular literature but in time you will likely find yourself seeking out even the more obscure technical journals where much key information lies entombed. The extent to which you can do this may depend upon how near you live to a college or university because few public libraries carry the scientific journals you will seek. Even at a university you may have to ferret out a departmental library or even a professor's private library to find what you want.

Using the behavioral pattern headings listed in Chapter 8 as an outline (see Appendix A) you may well wish to record the details about your study species from your readings. Thus a behavioral profile or ethogram will begin to emerge. This information will help you to get a picture of what the characteristics of good habitat for a study site would be, see what behavioral patterns and postures are known so you can try to spot them for yourself in the field, and determine what the major areas of ignorance about the species are so that you may seek to illuminate them through your studies.

The books and articles listed at the end of each chapter and in the Bibliography of this book cover a number of essentially nontechnical volumes on the behavior of a range of species as well as a listing of journals that regularly carry information about animal behavior. These writings are good starting points for your background digging. Almost all of them also carry their own bibliographies, which, if they are pursued, will lead you deeper and deeper into the mysteries and information about various species.

SHARPENING AND FOCUSING

At first, observations in the field tend to be quite general and anecdotal. Such information is useful in building a dim image of a species' behavioral repertoire. It is a beginning, but it needs sharpening.

In reporting on his studies of chulo behavior, Bil Gilbert writes:

> Everything we observed contributed to our learning, and in most cases the significance of a given phenomenon was not apparent until we had repeatedly observed it, and were able to relate it to other observations. . . . Our understanding improved as a result of slow accretion of observations, but gradual as the process was, we were aware of and pleased with it.

Each new action is fascinating in and of itself but we need to go on to determine if it is common and basic, or unusual, or even unique to the particular individual. Does the response of A to B's behavior represent coincidence or was it distinctly triggered by what B did? Does B's act always trigger the same response in others? If not, under what conditions does it?

Gathering data is not always easy, and like any skill, it takes patience, discipline, determination, and practice. A good example of the trials and joys of getting started in systematic behavior watching is found in the following excerpts from an article by Shoshana Satter. Satter, at the time, was a Yale student who had been assigned to study the behavior of the campus gray squirrels.

My method of research was simple: Follow one squirrel and record what it was doing every minute. Its behavior was assigned to one of eight categories: feed, clean/groom, rest, assume alert posture, move, dig, forage, nest build. Later I calculated the time spent at each activity for each hour of the day and graphed a daily activity pattern. Of course a reliable pattern would require approximately the same number of observation hours for each hour of the day that the squirrels are active. My observations were squeezed between classes, and thus were not equally spaced throughout the day. Also recorded in as much detail as possible, were each of the rare instances of social behavior. . . .

I was aware, often painfully, of the passing of each minute on my stop-watch. I tried anything to keep my mind occupied, planning all my conversations for the next week or inventing isometric exercises to keep my limbs from freezing (I couldn't move them, for fear of disturbing the squirrels). What, I wondered to myself, would Niko Tinbergen or Jane Goodall do at a time like this? . . .

My data hours, when computed according to instructions, numbered fewer than 100; several hundred hours are needed for significant results. Yet the experience was worthwhile in other ways. Time spent watching animals sharpens one's powers of observation. One must be still and wait for the animal to move, so that the observation hours are like meditation. One feels the excitement of participating in a scientific study in the most basic way. I started out knowing nothing about gray squirrels; pencil, paper, and stopwatch were my only equipment. Little by little, I collected information and began to formulate my own questions. I was a detective collecting clues, and each new bit of information became a piece fitting into the puzzle.

Answering many of our wildlife questions will demand that our observations be quantitative as well as qualitative. We need to record how many times a behavior occurs; how often conditions are the same; time of behavior, and so on. Only from a mass of such data can clear patterns begin to emerge that allow us to make valid and reliable statements about what a species does. In this vein Gilbert wrote:

> There being no Chulo grammar or dictionaries, it being a matter of complete indifference to the natives whether we understood their language or not, we learned what we did of Chulo by spying or eavesdropping. When we heard a new sound or gesture, we tried to remember or better yet, record it on tape or film, to make some note about the circumstances in which it was used, the response of the other animals to the sign. When we reached the point that we could predict the reaction of one animal to a sign made by another, we felt we had more or less made it on our own.

When making a prolonged observation of an animal or group of animals it is often useful to make regular intermittent observations. Set up your observations as a time log. In the left-hand column note the exact time (a digital watch is handy for this) and then write down what is happening. Do this over and over at fixed time intervals. You may also want to note how much time is devoted to certain behaviors. A stopwatch is a handy piece of equipment for this. As Satter's comments suggest, the watch may appear at times to be a dictator but it can help keep discipline over some of the less exciting periods of a wildlife stakeout.

The important thing is to have good reliable observational data. Beware of suggesting why something occurred or what its purpose was. Valid statements on such things usually must be based on careful experiments. It is not unusual for good field observers to be incorrect in their conclusions while their careful observations remain useful to others who may draw quite different conclusions from them. Be sure that if you wish to venture hypotheses based on your data that you clearly separate verifiable observations from your opinions or "conclusions."

The context of the behavior observed is very important. For example, two gulls may be threatening one another when all of a sudden one turns and begins to preen. Such inappropriate behavior is known as displacement. Or in a similar situation one individual may back down and then go off and attack a subordinate. This is redirected aggression. Such actions make little sense unless seen in their full context.

OBSERVATIONS
OF CAPTIVE WILDLIFE

Observing captive animals is often more convenient than dealing with the uncertainties of finding and observing free-roaming specimens, particularly of secretive species. However, the conditions of captivity often alter behavior patterns raising a host of questions about the validity and reliability of statements about a species' behavior based solely on captive observations.

Working with some smaller species such as invertebrates, fishes, reptiles, amphibians, and some small mammals where it is possible to create mini-habitats that closely approach the natural environment, an observer can gather good and reasonably reliable information. In fact with some species it may be the only reasonable way to provide relatively continuous observation over a substantial span of time. To be able to trust the validity of your observations in terms of the normality of the behaviors the mini-habitats must reproduce as exactly as possible the structure of the normal environment and provide adequate space for a territorial species to establish a territory.

Species also vary in regard to the impact the presence of an observer has on altering their behavior. Some species, particularly among invertebrates, are little affected by the presence of a human observer. Apparently, they perceive the observer as just another relatively harmless mega-object in their mini-world. Many others, particularly birds and mammals, generally have their behavior considerably altered by the observer's presence. This may be reflected in a fear response, or if the creature is tame, in incorporating the observer into the behavior inappropriately. To get valid and reliable information about a species, it is a key maxim of wildlife watching that the observer must have little or no influence on the behavior of the wildlife.

For those beginning behavior watching, zoos and aquariums can provide valuable insights and good opportunities for extended observations, particularly with recent trends for these institutions to work harder to create more realistic habitats for their specimens. At such institutions the observer can develop and sharpen observational and notetaking skills. However, you must realize that in many aspects the behavior you see may not honestly reflect the normal behavior of the species. Zoo and aquarium behavior watching is merely an *hors d'oeuvre* for field observation.

Captive conditions are often utilized to answer more definitively the how and why questions about behavior just because they do alter behavior. The scientist can control certain variables in the environment and record the behavioral response. Through such experimentation it is possible to focus on narrow aspects of behavior without worrying about how captive conditions alter the behavioral repertoire generally. There are those who question the validity of these studies as well, believing that if you do not know how all the behaviors are interrelated, you can't tell how altering other behaviors affects the more limited one being experimented with. Actually these are subtle arguments that have to be approached on a species by species basis.

HARD AND SOFT CAPTIVITY

In essence there are two kinds of captivity—hard confinement and soft confinement. Hard confinement means that the animal is physically confined to some type of cage or enclosure. It is the most frequent type of captivity. Soft confinement is psychological bonding to the observer through imprinting or habituation. Imprinting involves handling the young from birth through the critical development period when they make a psychological bonding with the object that rears them. Under normal conditions, this would be a member of its own species. Habituation means that the animal has slowly become accustomed to the presence of a human or other potentially dangerous creatures, and accepts it as a nonthreatening adjunct to the environment.

Psychological bonding often makes it difficult for the animal to relate normally to others of its kind, but it will still exhibit many normal components of its behavioral repertoire. The bonding does allow the observer to give the animal semi-, or even total, freedom and to move about with the animal without undue impact on much of its behavior. Behavior patterns most apt to be disrupted are those which must be socially learned from the parents, and sexual orientation. All too often the imprinted animal will make sexual displays to humans rather than to its own kind.

Herb and Lois Crisler made use of psychological bonding in studying wolves in Alaska. Their exploits are charmingly told in *Arctic Wild*. Douglas Pimlott also used this approach with wolves in a mix of hard and soft confinement. Unfortunately the technique usually involves a lifelong dependency of the animal on the humans and the animals often end up tragically at the hands of less trustworthy people. The technique seems most successful with predatory species. Peter Krott used it to study wolverines in Europe (see *Demon of the North*); and in Africa, Joy Adamson studied lions, cheetahs, and leopards using the soft confinement approach. Her various books (*Born Free; Pippa; Queen of Shaba*) point up the weaknesses as well as the strengths of this approach.

The naturalist Sam Campbell described the behavior of several porcupines that he raised and released on an island and observed over a period of years. Whereas *How's Inky* and *Too Much Salt and Pepper* are humorous accounts, they indicate what can be learned under such conditions. I have reared a number of porcupines under hard captive conditions but with much personal interaction with the animals. Some of my observations point up some of the disruptions of normal behavior that can occur. The literature generally describes porcupines as slow, stupid creatures. If you watch the animals in the wild you don't see much to dispute such a description. However, almost all the young captives exhibited considerable curiosity and much more "intelligence" than would be expected. However, their captive environment, particularly for those given fairly free run of the house plus the attention of the caretaker, was a much more stimulating environment than the wild environment and it fostered capacities not normally brought to play in the wild. Also, whereas most wild porcupines are normally loners throughout the year, all but one of my captive-reared animals have been very affectionate and remained so throughout their lives. But imprinting presented problems. One female captive never did accept another porcupine as a mate. She did do the rather comical courtship circle dance—but for me and me alone. It afforded me good opportunity to closely observe the behavior but it was frustrating in several ways. First, because there was no learning about how the display was received and responded to by another porcupine; and second, because it meant that the female would spend her life unfulfilled.

We can see that captive observations are potentially useful but have distinct limitations that must be constantly kept in mind. Behavioral data from confined specimens is most apt to be valid and reliable if

- the enclosure is large enough to represent the normal daily range of the animal and/or permit the establishment of territory where this is important.
- the materials in the enclosure are essentially the same as would be found in the wild.
- the temperatures and moisture regimen are essentially the same as in the wild and follow seasonal variations.
- the day/night cycle is the same as in the wild and is continuously adjusted with the passage of the seasons.
- the diet is essentially the same as in the wild.
- the animals are wild caught or reared without psychological attachment to humans or excessive stress from the perceived close presence of people.

Departure from these guidelines is likely to cause alteration of some behaviors. One must temper one's judgment about the normality of behaviors observed according to which of the above factors are altered and to what degree.

For example, it has been reported in the literature that within the vast freetailed bat colonies of the Southwest that the young gather in so-called nursery clusters and are fed by any female that lands, not necessarily the biological parent. This is very unusual behavior. I was curious whether the same might be true of the large colonies of little brown bats in my area. I already had observed that the young gathered in clusters of ten to thirty or more. Conditions for prolonged observation in the colonies are less than ideal. Most of the colonies I had under observation were in attics and barns where the temperatures averaged around 100° and the ammonia fumes from accumulated bat droppings were overpowering. In addition, most of the animals managed to stay wedged in cracks or in spaces between the siding and the studs. Hinged doors gave some access but not enough for serious observation. Captive studies seemed to be the only way to get some answers.

Pregnant females were captured and allowed to give birth in separate containers. Each youngster was marked and left with its mother for several days. Then, since I did not have a flight cage at the time, and thus could not allow for a normal nursery colony, I moved the young from container to container to see if the females would feed youngsters that were not their own. A great many species would not; they would either ignore them or actually kill them, but in no case with my little brown bats was a young rejected by the females. All thrived. Could we now say that like the freetailed bat, the little brown bats feed young indiscriminately in nursery colonies? Absolutely not. We knew from field observation only that the young did form such clusters but our captive observations reveal only that, under the very artificial conditions of captivity, female little brown bats will feed young other than their genetic offspring. Only careful and difficult observations of marked females and their offspring in the wild or of a generously sized group in a large flight cage/observatory will tell us if the females will feed other than their own young freely of their own accord and if so, whether this is a normal or abnormal occurrence.

Many fish, insects, invertebrates, and amphibians lend themselves to captive observation because most of the guidelines listed earlier can be met. Glass aquaria generally make suitable containers for these and in most cases the larger the better. Smaller tanks are often chosen for cost and convenience but they tend to prove too small in the long run for proper behavior watching. If the animals are bothered by the observer's presence, viewing screens and/or baffles can be used as in Figure 9.1.

PERMITS

Before undertaking any captive behavioral studies check with the proper authorities to see if a permit is required and if so, apply for one. You will generally need to indicate how you propose to conduct the study, how

Figure 9.1.
Aquarium with behavior-observation hood.

many captives you wish permits for, and for how long you plan to retain them in captivity. If you plan to hold any of the larger vertebrates for more than a very short while, you will probably also have to conform with the U.S. Department of Agriculture animal care standards for exhibit or laboratory animals. All this may seem to be a nuisance, and it is, but it is intended to protect the welfare of the animals and limit the number of uninformed, thoughtless people who needlessly destroy thousands of animals each year because they want a wild pet whose physical and psychological needs they do not understand.

Authorities need to know what you will do with the captives ultimately. Will they, indeed, can they be released to the wild or will they be so conditioned to humans that they will have to be held captive all their lives or be humanely put to death?

ANALYZING YOUR OBSERVATIONS

Every species is constantly interacting with its environment. As that environment goes through changes, the species either adapts or becomes extinct. The ability of a species to adapt to change lies in its range of genetic variability. Each individual is slightly different from others of its kind. There is a range of individual variation that will make an acceptable fit with current environmental conditions. More extreme variations are nonadaptive and individuals exhibiting such variation will either die without issue or leave far fewer offspring with their genetic structure.

Variability is not limited to physical structures; it involves behavioral patterns as well. This should not be surprising since the two are so closely intertwined.

In some groups of animals, such as the insects, we think of most of the behavioral patterns as basically being genetically fixed, instinctive, and with little or no capacity for modification through learning. Ethologists generally refer to such behaviors as "fixed action patterns." But living things are not stamped from production lines. Close study of insects such as the solitary wasps reveals considerable individual variation on a particular behavior pattern. This only becomes apparent by carefully recording the details of given patterns of behavior for a significant number of individuals.

For species less confined by fixed action patterns than insects, determining what behavior should be considered normative for the species becomes even more complex. The more careful observations one makes about a large number of individuals of a given species, the less dogmatic one tends to become in stating what a given species will or will not do under given circumstances. You learn that there is generally a normal range of behavior and a fringe of variability usually passed off as idiosyncratic behavior. Actually it is in this fringe variability that the potential lies for the species to adapt to gradual environmental changes. What actually happens is that the range of variability that is an acceptable environmental fit will shift toward one extreme or the other. George Schaller suggests that "species may be so adaptable that they may modify their social organization to meet local conditions, and thus in turn may influence the expression of certain kinds of behavior, such as frequency of aggression, making it difficult to generalize about a species."

Many authorities believe that every structure or behavior must have a real purpose and they seek long and hard to establish that purpose. However, it seems that there is considerable merit to a slightly different viewpoint that suggests that a variant doesn't have to have a firm purpose at present; it need only not interfere with survival. Such variants might be considered preadaptive to possible environmental shifts.

Schaller takes something of a middle ground, suggesting that "every behavior pattern can no doubt be explained by the selective forces that shape and maintain it, but these are not always apparent. Advantages may have concurrent disadvantages which prevent a pattern from being perfected and which obscures its survival value."

This little digression serves only to focus on the fact that, being human, we are seldom satisfied with gathering answers only to the "what," "where," "when," or "under what conditions" spectrum of questions. We are constantly plagued with how and why. Of the two, "how" is the safer question and can often be answered by careful experiments. Such experiments are not beyond the realm of some amateurs but most demand the general education and/or skills of a professional scientist if the resulting answers are to stand up under careful scrutiny.

It is wise to heed the caution in Niko Tinbergen's favorite phrase— "as far as we know." This pioneering student of animal behavior constantly pushes his own students to think long and hard before they make a firm statement. Is that statement really justified by sufficient data? Have all the possibilities been tested or explored? Are they rushing ahead to conclusions prematurely? All wildlife watchers can profit from this cautionary advice.

Some experimentation can be relatively simple and involves manipulating variables, perhaps using physical models that accentuate certain features, or altering some feature of the environment. Look to the writings of Niko Tinbergen for classic examples of such simple yet sophisticated experiments. However, most "how" answers require the study of physiological and/or biochemical factors that demand sophisticated equipment and skill as well as large investments of time. Description of these procedures is well beyond both the scope of this volume and the commitment of most amateurs.

"Why" questions are the most treacherous ground because they often move from observable fact to faith. Facts are supposed to be neutral but they seldom are; they have a valence depending upon the use to which they are put. The same fact may be used to support diametrically opposite explanations. Valid "why" explanations in today's world are the result of long and dedicated scholarship and the development of mutual professional respect. And even then, the later work of others with new credentials may cause a long accepted explanation of "why" to be strongly modified or even reversed.

In order to move away from purely descriptive information to statements about the normality of various behavior patterns or their effectiveness of adaptive fit to the environment or similar interpretive statements, it is important that you be able to organize your observations so that they can more easily be examined for patterns. In general this means arranging it so that at least elementary statistical methods can be applied, and such results displayed in simple charts and graphs.

It is a truism that people that have a strong love of working with living things tend to have small love for, and little skill in, things mathematical. Thus the thought of using statistical methodologies to help analyze their observational data tends to put them off, or at least, to give them a good case of butterflies in the stomach. I know because I clearly fall into that category. However, the availability today of the hand calculator, and even the home computer, takes some of the pain and apprehension away.

Several examples may indicate the role of some basic quantitative data. The first involves a species' preference for a given habitat or community. Species can generally be classified into one of the following three categories:

1. *Exclusive* (those confined very strictly to one kind of community)
2. *Characteristic* (those that are closely identified with a certain community)
3. *Ubiquitous* (*or Indifferent*) (those that show no particular affinity to any community)

To get a solid handle on how particular species being studied fits into this classification, we can establish each species' frequency of occurrence and a coefficient of community for several habitats or communities.

First, data must be gathered through a number of weekly, day-long, or at least half-day-long trips to the study area that has been mapped for community types. For each sighting of a target species, location, sex, and activity are noted.

Frequency of occurrence of the target species in a given habitat or community is simply determined by calculating the percentage of times that each species is observed in a given habitat out of the total number of census trips to that habitat. Thus if the tufted titmouse is observed in the oak woods area forty-two times out of forty-eight weekly trips to that habitat, then the frequency of occurrence would be 42/48 × 100 = 87.5 percent frequency of occurrence for the tufted titmouse in your area. Similarly, if during the same study the titmouse shows up only fourteen times in the nearby hemlock grove, its frequency for that community would be 14/48 × 100, or 29 percent. Note that frequency of occurrence by habitat may vary by season and geographic area; therefore, be careful in stating what the frequency of occurrence means until you have gathered the data over several years and compared it with several other regions.

The coefficient of community is derived by dividing the number of species (of a target group of animals, such as, birds, amphibians, or beetles) common to two different habitats or communities by the total number of species of that group found within both habitats. For instance, if thirty of the same species of birds were found in both mixed oak and mixed hardwood habitats, and if the two habitats together had a total of seventy different bird species, then the coefficient of community between the two habitats would be 30/70 = .42. In the unlikely event that the two habitats had identical bird life in both habitats, they would have a coefficient of 1.0.

The important thing to remember is that your observations generally will represent only a very small sample of the behavior of a species. Your personal observations on a limited population can give very skewed results. For example, for a number of years friends of mine and I have raised dairy goats. Each year, as the kids are born, some breeders seem to get a run of luck and all female kids are born; other less fortunate breeders get mostly bucks. This leads to all sorts of speculation about factors that might affect the normal 1:1 ratio of males to females that should be expected. I set out to discover what was really happening. A questionnaire was sent to all the goat breeders in a wide area that asked them for records of each breed and the number of males and females born in each of a period of years. When over a thousand animals had been analyzed, the ratio was almost exactly 1:1 males and females. Breaking it out by breeds, those breeds with the most animals to include came closest to 1:1 ratio and those with the fewest animals reported were most divergent. It was a good reaffirmation of the fact that the more data available the lower the margin of error.

At all times it must be remembered that there is a difference between the natural or real population and the sample population used for statistical analysis. Statistics allow inferences and observations about the natural population based on the sample population. Thus, great care must be taken in selecting the sample. The more truly random and the larger the sample, the greater the likelihood that the results reflect the nature of reality in the natural population.

FIELD EXPERIMENTS

As you make observations in the field, questions will naturally arise. Some of these questions can only be answered by careful laboratory experiments, but some can be answered through creative field experiments. For example, if you wonder what changes in its territory the animal will respond to, you can carefully make various changes, one at a time, and observe how the animal reacts, how often, and for how long.

A number of investigators have suspected that, in social interactions, behaviors were not triggered by the whole animal but only by certain segments. These are called triggering objects, or *releasers*. Tinbergen noticed, for instance, that baby gulls would pick at the red spot on the adults' bill. This would result in the parent regurgitating food for the young. Using cardboard cutouts of various shapes—some realistically gull-shaped, others totally un-gull-like—he was able to show that indeed the red spot was the releaser for at least one aspect of care soliciting in young herring gulls.

How do members of a species recognize each other for courtship, socialization, and other intraspecific interaction? Are there key markings that make a difference? Does a female flicker with painted moustaches still gain acceptance by its mate? Does a striped fish that will court a model painted like itself also court it if it is changed to have more or less stripes? What causes birds to mob a predator—its shape, its size, its eyes? Can you create a model that increases the intensity of mobbing behavior?

What are the boundaries of a bird's territory? If the bird will react to a mirror, can you slowly move it until it is at a point where the bird ignores it? Is this a boundary? Can the mirror be moved in different directions and the basic area of the territory be so mapped?

All experiments raise some ethical questions. At one level of intensity an experiment may be only a minor annoyance to the animals. The researcher gets data and puts things back to normal. Of course, to get reliable data the experiment must be repeated for a statistically adequate sample. The line between minor annoyance and dirty trick is sometimes very fine. For example, the female flicker with moustaches may be fully rejected by males until the next moult, which is not only cruel to the individual, but it will also mean that she is lost from the breeding population for a season.

Before instituting any field experiment to test a hypothesis that arouses your curiosity it is necessary to project what the negative impact of your actions could be on individual animals and the local population of the species. If the activity is liable to cause the experimental animal to

- receive unusual aggressive response from others of its kind
- be an easier target for predation
- be unnaturally excluded from the breeding population
- cause severe or prolonged pain to be inflicted directly or indirectly
- devote significant time to the experimental activity such that it saps its energy or takes it away from its normal round of activities

then it is not a suitable experiment. To satisfy human curiosity is not justification enough for such experimentation. Experimental activity should have a very minimal impact on the normal activity of the wildlife.

ANALYZING DATA

In analyzing your observational or experimental data, seek help from professionals at local colleges, universities, museums, nature centers, government research facilities, or similar sources. If you are serious and persistent in your efforts you can usually turn up a professional to share your interests and provide guidance and limited instruction. They can often help you locate technical publications as well. A number of these organizations also host amateur naturalist groups of one sort or another where you may be able to share your observations and interests as well as recruit field companions if so desired. Many of these clubs publish bulletins and journals where you may want to publish some of your observations or findings.

There are also the professional journals as sources to publish your serious work. They will publish the efforts of amateurs as long as the work meets professional standards. Most of these journals are refereed, that is, each paper submitted is reviewed by a panel of judges for its adherence to standards of valid and reliable data gathering and analysis. Check recent issues of the journal to which you would like to submit for instructions to authors, or write to the current editor for such information. Follow the formalities suggested for that publication rigorously. They are not interested in your skills as a creative writer; they want their traditions and guidelines met. Remember also that each article is a contribution to science. The authors receive no monetary rewards. Also note that because of the referee process and limited space in any given issue of that journal, your article may not appear in print for well over a year after it is submitted. Some of these journals have a section for Notes which are usually fairly brief reports of interesting or significant observations. Amateurs' observations are most likely to gain entrance there.

Behavior watching is a very satisfying activity that covers a broad developmental range from initial casual eavesdropping on wild neighbors, to expanding knowledge about many wild neighbors, to indepth involvement with a specific species, to abstract involvement with the meaning of comparative behavior of species. It can satisfy a spectrum of emotional and intellectual needs for the observer, and most of the time it is just plain fun!

FURTHER READING

ALDEN, PETER, and JOHN GOODERS. *Finding Birds Around the World*. Boston: Houghton Mifflin, 1981.

ALTMANN, J. "Observational study of behavior: sample methods," *Behavior*, 49 (1974), 227–67.

BEVERIDGE, W. I. B. *The Art of Scientific Investigation*. London: Heinemann, 1957.

BISHOP, O. N. *Statistics for Biology*. Boston: Houghton Mifflin, 1966.

COUNCIL OF BIOLOGY EDITORS. *CBE Style Manual*, 3rd ed. Washington, D.C.: American Institute of Biological Sciences, 1972.

CROXTON, FREDERICK E. *Elementary Statistics with Applications in Medicine and The Biological Sciences*. New York: Dover Publications, Inc., 1959.

EDWARDS, ERNEST P. *Finding Birds in Mexico*, 2nd ed. Sweet Brier, Va.: E. P. Edwards, 1968.

GEFFEN, ALICE M. *A Birdwatcher's Guide to the Eastern United States*. Woodbury, N.Y.: Barron's, 1978.

HEDIGER, N. *Studies of the Psychology and Behavior of Captive Animals in Zoos and Circuses*. New York: Criterion Books, 1955.

HILTS, LEN. *Rand McNally National Forest Guide*. Chicago: Rand McNally, 1980.

PERRY, JOHN, and JANE G. PERRY. *The Random House Guide To Natural Areas of the Eastern United States*. New York: Random House, 1981.

PETTINGILL, OLIN SEWALL. *A Guide to Bird Finding East of the Mississippi*, 2nd ed. New York: Oxford University Press, 1977.

———. *A Guide to Bird Finding West of the Mississippi*, 2nd ed. New York: Oxford University Press, 1981.

RILEY, LAURA, and WILLIAM RILEY. *Guide to National Wildlife Refuges*. Garden City, N.Y.: Doubleday/Anchor Press, 1979.

ROSS-MACDONALD, MALCOLM, ed. *The World Wildlife Guide*. New York: Viking Press, 1971.

SCHNEIRLA, T. C. "The relationship between observation and experimentation in the field of behavior," *Annals of New York Academy of Sciences*, 51, no. 6 (1950), 1022–44.

SCOTT, J. P., ed. "Methodology and techniques for the study of animal societies," *Annals of New York Academy of Sciences*, 51, no. 6 (1950), 1001–1122.

SIMPSON, G. G., ANNE ROE, and R. C. LEWONTIN. *Quantitative Zoology (rev. ed.).* New York: Harcourt Brace, 1960.

SMITH, STUART, and ERIC HOSKING. *Birds Fighting: Experimental Studies of the Aggressive Displays of Some Birds.* London: Faber and Faber, Ltd., 1955.

STOKES, A. W., ed. *Animal Behavior in Laboratory and Field.* San Francisco: W. H. Freeman, 1968.

VAN TIL, WILLIAM. *Writing for Professional Publication.* Boston: Allyn Bacon, 1981.

CHAPTER 10

EXTENDING
YOUR SENSES

MOST PEOPLE SELDOM MAKE FULLEST USE of the senses they have and there is much we can learn about the world just by using the senses nature has provided us. However, since most wildlife rarely permits prolonged close approach within the range of optimum use of our unaided senses, we have profited from our technological capacities to produce devices that extend our senses. With the aid of such devices we can extend our ability to see over distance, capture sounds on tape, go below the surface of the water for extended periods of time, see more clearly in the dark, and record and/or track the travels of animals we cannot easily approach for visual contact.

In a society that puts a premium on gadgets, it is easy to be seduced into excessive concentration on the devices themselves and lose sight of the fact that they are only tools to enhance observation. Gadgets are not ends in themselves. In wildlife watching, as with all pursuits, it is easy to let the tools become status symbols, but as in other fields, some of the best work has often been done with the simplest equipment and a creative mind. The key to equipment is appropriateness. Choose tools that do the job you need done—no more and no less. Proper tools are a good investment.

VISUAL EXTENDERS

For most wildlife observation the single most important piece of equipment is binoculars. There are many brands on the market to choose from. As with many products you tend to get what you pay for. Inexpensive binoculars usually lack basic features of durability and optical quality. Binoculars that might be quite adequate and durable at sports events fare poorly under the much rougher conditions of the field. Once you move into choosing from the middle and upper price ranges of binoculars one's selection becomes a matter of personal preference and a fondness for one particular feature or another. Before making a choice you should decide what your primary kinds of observations are going to demand and select features that will meet those needs most effectively.

For the field observer the following qualities should always be sought: highest possible definition, contrast, resolving power and color corrections; dust proofness; shock and water resistance. The other qualities—power (magnification), weight, twilight factor, and field of view—provide the chief choices to be made.

MAGNIFICATION

A first decision usually revolves around the appropriate magnification or power of the binoculars. The number used to indicate the power—7×, 8×, 10×—refers to how many times larger the object will appear through the binocular than when viewed with the unaided eye. For wildlife observation purposes nothing under 7× is of much real value. However, increased power comes with a price; as the object is magnified so too is any movement by those holding the binoculars. Any binoculars above 9× can usually be hand-held for only a short time without motion distortion, and therefore, they will need to be used with a tripod.

Of course steadiness of holding the binocular is a function of weight and it is here that you have to make choices among different lens constructions and design features that reduce weight, but often ruggedness as well. Unfortunately those situations where one might most profitably use the greater powers are also those that are most apt to call for the most rugged construction.

EXIT PUPIL

A factor to be considered is the time of day you expect to be doing most of your observing. Daytime, open area, observing has one set of requirements; early morning, evening, and wooded area observation another. In choosing the appropriate binocular, consider the exit pupil feature along with what today is called the twilight factor.

In dim light the human pupil dilates; in bright light it contracts. For good viewing with binoculars the circle of light exiting from the ocular lens should be at least the same size as the pupil of the eye or larger. During normal daylight the pupil of the eye is about 2mm in diameter.

If you hold a pair of binoculars out at arm's length you will see a circle of light standing out from the black surrounding field of each eye piece. This is the so-called "exit pupil." You can determine the diameter of the exit pupil by dividing the diameter of the lens by the magnification. It is two figures that are used to designate a binocular such as 7×21, 8×24, 9×30. If you do the division for each of these examples you find that they all have approximately the same exit pupil size—about 3mm. Such glasses would be satisfactory in open areas during daylight. For glasses that will be useful over a broader range of light variability a choice of exit pupil around 4mm would be good—such as 8×30, 7×35, or 9×35 glasses. For low light observations where the human pupil dilates to about 7mm one turns to the so-called twilight glasses—the 7×50 or the 10×70. Lens coatings are also important in terms of the light-gathering efficiency of a lens and can increase that efficiency by 50 percent. Mathematically the light efficiency of a lens is equal to the square of the diameter of the exit pupil.

Twilight factor is a modern term for determining the visual performance and detail recognition in dim light. At the same exit pupil size, the greater magnification will give a better twilight factor for gathering in light. Thus a 10×40 glass would have a better twilight factor than an 8×32 glass, although they both have the same exit pupil size. The twilight factor is calculated as the square root of the magnification times the diameter of the objective lens. For people who wish to study mammals, many of which are most active during the twilight hours, the best twilight factor is an important consideration.

ANGLE OF VIEW

Looking through binoculars is essentially like looking through a tube; the longer the tube, the smaller the angle of view, that is, the less area you can see out the other end. This is what makes it difficult to sight a spotting scope because it has a relatively small angle of view, and an object at a distance need move only a small amount to be out of the scope's view. New methods of arranging the lenses internally in binoculars have effectively "shortened the tube" and increased the angle of vision while still maintaining a high magnification. Of course this is generally accomplished at increased cost. However, a large angle of view is of great advantage in watching wildlife. It will come down to a choice of how much more the cost is for each unit advance in the angle.

In comparing binoculars for angle of view, the traditional measurement is how many meters you can see in the field of view at a distance of 1,000 meters. The data on the binocular would indicate something like 130m at 1,000m, or 7.4°. If the data on the binocular is given only in degrees you will have to do a little basic math to get the comparative field of view at 1,000m. This is done as follows:

Since
1° at 1000m = 17.5m,
we multiply the stated degrees by 17.5m.

Thus 7.4° × 17.5m = 129.50m at 1,000m.

We can only compare two glasses of the same optical data for field of view such as two 7×50's or 8×30's. If one brand has a 7.4° angle of view it will cover 130m at 1,000m. If the other brand has an 8° angle of view it will cover about 140m at 1,000m. That is, the second one will allow inclusion of about 10m more. This could be valuable if you don't have to pay too high an additional price for it.

In shopping for binoculars it is useful to fill out a chart such as that shown below for the various binoculars you are comparing. The figures in the example give an idea of what you will find but different models differ from manufacturer to manufacturer. Swift's 7×35 will not necessarily have the same statistics as a 7×35 from Bushnell. Indeed there may be some variations among different models of 7×35 binoculars offered by a single manufacturer, as with the two 7×35's in the accompanying table.

Magnification (M)	Objective lens diameter (D)	Exit pupil diameter (D/M)	Weight (W)	Relative brightness $(D/M)^2$	Angle of view	Field in ft. at 1,000 yds. (F)	Relative field (M × F)
6	30	5.0		25	8.5	450	2700
7	35	5.0	29 oz.	25	7.3	500	3500
7	35	5.0	20 oz.	25	7.3	380	2660
7	50	7.1	27 oz.	50	7.3	380	2660
8	30	3.75		14	6.3	330	2640
8	30	3.75		14	7.4	390	3120
8	30	3.75	19 oz.	14	8.5	450	3600
8	40	5.0		25	7.2	375	3000
10	50	5.0	26 oz.	25	7.0	370	3700

OTHER OPTIONAL FEATURES

There are, of course, many features that can be considered in the final choice of your binocular, such as external vs. internal focusing or the type of color correction used. These are fine points to be discussed between you and the salesperson. Each person has his or her own special opinion on what is best and it often comes down to how much money you are willing to invest. Good binoculars, given reasonable care, even with heavy use, are a lifetime investment. Nothing but frustration is gained by taking the cheapest way out.

Those who wear eyeglasses will want to be sure that their binocular has rubber eyecups that roll back so that the instrument is at the proper distance from the eye, giving you the full angle of view for which the binocular was designed. It makes little sense to pay for increased field of view and then lose much of it by having to hold the binoculars too far from your eyes because of your glasses. Binoculars are generally designed so that the eyepoint is 11mm behind the eye pieces. Glasses tend to extend that distance, reducing the useful field of view.

Your method of carrying the binocular should also be a matter for concern. Small, compact binoculars are little problem since they can be tucked into a pocket, but larger ones can be a literal pain in the neck. Carried by a neck or shoulder strap they sometimes keep a steady pressure on nerves or blood vessels. Also, binoculars carried in such a manner have a habit of bouncing when you move, which creates noise and jars the lenses. And if you run, there is the risk that the glasses will swing out and bang against a tree or rock. This is good neither for you nor the binoculars. For these larger glasses I recommend the use of a harness, which is readily available at most camera stores. It goes around the chest and over the shoulders, and gives better distribution of weight. It has a rubber band system that can be slipped over the glasses when they are hanging down to keep them snugly against the chest without bouncing even if you have to break into a run.

SPOTTING SCOPES

For certain kinds of observation, such as watching waterfowl off the coast, shorebirds, and shy mammals in open terrain, binoculars frequently are not sufficient. One needs greater magnification. The tool most used is some form of telescope. Telescopes used for astronomy are optically contrived to gather as much light as possible and every lens element causes some loss of light. Astronomers don't mind if the image is upside down; therefore, they often eliminate the lens that would reverse the image in their scopes. Those used for wildlife watching, generally known as *spotting scopes*, add the lens and accept some small decrease in light-gathering ability.

The factors we have discussed in the section about binoculars generally apply to spotting scopes as well since they are similarly constructed optical instruments. The greater the power, or magnification, of the spotting scope the more it magnifies user motion. Thus all spotting scopes demand some form of sturdy steadying device. This is usually a tripod, although some people use their automobile hood or a handy tree. There are special tripods that attach to, or rest on, a car window rail, which permits the car to be used as a blind.

The field of view of spotting scopes is quite limited so that locating and keeping an animal in view can be frustrating. Spotting scopes are generally of more use to an observer that just wants to quick view the animal than for someone wanting to make extended observations. They are most useful for behavior observations at dens or nests where, because the animals tend to concentrate their action, the scope can be set up and left in one fixed position.

Most commonly used spotting scopes are 20× with a 3mm exit pupil. Other higher magnification eyepieces are available to interchange with the standard 20× on some models. Variable magnification or zoom lenses are also available. There is an appeal to these zoom lenses since you can conveniently locate and center the object at the lower magnifications with its greater field of view and then increasingly enlarge the magnification. However, doing this creates a variety of optical problems. Older or current inexpensive models will give you a sharp picture at one particular magnification but increasing distortion as you vary the power. A great deal of such distortion has been eliminated in the newer more expensive models.

However, one factor remains relatively unimproved and that is relative brightness. If your scope is 15× with a relative brightness of 16, as you zoom up to 30× your relative brightness will drop to 4, and if you zoom up to 60× your relative brightness will be only 1. Unless your subjects are in good bright light your highest magnifications may be virtually useless. Consider well what conditions you will use your scope under and if the frequency with which you will be able to use the highest power is sufficient to justify the considerable extra cost.

PROTECTIVE GLASSES

The wise wildlife watcher wears some form of glasses while afield whether or not prescription glasses are normally worn. Glasses help protect the eyes from projecting twigs, blowing debris, and excessive light. In choosing the glasses the important thing to consider is their role in cutting down excessive light and the scattered light that causes glare and internal reflections.

Sunglasses are the most useful type of protective glasses whether or not you wear corrective lenses. Their main purpose, of course, is to reduce excessive brightness and glare. They also obscure your eyes and thus the eye contact that is often frightening to animals you may be watching. Good sunglasses should be dark enough for the conditions, but not any more so, for that cuts into the clarity of view. This means that you may wish to have several pairs of glasses—one for each major set of conditions. Check the manufacturer's description for percent of light absorption. In very bright areas such as beach, desert, open water, and snow a very dark lens with 85 to 90 percent absorption is appropriate. For fields and shrubby areas without much reflection, look to a light absorption factor of 75 to 85 percent. In shady areas such as forests and ravines, no more than 60 to 75 percent is necessary; and in twilight hours or on overcast days 30 to 50 percent absorption is normally adequate.

Nowadays you can get photochromic lenses that change their density with the amount of ultraviolet light present. This gives you a broad range of light absorbency in only one glass. However, these are not sunglasses. Depending upon temperature and the amount of sunlight, they will maximally absorb 50 to 60 percent of the light. Thus if you work mainly in wooded areas and in the twilight hours they may be useful, but in brighter conditions you will still need sunglasses.

Avoid fashion tints. Stick with neutral tones such as gray or gray-green. These lenses transmit the wavelengths most useful for seeing and absorb those that help us very little. They also do not distort the color balance of the things you see through them.

Of course, there are also drawbacks to glasses. In protecting you from reflections they themselves reflect light and may give you away during a stalk or in some types of blinds. You must be very alert for this and remove them in appropriate situations. They are also sometimes clumsy when you are trying to use binoculars. I prefer glasses in a frame that permits the lenses to flip up out of the way. This eliminates the need to keep putting the glasses on and off. For all glasses, a safety cord that attaches to the ear pieces and goes around the back of the neck is very useful in the field.

Plastic lenses are light and inexpensive but they are seldom a good buy because they scratch easily and the tints are often unstable. Plastic lenses do not absorb ultraviolet rays unless they are specially treated, and only a few brands are. This is all true of mass-produced sunglasses but not of plastic prescription lenses.

Polarizing glasses are particularly useful when working around water because they will help eliminate the surface glare so that you can see the creatures below the surface. Polarizing lenses allow only light arriving in certain planes to enter and thus work best only at certain angles. You have to be aware of this and adjust your position accordingly. Polarizing glasses tend to have a strong mirror-effect from the other side, thus they are liable to give a telltale light flash when used during stalking.

PARABOLIC REFLECTORS
AND TAPE RECORDERS

Sounds that animals produce are an important part of their behavior, particularly their social behavior. Today it is possible to acquire devices to record these sounds at relatively affordable prices. The most important device is a tape recorder with sensitivity to a wide range of frequency of sound. Many excellent, inexpensive tape recorders are designed to be within the range of the human voice but they are not able to pick up higher or lower ranges of frequency. However, many animal sounds, such as bird calls, fall in the higher range and some, such as whale calls, may be in the lower range. Recorders with the extra sensitivity, usually designed for good music recording, will be more expensive.

Most serious field recordists still prefer ¼-inch open reel tapes to cassette machines. Those made by Nagra, Uher, and Yamaha are probably more widely used than any others for this purpose.

A small compact cassette recorder will generally be suitable for recording notes and getting general recordings of common birds and amphibians. Such are suitable for playing back bird calls and animal distress calls that will lure creatures to an observer. But for accurate work, the open reel machines with their wider tape and higher tape speeds are needed. All recorders used in the field will need regular daily checkups since they are more vulnerable to dirt on the recording heads and to jarring that loosens vital connections. Few things are more frustrating than playing back a recording only to find that although the tape ran through the machine, nothing was recorded.

A good quality microphone is of almost equal importance to a good recorder. There are two major categories of microphones—low impedence and high impedence. For the wildlife watcher, low impedence mikes are generally preferable since they can be used with long extension cords between the microphone and the recorder. This permits mounting a microphone near the animal while having the recorder with its disturbing operational noises some distance away. A directional mike is generally more useful for our purposes than an omni-directional one, for the latter picks up too much unnecessary ambient sounds. Dynamic, rather than ceramic, microphones are another preference since they have a higher frequency range. The frequency reponse should be as uniform as possible over a range of at least 50 to 15,000 Hertz. The quality of the microphone will have a great deal to do with the quality of the recordings. Microphones that come with a portable cassette recorder are seldom suitable for field recordings.

In most outdoor work a wind screen is a necessity if the sound is not to be distorted. These can be purchased but you may wish to make your own according to a design reported by the naturalist Charles Laun

(Figure 10.1). You will need twenty plastic drinking straws, plastic cement, and various odds and ends. Leaving one straw full length, cut each succeeding straw ¼-inch shorter than the one you just cut. A sharp razor blade is a good cutting tool for this. Encircle the longest straw with the next six shortest straws and cement them all together with one end even. Use a rubber band to hold them together until dry. In a similar fashion of declining lengths, glue the next row of straws in place and let dry. Proceed similarly until all the straws are in place.

Next make a sleeve that will be able to connect the baffle you have just made with the microphone. You may be able to adapt a plastic bottle with both ends removed for this purpose, or else use masking tape to build a collar and fasten it in place.

In the field you will wish to record a particular song or call. If you use a microphone, even a directional one, you will pick up a great many other sounds along with the one you wanted. At the time of recording you may even be unaware of the other ambient sounds because your mind is capable of screening out those sounds as you concentrate on one in particular. Unfortunately when you hear your tape the other sounds will be all too apparent.

The tape you use is also important, particularly on open reel machines. You will need to match a tape to the machine, balancing the whole system of recorder, microphone, and tape. Once the system is balanced, always use the same brand and model of tape. Open reel tapes come in three standard thicknesses—.5 mil, 1 mil, and 1.5 mil. Most field workers prefer 1 mil tape since .5 mil tends to be too thin, with frequent play-through of sound, and 1.5 mil is thick enough that it often doesn't press firmly against the recording head. Choose a tape model with either low noise/high output or low noise/low print.

There is a broad range of choices among cassettes, but in making your selection look for a cassette with the widest possible dynamic range, best frequency response, and best signal to noise capabilities. It is generally best to avoid the 90-minute cassettes, in spite of their apparent convenience and economy. They are apt to cause frictional drags that will distort the sound.

Sound travels in all directions from its point source. To really select out one sound you need some way to focus on the signals coming from

Figure 10.1.
Drinking-straw windscreen for microphone.

that source while blocking out most of the other sound signals. This can be achieved with a parabolic disc reflector. The disc intercepts only a sector of the radiating sound and reflects it to a single focal point. At this point a microphone is mounted to catch and record that sound. Other sounds either by-pass the reflector or are focused elsewhere than into the microphone.

Early parabolic reflectors were heavy, unwieldy polished metal affairs that were both clumsy and tended to reflect light as well as sound, thus frightening some of the wildlife. Today the reflectors tend to be made of clear plastic which is both lighter and cheaper. Not only is it less likely to reflect light but it also lets the operator look right through it, making it possible to help focus the instrument by sight as well as sound.

The distance at which you can detect a sound with the parabolic reflector varies with the diameter of the parabola. Doubling the diameter may more than double the detection distance. The actual range will depend upon the size of the parabola, the sensitivity of the microphone and the recorder's amplifier, and the amount of external noise. Indeed this last factor is generally the most limiting.

If a commercial parabolic reflector is a bit expensive for you until you are sure you really want to dig in more deeply to sound recording, you may wish to "Rube Goldberg" it, using again the recommendation of Laun (Figure 10.2). For a parabolic reflector he uses an old aluminum snow saucer. He bolts a pipe flange and ⅛-inch pipe to the saucer to serve as an attachment for the microphone. The mike is mounted to the pipe, using a chemist's test tube clamp. This allows the mike to be moved along the pipe until the focal point (the point where the sound is loudest) is located. A U-shaped drawer handle is bolted to the reflector along with an L-bar that will permit the entire device to be mounted on a camera tripod.

NIGHT AIDS

Given the limitations of human night vision, nocturnal observations mean some type of light enhancement or modification. The military has developed infrared spotting scopes and more recently low-light intensifiers. Unfortunately for the amateur naturalist, these are still far too

Figure 10.2. Homemade parabolic reflector for animal sound recording. (A) aluminum snow disc; (B) test-tube clamp to hold microphone to pipe (slide along pipe to proper focal point); (C) ⅛" pipe flange bolted to disc to hold pipe.

expensive for most individuals to purchase. They are also relatively clumsy to use and their resolving power for small objects leaves much to be desired.

The wildlife watcher will generally have to remain content with portable light sources with red filters. Electric headlamps with a belt pack of batteries are generally available from sporting goods stores and catalogues. Personally, I prefer the type that allows you to change the focal point of the beam. For these headlamps you will have to provide your own red filter. I use the gels that are available for theatre lights. Cut a disc of the material, using the glass cover of the light as a template. Place it behind the glass and hold it in place with the bulb reflector. The same can be done with most hand flashlights. The obvious advantage of the headlamp is that it is always beamed where you are looking and it keeps your hands free for note taking, using binoculars or other equipment. The disadvantage of the headlamps, and flashlights as well, is the relatively short life of the batteries. Sometimes it seems that action gets going just about the time batteries start slowing. Always carry extra fresh batteries. If you do much night watching, investment in a battery recharger may well be worthwhile.

Another disadvantage of the headlamps is that the candlepower is relatively low so that light penetration into the distance is quite limited. One must remember that light intensity falls off proportional to the square of the distance. Thus at twelve feet you will have only one-sixteenth the light you have at four feet, and at eight feet you will have one-fourth the light you have at four feet. For the headlamp to be useful you have to be able to get close to your subject.

For more light penetration at a greater distance you need more electricity for more candlepower. This can be achieved with the help of a car. A number of high intensity spotlights are available that plug into the car's cigarette lighter. Several of them are already available with a snap-on red filter. Such spotlights will drain your car battery quickly so you must compensate by keeping the car idling or monitor the use of the light carefully so that you don't find yourself stranded in the middle of nowhere with a dead battery. If you opt to use such a light, check with your state game laws. In some states such lights are completely outlawed; in others the legitimate use is carefully proscribed. These lights can also be used with some boats and since wildlife often congregates around water, they are a useful addition to the craft. Some portable battery packs are now on the market but these lights drain them fairly rapidly, reducing their usefulness and practicality.

Another strategy for nocturnal observation is a bit more remote. It involves the use of fluorescent powders. These can either be fed in baits where they will pass through the digestive tract and show up in the scat or they can be scattered around bait stations where it will be picked up on the feet and deposited literally as the animal makes tracks.

The trick is to locate the animal's route via the powder. This is done with an ultraviolet light. Whenever this light hits a particle of the powder, the powder glows. Portable neon camping lights are the base for your tracking unit. Simply replace the normal neon tube with an ultraviolet "black light" tube of the same length. You are then ready to go forth and follow the glowing tracks. Sometimes the creature at the end of the trail is a real surprise. You may be equally surprised at the wild and crazy pathway the animal has taken.

UNDERWATER

Dealing with observations below the water surface demands equipment of varying sophistication, depending upon how far you intend to enter into the world of water.

If you wish to watch from dry land you will encounter problems of reflection that may frustrate your efforts. This frustration can be reduced by wearing polarizing glasses. In reality it is not quite as simple as just putting on the glasses and looking. Water has a polarizing angle of 53° and polarizing lenses, to be effective, must be positioned at right angles to that. This means you must be conscious of your angle of view to the water if you are to get maximum effectiveness from the glasses.

For those who are willing to wade about in shallow waters but want good underwater viewing, a simple waterscope can be constructed. There are a number of designs, including those shown in Figure 10.3. They basically involve a piece of glass secured below an opening in a black-lined tube or tunnel with a silastic adhesive. The glass is put in below the opening so that water pressure will work to hold it in place rather than to force it loose.

The more advanced design with the mirror set at a 45-degree angle allows a much broader viewing area and better handling control of the scope. It can easily be used for photography as well, and even for getting pictures above and below the surface at the same time.

The next level of involvement is snorkeling, that is, covering your eyes and nose with a glass face mask and breathing through a tube held in your mouth. (That is, you breathe through the tube while it sticks above the surface.) To go below, take a deep breath and dive. A little

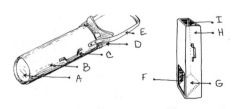

Figure 10.3. Waterscopes. *Left:* (A) glass or clear plastic viewport; (B) aluminum or plastic pipe; (C) screen-door handle or door pull; (D) old snorkeling face mask; (E) carrying strap. *Right:* (F) viewport; (G) mirror set at 45 degrees; (H) waterproof plywood with marine spar or polyurethane finish; (I) flat black painted interior.

water will enter the tube but air pressure keeps most of it out. As you resurface, give a short, forceful blow to expel the small amount of water and then resume breathing through the tube. Snorkeling takes a bit of getting used to because you must discipline yourself to breathe *only* through the mouth, but almost anyone can become proficient at it within a few hours. Most snorkelers use foot fins to add power to their swimming; they are, however, not essential.

Snorkeling provides great opportunity for prolonged and clear underwater observation. You need only float or swim slowly and peer out through the faceplate. It can be quite addicting. Consequently one must beware of acquiring a severe sunburn on the back—particularly on the back of the legs behind the knees.

Good snorkels are J-shaped with a straight tube and no water-excluding ball valves or similar devices. The mouthpiece should be comfortable for you and allow a good seal. The face mask is the key to the joy of snorkeling because it permits you to see underwater without the distortion from water pressure on your eyeballs. In selecting a face mask, put it to your face and breathe in; if it is a proper fit it will cling to your face by external air pressure alone. If it won't hold that way, it means that water would probably seep into the mask. A leaky mask isn't fatal; it's just disconcerting and annoying. Almost all masks leak sometimes. To get the water out while you are underwater, force air out through your nose, lift the seal at the lower edge of the mask, and let the air pressure expel the water. Better masks have a special purge valve to make this process easier. Such masks are a good investment.

Not many years ago a person who wore glasses was disadvantaged under water because he had to leave his glasses topside. Today faceplates can be purchased that are ground to prescription or that can have prescription lenses bonded inside them. These are expensive but worth the price if you get hooked on the delights of our water world.

All underwater viewing involves image distortion of size and distance due to the differing optical properties of air and water. Because of the optical effects of the water and the air in the faceplate, there is about a 25 percent magnification of perceived image size. Thus objects appear to be closer to the observer and larger than they really are. For instance, a lobster that appears six feet away is actually eight feet away and is really 25 percent smaller than you think. It takes experience and practice to accurately judge size and distance for underwater note taking (or judging legal-sized lobsters). The optical distortion under water also narrows peripheral perception so consider getting a face mask whose design offers as much peripheral view as possible.

The next step from snorkeling is scuba diving. This involves taking your own air supply with you so that you can remain well below the surface for up to an hour or more. Scuba involves complex equipment whose use and safe maintenance takes both money and careful training.

No one should attempt SCUBA diving without taking an appropriate training course that leads to basic certification. Although the equipment and training is both expensive and time-consuming, SCUBA diving is a skill that literally opens new worlds and lets the amateur naturalist explore the lives of species that he or she could get to know in no other way.

One drawback of most SCUBA gear is that air bubbles are constantly being released and with some shy species these are a disturbing factor that limits close approach and extended observation. New respirator designs eliminate the bubbling and although they have other drawbacks of their own, they should be investigated if you are intent on extended underwater observations.

FIELD COMMUNICATIONS

When you are working in cooperation with other observers, it is desirable to keep in communication in order to alert each other to the movements of a species under observation. Thus one observer can let an individual or group of animals move out of his immediate visual range and into the view of a cooperator without someone's losing contact. The animals are not stressed by pursuit yet remain under constant surveillance.

The easy availability of citizen band portable radio units makes such efforts possible today at moderate cost. The walkie-talkie units are generally the least expensive but their range tends to be limited and strongly influenced by the terrain. Portable/mobile CB transceiver units, although generally a bit more expensive, have a greater versatility. They generally operate not only on standard batteries, but can also be used with car batteries. Many more features are available for these transceivers than with the basic walkie-talkies. Automatic noise limiters (squelchers) are a real benefit because they eliminate the sudden weird noises that alert or spook wildlife. Look carefully at the wattage a given unit will deliver on portable power and whether or not there is a low power energy conserver. A unit in the field with inadequate or no power is useless. A unit with Nicad batteries and an AC battery charger can be a considerable advantage if you intend to use the units with any regularity.

DOGGING IT

Modern people have lost a great deal of whatever sense of smell our species once had. Other mammals, however, have and use a keen olfactory sensitivity. Actually there is no simple device we can use to enhance our ability to follow scent trails, but we can enlist the aid of dogs.

Dogs are not effective with all species but they can be trained to focus their attention on specific species. If you use a trained dog, it is possible to plot the movement of individuals of the target wildlife. This information can be plotted on a map which will help build a picture of the daily range of the animal and ultimately its territory. Using this basic information on movement, den locations, and so forth, it will be easier to establish key locations likely to provide more direct observation through use of blinds and other strategies.

Radio tracking of a wild species involves capturing, drugging, and ultimately recapturing the individual to boost waning battery power or retrieve the instrumentation. Some basic approximations can be gained by instrumenting the dog, putting the dog on the animal's trail, and plotting the dog's movements as it follows the wild animal's route. There are problems, of course, because dogs will sometimes pursue the spoor of a different individual, or even species, if it crosses the track the dog was originally pursuing. A great deal depends upon the individual dog and how skilled and well trained it is.

A serious amateur butterfly watcher friend of mine trained her Brittany spaniel to point butterflies. She was working on the life history of a butterfly that lives only above timberline in the White Mountains of New Hampshire. Her studies were being frustrated because the butterfly's habit was to fly up and away, then settle quickly to earth among the boulders. Its protective coloration came into play once the wings were folded, making it instantly invisible among the rock lichens. The butterflies generally remained hidden until their flight distance was violated and then they were again up and away.

The spaniel quickly learned to chase the fleeing butterflies and come to point where they landed. The observer could then spot them with field glasses or move in carefully to collect them. Without the dog and her unusual help, the studies of this species would have been quickly frustrated. Butterfly pointers may be exceptional, but it does point up the potential of a good dog in some aspects of wildlife watching.

REMOTE SENSING
AND RADIO TRACKING

From time to time it is useful to be able to get information about an individual you are studying at times when you cannot be available to do the observation directly. The scientific literature has many examples of specialized devices for doing this, but most are outside the realm of most amateur research.

One reasonably practical form of remote sensing is camera trapping. Until recently this was rather clumsy and only one shot at a time was possible without the observer resetting the shutter release and advancing the film. Recent improvements in 35mm camera equipment have made multiexposure camera sensing much more feasible. The key pieces are the battery-operated autowind units that advance the frame each time the shutter is tripped and strobe lights that automatically recycle. By rigging up a photo-electric cell and a solenoid cell to trip the shutter, a series of shots can be taken each time a creature cuts the light beam. The numbers on the film frames will verify the sequence in which they were exposed. If you want to establish the times of activity, set up a battery-operated clock so that it will be included in each shot; thus you will know who passed and when.

It is important to try and make the set-up as unobtrusive as possible so that it has minimum impact on the normal activity along the runway, den, or nest upon which the camera is focused. It is desirable to use a telephoto lens of about 135mm so that the camera does not have to be too close to the animal. This reduces the disturbing effect of the sound of the shutter and autowind.

Radio tracking and radio telemetry are discussed briefly in the section on marking wildlife. Both are interesting technologies for extending our senses but they basically belong in the hands of professionals. The ethical considerations of having animals bear the collars and harnesses and even electronic probes needed to gather information, clearly mandate a very carefully mapped and executed research plan.

FURTHER READING

ABBOT, J., and R. COOMBS. "A photoelectric 35mm camera device for recording animal behavior," *Journal of Mammalogy*, 45, no. 2 (1964), 327–30.

BANDER, ROBERT B., and WILLIAM W. COCHRAN. "Radio-location telemetry," in R. H. Giles, ed. *Wildlife Management Techniques*. Washington, D.C.: The Wildlife Society, 1971.

GANS, C. "An inexpensive arrangement of movie camera and electronic flash as a tool in the study of animal behavior," *Animal Behaviour*, 14, no. 1 (1966), 11–12.

GREGG, JAMES. *The Sportsman's Eye*. New York: Collier Books/Macmillan, 1971.

GULLEDGE, JAMES L. "Recording bird sounds," *The Living Bird*. Ithaca, N.Y.: Cornell Laboratory of Ornithology, 1976.

LENHOFF, E. S. *Tools of Biology*. New York: Macmillan, 1966.

LOVELESS, A., et al. "A photoelectric-cell device for use in wildlife research," *A.I.B.S. Bulletin*, 13, no. 4 (1963), 55–57.

MIYAZAKI, MANABU. *Animal Paths*. Japan: Kyoritsu Publishing Co., 1979.

REICHERT, R. J., and E. REICHERT. *Binoculars and Scopes and Their Uses in Photography*. Philadelphia: Chilton Co., 1961.

STRYKOWSKI, JOE. *Diving for Fun*, 4th rev. ed. Northfield, Ill.: Dacor Corporation, 1974.

TOMBS, D. J. "Wildlife recording in stereo," *Recorded Sound*, 54, (1974), 278–89.

SOURCES

FOR SPOTLIGHTS, HEADLAMPS, PORTABLE CBS, BINOCULARS, SPOTTING SCOPES, AND OTHER WILDLIFE TOOLS NOT AVAILABLE LOCALLY, TRY:

- Gander Mountain, Inc.
  P.O. Box 248
  Wilmot, Wisconsin 53192.

CHAPTER 11

YOU OUTDOORS

ACTIVE WILDLIFE WATCHING BEYOND YOUR BACKYARD requires an increasing amount of conditioning and fitness. You may find yourself walking many miles a day over rough terrain; stalking, with its component of periodic "freezing," means holding uncomfortable, cramped poses for extended periods; even sitting in blinds demands mental and physical fitness. In addition, nature is not all sweetness and light. Weather can cause considerable discomfort, and occasionally, real danger. Several groups of insects cause irritation and some plants and animals are poisonous and represent a potential hazard. And most frightening of all is getting "lost"; such disorientation can happen particularly when concentrating closely on following wildlife in extensive areas of rather uniform habitat.

The purpose of this chapter is to provide hints on basic physical conditioning and to share fundamental information about common outdoor hazards so that you can deal with them calmly and effectively if you become involved. There are a number of references that will give much more detail and there are a variety of self-help courses available in most communities that provide some real hands-on experience with aspects of conditioning and first aid that are extremely valuable.

PHYSICAL AND MENTAL
CONDITIONING

It is easy to forget how sedentary our lives have become. Muscles that can carry us tirelessly mile after mile when well conditioned, very quickly get out of shape if not exercised regularly. If you intend to put in all day on some weekends or to do extended wildlife watching during your vacation, start well ahead with regular daily walks, or jogging if you prefer, to build up your muscle tone and stamina. You should be able to walk five to seven miles easily without experiencing muscle aches or cramps and without getting winded if you expect to be able to put in significant time stalking wildlife. If you are not well conditioned you will find yourself easily exhausted and napping away your observational time, and become so uncomfortable that wildlife watching will be little fun. Each wildlife watcher must be aware of his or her own current physical and psychological limits and take care not to go beyond them. If you are unhappy with those limits, program yourself to improve them.

Regular walking and some setting-up exercises are basic and will be enough for most things, but you must be aware that often you must not only carry your own weight but also that of such paraphernalia as portable blinds, tree stands, or photographic equipment. It is amazing how much that extra weight can take out of you even when you are otherwise in pretty fair condition. If you do regularly carry such burdens, do your working out with a pack of roughly equivalent weight to build in the extra conditioning.

Physically, strength is not all that is needed outdoors; flexibility and agility are necessary too. A regular program of simple calisthenics and stretching exercises will help with these aspects. Work also on breathing exercises which help not only physically but also psychologically. When you are out of condition it seems to be another one of Murphy's famous laws that at about the time your endurance is fading, interesting wildlife activity gets going.

There are many books available on fitness that range widely from the sensible to the faddish. Over the years the Royal Canadian Air Force Exercise Plans and those derived from them have proven to be very sound. They are based on a series of gradual progressions that generally assure a safe development of strength, endurance, and general fitness over a reasonable and sensible period of time. The program also indicates the appropriate rate of progression for different age groups. Older people may not be able to perform as vigorously, or progress as rapidly, as teenagers, but given a little more time they can achieve complete fitness for even vigorous wildlife watching. For example, the amateur eagle researcher Charles Broley began climbing ropes to band nestling eagles after his retirement from banking. He continued this activity well into his seventies.

The ancient Greeks spoke eloquently of the value of a sound mind in a sound body. This is an important maxim for today as well. Nature study itself is a great contributor to mental relaxation and release of tension. However, working closely with wild animals is often possible only when the observer is not radiating olfactory and visual clues of tension. Animals, ever more sensitive to such subtleties than most of us, respond to the signals by fleeing or maintaining an extended flight distance. The same animals may well permit quite close approach of humans whose emotional state sends signals of calmness, relaxedness, and thus no threat to the wildlife. Such differential acceptance by other animals is not reserved for relations with humans. Many naturalists have noted how prey species in Africa can recognize a satiated lion out for a stroll and allow that animal relatively close approach, while quickly fleeing from the same lion at a later time when it is hungry and on the prowl.

To get your mind and body in a properly relaxed state for success-ful wildlife watching it is often useful to evoke the "relaxation re-sponse." This process is described in Chapter 5 in the section on the use of blinds, but the technique itself can be used almost anywhere. After having fought traffic to drive to an observation area, take a few minutes to decompress by using this technique. You will be surprised at the positive effect it has on your wildlife observing. Evoke the response at any time when the frustration of daily living may have set you up for inadvertently signaling your tensions to those you would observe.

Another exercise that I often use to heighten my awareness and reestablish my sense of oneness with the natural world involves spread-eagling myself on the ground face and palms down. The cool-ness of the earth penetrates my undersides while the warmth of the sun strikes my back. The odors of the earth rush in. My fingers sense the texture of the substrate. At first I let my mind take in all these sensory experiences; then I close my eyes and focus on the thought that I am gradually sinking into the ground. I let all my muscles relax until I really seem to be settling lower and lower and lower. I then mentally focus on determining that point inside my body where the warmth penetrating from above seems to meet with the coolness from below. At this point I feel almost as if I cannot move as I am now integrated into the flow of things. After a few moments of this, I concentrate on returning to activ-ity. This must be done slowly because if you jump right up you may feel temporary faintness. In reality this is only a variant way of inducing the relaxation response, but it is very rewarding.

If your observation time is sporadic, it is helpful to do some of the exercises mentioned in Chapter 2 to sharpen your seeing ability before each outing. This is comparable to doing warm-up exercises before jog-ging or other vigorous physical pursuits.

DEALING WITH HAZARDS
AND NUISANCES

For most wildlife watchers the main problems they face outdoors will be of the nuisance variety but those who roam further afield, particularly in wilderness areas or habitats with which they have little familiarity, may face some real hazards. It is really inexcusable today for any literate person to set forth into unfamiliar areas without informing himself or herself about the nature of such nuisances and hazards and how to cope with them if they are encountered.

Insects and Their Relatives

Given that insects are about 80 percent of all living things, it is surprising that such a small percentage directly attack humans. However, it does seem that those few amply make up for all the others. Members of the dipteran family probably cause more misery to wildlife watchers than all the others combined; this family includes mosquitoes, blackflies, greenhead flies, deer flies, tsetse flies, and a number of other equally annoying creatures. Besides from the irritation they cause, a number can transmit serious diseases to people; a number of them are shown in Figure 11.1.

MOSQUITOES.   These creatures lead the list of serious annoyances to the wildlife watcher. There are hundreds of species and one or more is found in virtually every major land habitat. Not all species bite people, but every habitat seems to have at least one species that is willing to sample your blood and buzz in your ear. These insects generally pursue concentrations of carbon dioxide, following it from low concentrations to high ones. This usually leads them to an active living creature. They zero in over the final distance visually. Most species are most active at dawn and dusk.

Humans vary widely in their attractiveness to mosquitoes. Two people afield together may find that one is black with them while the other is bothered by only a few. Insect repellents are the simplest answer to mosquito harassment, but just as people vary in their attractiveness to these pests, the value of a given brand will vary from person to person. Unfortunately the odor of mosquito repellent is often as alerting to mammals you might want to observe as is human scent itself. For some people large doses of B-vitamins will act as a systemic mosquito repellent. The excess vitamin is excreted through the skin's pores and repels the insect. No repellent keeps them far enough away to eliminate the ominous buzzing or the swarming in front of your face.

If you want to avoid repellents, a hat and headnet are useful. If you will be using binoculars, replace the netting in front of your eyes with a rectangle of clear acetate. Combine all this with long sleeves and pants and the nuisance is reduced. The trade-off is often the discomfort of heat. This can be alleviated somewhat by avoiding man-made fibers that do not breathe. Stick to cotton and wool.

When it bites, the mosquito automatically injects a bit of its saliva. The human body reacts to this foreign protein by welting and itching. After a few bites from a given species the human body usually produces

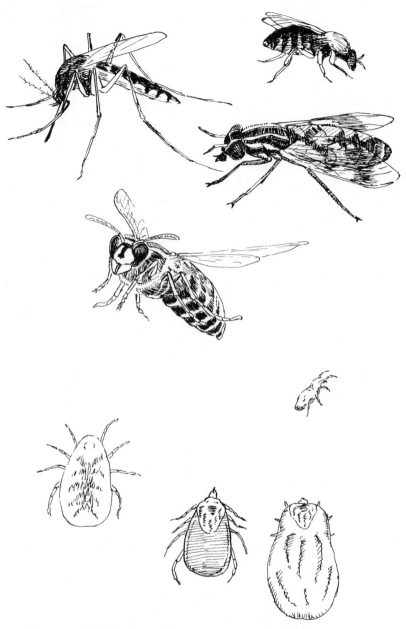

Figure 11.1. Wildlife observer's nuisances. Top right, black fly; top left, mosquito; mid-right, deer fly; mid-left, whitefaced hornet, with chigger at right; bottom left, soft tick; bottom center, hard tick; bottom right, hard tick engorged with blood.

an antibody and future bites from that species welt and itch less or not at all. Unfortunately each different species' proteins must be dealt with separately; immunity to the saliva of one does not provide immunity to all. Various species hatch at different times throughout the season. New welts usually mean that a different species has emerged in your area or that you are in the range of a species that you don't normally encounter.

Dabbing the welts with ammonia or damp baking soda will often relieve the itching. Afield you can use a poultice of crushed stems and leaves of jewelweed or touch-me-not (*Impatiens pallida*). This juicy plant is widely found in damp rich soils and it is useful to know where it grows in your area.

BLACKFLIES.   These humpbacked little flies are basically creatures of streamsides. Members of the family *Simuliidae*, they occur from the tropics to the arctic but are most numerous in temperate and subarctic regions. Their larvae swarm by the hundreds of thousands on the rocks of flowing waters. The adults swarm over the people, getting in ears, nose, mouth, and generally driving a person crazy. The bite is not usually painful in itself, but the saliva causes strong allergic reaction in many people and also has an anti-coagulant substance. Often a person will return from a visit to blackfly territory unaware of having been bitten, yet looking like the victim of an axe attack as blood trickles down face, neck, and ears.

As with mosquitoes there are a number of different species of blackflies. All will swarm about man but not all will bite. There are usually several broods each year, but they are most numerous and irritating in June and July. Head nets and long clothing are about the only way to tolerate these insects if you must frequent their haunts. Repellents will hold them at bay for a while and some people coat their skin with grease as many native American peoples did.

BITING FLIES.   A number of species of flies of the tabanid family can give sharp, nasty bites and nothing can disrupt a careful stalk like the involuntary swat at the fly that just delivered a hot needle jolt to your concentration. Deer flies are a pest of open woodlands. They seem attracted to hair oils and generally like to alight on the highest part of one's person. They are slow and can be easily swatted but that motion may well give you away. Merely wearing a cap or other hat will usually keep them at bay. If you forget your hat and there is bracken fern about, pick one and put it on your head with its stem pointing skyward. The fly will usually alight on the stem and the fern frond provides you some camouflage. You may feel a bit ridiculous but it is surprising how well it works.

Observers working in beach areas may encounter the greenhead fly during July. When these flies are abundant they own the territory. Since they like to gather in shaded areas, they make blinds totally unusable at that time; they also like to get inside parked autos. The stiletto-like mouthparts deliver a painful bite that is impossible to ignore.

BEES AND WASPS.   Bees and wasps are among the most interesting insects to study in their own right. However, many can deliver potent stings that affect different people in different ways. For most people it is a painful experience that dissipates after a couple of hours but for others it triggers a very strong allergic reaction that can induce extensive swelling, a state of shock, collapse of the circulatory system, difficulty breathing, and occasionally even death.

The active wildlife watcher is always at risk of stumbling accidentally onto a yellow jacket or bumblebee nest hidden in the grass, or a paper wasp nest in the shrubbery. The results can be very painful. It takes great control, but one should not run in panic from the area because this causes the wasps to pursue at greater length. Move swiftly and steadily away and don't swat wildly at the pursuers. Dark clothing seems to anger the insects and if you are wearing such clothing for camouflage purposes, be extra cautious. Light-colored clothing seems to disturb them less. The best way to avoid trouble is to be alert and avoid the social wasps.

Anyone with a strong allergy to their venom should not go afield without proper medication as recommended by their physician. Keep it handy in an emergency kit. If you use good sense, bees and wasps should not be any problem. Just remember:

1. Stay away from bee or wasp nests because most will not sting you unless you molest their nest.
2. In areas with a great many bees and wasps, move slowly. The wasps are sensitive to air movement and sudden motion.
3. Avoid hair oils, perfumes, and colognes that have floral odors, for these attract the insects.

CHIGGERS.   These tiny red mites of the southern states swarm in the grass in late summer. They crawl up their victim and wedge themselves in where they find tight contact such as around the top of socks or underwear waistbands. They burrow under the skin and cause intense itching which will persist for weeks. Dust your clothes at ankles, waist, and so on, with a chigger repellent such as powdered flowers of sulphur or those containing diethyltoluamide, to keep these little devils away. If you find yourself the victim, apply clear nail polish to each welt. This seals off the breathing hole and the creature dies. It will be absorbed by your body since there is no way to remove them once they burrow in. Frequent washing of your field clothes and showering immediately upon your return from your wanderings will reduce the chance of their getting firmly attached in you.

TICKS.   Ticks of a variety of species live in fields, brush, and woods. They climb to the tips of vegetation and wave their tiny claws hoping to catch a passing victim. They are strongly attracted to concentrations of carbon dioxide, consequently they are more likely to be encountered in concentrations along roadsides and the edges of parking lots where this gas is released from autos.

Ticks fall into two major groupings—hard, or wood, ticks, and soft ticks. The bites of these animals are not painful but they may become infected and some species can transmit diseases serious to humankind such as tularemia and Rocky Mountain spotted fever. Those two diseases are primarily transmitted by species of wood ticks. Soft tick species tend to transmit relapsing fever.

Wood ticks move slowly and take several hours to decide on a site to make their attachment. They then rasp their way through the skin to the layer where they can tap into the victim's blood supply. If you run a detailed check of your body several times a day during tick season, you can usually remove any wood ticks before they attach themselves. Soft ticks, to the contrary, bite much more quickly and often have drunk their fill of your blood within ten to thirty minutes of having come aboard.

It is important to remove the whole tick to prevent infections. If tweezers are used to pull them off, the head often breaks off and remains in the skin to fester. The key is to make the ticks back out of your skin of their own accord. Some people do this by applying a lighted cigarette to the body of the tick. It does work but you risk burning yourself. To the same end you can smear the tick with heavy oil (mineral, machine, or salad) or clear nail polish. This blocks the tick's breathing pores and it will back out in anywhere from a few minutes to half an hour. Then it can be removed with the tweezers. Scrub the area of the bite with soap and water to help remove any germs from the skin.

To help prevent ticks from getting to your skin, when in tick country it is a wise precaution to wear trousers with legs tucked inside the tops of your boots, or if wearing shoes, slip the socks over the trouser legs. Elastic bands impregnated with repellent are now available to help hold pant and shirt cuffs and keep the ticks out.

A key place to check for ticks is in the hair at the base of the neck. Tick bites there have put people into a mysterious coma. Once the tick was found and removed, the victims returned to normal within a very short time. Tularemia, which is the most common disease transmitted by ticks, is marked in humans by formation of an ulcer at the site of the tick bite. Then there will be an inflammation of the lymph glands, a headache, nausea, chills, and a fever. Any indication of such symptoms should result in a visit to the doctor for an immediate examination. Recovery from this disease may take up to three months but there is usually permanent immunity thereafter.

SPIDERS.   These creatures are the source of more phobia than any other animal except snakes. Rationally there is no justification for such a phobia; most spiders are entirely harmless to humans. A person is just another object to crawl over. However, if attacked, the spiders will defend themselves by biting. Attack to a spider means being picked up between the fingers or being sat or rolled upon. If bitten some people will show a slight allergic reaction to some species, but only two North American species are dangerously toxic to humans—the black widow and the brown recluse (see Figure 11.2). Children are more at risk from the toxins of both these species than are adults.

The black widow is recognized by its shiny black, round abdomen with a bright red hourglass pattern on the underside. The brown recluse is brown of body with a dark, violin-shaped marking on its cephalothorax. Both are shy species that spin their webs in sheltered spots. Unfortunately, such spots include outhouses and wildlife blinds. It is quite easy to inadvertently sit on one in such places and provoke a bite.

Symptoms of a black widow bite include a slight local reaction at the bite site, followed by severe pain caused by a nerve toxin. There will be profuse sweating, nausea, painful abdominal cramps, and difficulty in breathing and speaking. Most victims recover but to a very few the experience can prove fatal. The bite of the brown recluse induces a very different set of reactions. There will be a severe local reaction to the venom which results in an open ulcer within a week or so. The victim's red blood cells will be destroyed and there will be other blood changes. There may be a generalized rash within a day or two, along with chills, fever, joint pains, nausea, and vomiting. Prompt medical attention is advised.

SCORPIONS.   These miniature-lobster–like creatures with long, upturned tails ending in a stinger are easy to recognize. There are more than seventy species in North America. Most of these are not dangerous. Scorpions do not attack people but if they are disturbed they will inflict a sting that can be quite painful, and from some species, toxic. Scorpions avoid light during the daylight hours and may take refuge in shoes or the folds of clothing left on the ground. This puts them in a position to be accidentally disturbed by people.

Figure 11.2. At right, Brown Recluse Spider (note violin-shaped marking); left, Black Widow (female; extreme left shows underside with hourglass marking).

The venom of most scorpions produces only a local reaction, that is, swelling, discoloration, and a painful burning sensation. This should be treated with an ice pack. However, there are two scorpions in this country that possess a systemic venom that spreads through the body, affects the victim's nervous system, and may even cause convulsions (see Figure 11.3). These two species can be found from Florida and the Gulf Coast west to Arizona. Both of these are members of the genus *Centroides*. They are slender scorpions of a yellowish, straw color over the whole body. *Centroides sculpuratus*, the more dangerous species, is plain colored, while *Centroides gertschi* has two irregular blackish stripes along its upper surface. The pincers of these two species are very slender, about six times as long as broad. Young are about ½-inch long and are commonly about two inches long as adults, although specimens three inches long are not uncommon.

Stings from these species do not produce swelling or discoloration at the site of the sting. A prickly-pin sensation is felt immediately and this may become quite painful. The prickly-pin sensation and numbness travels along the limbs. Sometimes the victim feels "electric" sensations throughout the body. As the venom spreads, there may be a tightness in the throat that makes the victim want to keep clearing his throat. Speech becomes impaired, and the victim becomes very restless. This can lead to convulsions or sneezing spasms accompanied by frothing from nose and mouth.

The important part of first aid for scorpion stings is to retard the spread of the venom in the body. This involves a constricting band between the sting and the heart but not at any joint. The band should be tight, but not so tight that a finger cannot be inserted beneath it. Place ice on the sting and then wrap the whole area in crushed ice or use a spray refrigerant like ethyl chloride on the area until you can get to a supply of crushed ice. The ice pack should be kept on for about two hours. The victim should be taken to medical facilities for antivenin if the sting is clearly from a *Centroides* species. If at all possible, kill the scorpion and bring it with the patient so that positive identification can be made. Use of antivenin in the case of a sting from a scorpion lacking systemic toxin can prove harmful to the victim.

Figure 11.3. Left, poisonous Centroides scorpion (note long, slender pincers); right, nonpoisonous scorpion (compare with other's pincers).

POISONOUS SNAKES.   Most of our snake species are harmless, but a few are venomous. In North America, all the venomous snakes, except the coral snake, are members of the pit viper group. This includes a number of species of rattlesnakes, the copperhead, and the water moccasin. The alert wildlife watcher is unlikely to be bitten, but since these species tend to remain motionless and are protectively colored, it is possible to accidentally invade their space and startle them into striking. Over half the venomous snake bites in this country each year occur in Texas, North Carolina, Florida, Georgia, Louisiana, and Arkansas.

It is important to understand that fear and panic are more dangerous than the bite of the snake itself. The effects of the poison will not be felt immediately and the situation can be dealt with successfully if calm can prevail. The first thing to do if bitten is to assess the seriousness of the situation. The factors that determine that are

- the amount of venom that was injected and where the bite is located in terms of how it affects the speed of absorption of venom into the circulatory system. About 30 percent of snakebites show no signs of venom injection.
- the size of the victim.
- how long it will take to get to a place for antivenin therapy.

If the bite is from a pit viper it will tend to swell rapidly and be extremely painful. There will be marked general discoloration of the skin. As the poison takes effect there will be general weakness, rapid pulse, nausea and vomiting, shortness of breath, dimness of vision, and shock.

The objectives of any first-aid measures with snakebite are to reduce the circulation of blood through the bite area to delay the absorption of the venom; to prevent aggravation of the wound; and to sustain respiration. This means getting the victim to a hospital quickly, while keeping the victim from moving around, preferably keeping him in a horizontal position. Try to keep the bitten area at, or below, heart level. As long as you can get the victim to a hospital within four to five hours, this is usually adequate first-aid procedure.

However, if the delay in reaching a hospital is likely to be longer, and mild to moderate symptoms develop, apply a constricting band two to four inches above the bite but not around a joint such as elbow, wrist, knee, or ankle, nor around the head, neck, or trunk. The band should be 1 to 1½ inch wide and should be loose enough to slip a finger underneath. Be alert for swelling and loosen, but don't remove, the band if it becomes too tight. Periodically check the pulse in the extremity beyond the bite to be sure the flow of blood has not stopped.

If severe symptoms develop, it may be necessary to make incisions and apply suction. This must be done calmly and thoughtfully. Unnecessary complications can occur through panic at this point. The constricting band should be applied and then cuts made in the skin through the fang marks.

- Use a very sharp sterilized knife or razor blade.
- Cuts should be no deeper than just through the skin and only ½ inch long.
- Cuts should be from fang mark to suspected venom deposit site which, because the snake strikes downward, is usually lower than the fang mark.
- Cuts should be made along the long axis of the limb. Do not make cross-cut incisions nor cuts on head, neck, or trunk.

Apply suction with a suction cup for half an hour. If a suction cup is not available, use your mouth. Mouth suction poses little risk to him who sucks unless he has mouth sores or cuts, but it is not recommended that the venom be swallowed. Rinse out the mouth before and after.

Although there has been work done on using icepacks or other refrigerants as part of reducing venom circulation, as is done with scorpion stings, instead of cutting and suction, the Red Cross does not recommend any form of cold therapy in the treatment of snakebite.

Some other concerns related to snakebite treatment need to be addressed. Shock is very likely to accompany snakebite, so keep the victim lying down and comfortable and maintain his body temperature. If breathing stops, mouth-to-mouth resuscitation will be in order, and if both breathing and pulse stop, cardiopulmonary resuscitation (CPR) will be called for if you know this procedure. The victim will want medicine to relieve the pain, but do not administer alcohol, sedatives, aspirin, or any medicine containing aspirin! Give only a pain-killer recommended by a consulting doctor. Wash the bitten area with soap and water and blot dry. Use dressings and bandages for only a short time.

Some people are allergic to antivenin and the effects of this can be worse than the bite. Doctors not used to treating snakebite should be reminded of this so that they are doubly alert for any problems.

Coral snakes are extremely unlikely to bite unless handled. Their venom is quite different from that of the pit vipers, although the first aid is about the same. A coral snake bite will manifest itself with only mild local swelling and slight burning pain, but will be followed with blurred vision, drooping eyelids, slurred speech, drowsiness, increased saliva and sweating, sometimes nausea and vomiting, shock, respiratory difficulties, paralysis, convulsions, and possibly coma.

In venomous snake country a snakebite kit and an understanding of snakebite first aid should be your constant companion. Hopefully you will never have to use either, but don't get caught without them.

MARINE ORGANISMS.   Several sea creatures must be treated with respect—moray eels, sharks, lionfish, sting rays, and the like—but of more general concern is careless or accidental contact with members of the coelenterata such as jellyfish, Portuguese man-o-wars, and stinging corals. Each of these creatures has stinging cells on their tentacles that discharge venom on contact. At best, encounters with these creatures are painful and, if contact is prolonged, the toxin can be dangerous or even fatal. The venom of these creatures produces burning pain and a rash. If a large dose of the venom is received there can be cramping, nausea and vomiting, shock, and respiratory difficulty. First aid involves wiping the affected area with a towel and washing it with diluted ammonia or rubbing alcohol to deactivate the stinging cells imbedded in the victim's skin. You can give aspirin for the pain. If the contact was extensive, treat the victim for shock and get prompt medical attention.

TOXIC PLANTS.   People vary widely in their sensitivity to various plants and a number of different species are known to cause skin rashes and irruptions to some individuals. Several members of the carrot family have been implicated but the most common offenders in North America are all members of the genus *Rhus*—poison ivy, poison oak, and poison sumac (Figure 11.4). These are the only ones we will discuss here. Poison ivy exists throughout the United States except in California and portions of adjacent states where it is replaced by the very similar poison oak. Poison ivy grows in three forms—as a low ground cover, as a shrub, and as a climbing vine. Poison oak generally grows in shrub form but sometimes as a vine. Both species have a leaf composed of three leaflets and drooping clusters of white fruits. Poison sumac is a 5-foot to 25-foot shrub of eastern wetlands. It has clusters of drooping white fruits like those of poison ivy, in contrast to the other sumacs that have upright bobs of fruit that start out greenish and turn bright red.

   All parts of these species contain a volatile oil which causes skin rash and blistering on sensitive human skin. A person's sensitivity to that oil may vary throughout his lifetime. Sensitivity, or lack of it, may be turned around during those periods of life with major hormonal

Figure 11.4. Left, poison ivy (note that leaflets can be smooth edged or slightly toothed); center, poison oak; right, poison sumac.

changes such as puberty and menopause. It doesn't pay to take chances. In addition, there is evidence that resistance to the oil decreases with exposure. For example, I had been blessedly immune to the stuff in spite of often careless handling of it. At the age of twenty-five I was engaged in digging out a muskrat bank den that happened to be in the middle of a poison ivy patch. In spite of a thorough washing with yellow soap afterwards, to my surprise and chagrin I came down with a massive dose of poison ivy that required medical injections to get cleared up. It was an unpleasant way to learn the truth about what I had been telling others for years.

If you come down with poison ivy rash and blisters, apply calamine or other soothing skin lotion. If the reaction is widespread on your body and the itching severe, seek medical attention. Today even extreme sensitivity to these plants need not drive you indoors because an allergist can provide desensitization treatments. Be sure you can recognize these plants in all their growth habits. It has been my observation that many of the people most affected by the plants can't readily recognize them in the field.

For most people, the results of contact with the oil are an itching rash and blistering which begin a few hours after exposure but which may be delayed twenty-four to forty-eight hours. In more extreme cases the victim may develop a high fever and become quite ill. After every exposure to any of these plants, remove all contaminated clothing and wash it. Wash your exposed skin with Fels Naptha or other strong laundry soap or liquid green soap. This generally will prevent the oil from doing its worst.

Physical Hazards

SUN.   It is easy to become so absorbed in wildlife watching that one loses track of how much exposure to the sun one has received. This is particularly true in open habitats, especially near the ocean. Snorkeling keeps you floating back up and the water helps magnify the sun's rays. The results can be a severe burn that may make it difficult even to walk. The wise wildlife watcher builds up exposure to the sun gradually until the skin has developed protective pigments (if it is genetically programmed to do so). In any case, it is also prudent to wear protective clothing and modern sunscreen lotions.

In hot climates, the sun not only burns with its rays but it also evaporates water rapidly. It is essential to maintain body fluids and increase salt intake appropriately to make up for the extra secretion and evaporation of sweat. This will help prevent heat exhaustion and heat cramps. Both conditions are unpleasant companions on a wildlife watching venture.

WEATHER.   Reading the weather is an art less well developed today than in days of yore. Today we tend to rely on professional weather forecasters and the mass media. Weather has a habit of changing rapidly and in places of variable climate it is wise to learn the signs of approaching weather shifts or violent storms. This is particularly true for mountain regions and regions near large bodies of water where weather changes may be quite localized and will not show up even in regular scanning of a portable radio for weather news. High wispy cirrus clouds usually indicate a change in the weather within twenty-four hours. Fluffy cumulus clouds are fair weather clouds, but when they seem to be boiling upward and spreading out at the tops into anvil shapes, look forward to heavy rain and probably thunder and lightning within a very short time. A sharp drop in temperature will often precede the storm by a matter of a few minutes.

To determine if an electrical storm is approaching or moving away, count the seconds between the flash of lightning and hearing the thunder clap. Each five seconds represents a mile of distance. Noting those time intervals every five or ten minutes should give you the information about the storm's direction of movement and relative speed.

It is always good insurance to carry with you a day pack with spare clothing that will let you cope with sudden temperature change—particularly in mountain country—or with precipitation. You can also carry materials to make a temporary shelter such as a plastic sheet and some strong twine. A pocket space blanket is always good insurance as is a container of waterproofed matches.

In many parts of the country it pays to keep a good emergency kit in your car. This would contain a folding stove, pot, emergency rations, and water. A sleeping bag and/or space blanket will help keep you warm. Your car may become your only home for a day or two if you are caught in drifted snow or cut off by flash flooding.

The most dangerous weather-related hazard is hypothermia. This is a rapid and progressive mental and physical collapse that comes about when the inner body core becomes chilled. It is usually brought about by exposure to cold, or to being wet and exposed to the wind, or by a combination of both of these. It is not just a winter phenomenon by any means, for most cases of hypothermia occur when the air temperature is between 30° to 50° F. Those most susceptible to it are amateur outdoorspeople who are not conditioned to physical stress and who are unaware of the potential danger posed by wetness, wind, and cold.

Hypothermia is a threat whenever the body is losing heat faster than it is producing it. It can be induced by becoming sweaty from exercise such as snow shoeing, cross-country skiing, strenuous hiking, or similar exertion, and then removing the outer protective shell of clothing so that the wind evaporates the moisture. It can happen after getting soaked in a sudden rain squall in the mountains or falling into a mountain stream or getting drenched by a cold ocean wave along a windy shore. If you are not aware of the danger such conditions create and do not take positive action, you could soon find yourself involved with exposure and hypothermia. You probably wouldn't even be fully aware of what was happening because the condition robs one of judgment and reasoning power.

Symptoms of hypothermia include uncontrollable fits of shivering; immobile, fumbling hands; vague slurred speech; pale skin; a lurching gait and frequent stumbling; drowsiness; and apparent exhaustion and inability to get up after rest. If you know the person well, you will also often perceive a personality change. If first aid is not given and the person does stop moving about, the internal temperature will continue to slide, leading to stupor, collapse, and all too often, death.

If you are involved with a person suffering from exposure, get the person out of the wind, rain, and all wet clothes as quickly as possible. Clothes that become wet lose 90 percent of their insulating value. If the person shows only mild impairment of functions, get him into dry clothes and a sleeping bag. Give warm, but not hot, drinks and have someone get into the sleeping bag with the victim to give added warmth.

If the person is semi-conscious or worse, try to keep him awake. Give the warm drinks if possible but keep the person naked in the sleeping bag. Have one or two other people strip naked and climb into the bag with the victim. This is no time for modesty; skin-to-skin contact and heat exchange is the most effective treatment.

Hypothermia is very dangerous. Normally, it can be avoided by using good sense. Put on rain gear before you get soaked. Carry it with you even on a sunny day. Put on warm clothes after an accidental soaking or even when exposed to falling temperatures before you begin to shiver. Wear a hat and learn how hats can help regulate body heat. Eat a good breakfast before setting out in the field, and carry some high-energy foods such as the gorp of the hiking fraternity (raisins, nuts, and M & Ms). Carry hot chocolate or soup with you to places where sudden cold or damp weather is known to strike. (Never use alcohol because it makes you lose heat faster.)

If you should accidentally get into a situation where hypothermia may strike, keep active until you can get the warm fluids and dry, warm clothing. Do calisthenics, walk—anything but stop and sit down— because once you cease activity, your body's rate of heat production instantly drops by 50 percent or more. In a matter of minutes this could slide you into early stages of hypothermia (marked by poor judgment) with the likelihood of your slipping deeper under its potentially fatal influence.

MOUNTAIN SICKNESS. Persons venturing forth in high altitudes are subject to mountain sickness until they have become acclimated to the change in pressure and the thinner air over a period of several weeks. The decreased oxygen of the thinner air can result in headaches, nausea, and a feeling of weakness. These symptoms can be intensified by exertion, cold, or drinking cold water. The degree to which you will be bothered will depend in large measure on the amount of difference between the altitude at which you normally live and the one you are visiting. At altitudes considerably greater than you are used to, walk slowly and rest several times an hour. Don't hesitate to lie down and relax fully. If the symptoms persist even with rest, go down to a lower altitude. It is better to let your body adjust to increasing altitudes in stages rather than to make a drastic change without gradual acclimatization.

QUICKSAND AND QUAGMIRES. In some parts of the country quicksands, quagmires, and mud and muck provide very insecure footings and inspire great fear because of the horror stories we have often heard since childhood. However, anyone who keeps their head can get out of such treacherous areas with reasonable ease.

In areas where such unstable footing is suspected, it is a good idea to carry a pole to probe questionable footing. Be particularly alert in areas where people talk of underground streams, rivers, or springs. Quicksands generally are found on flat shores, in silt-choked rivers with shifting water courses, and near the mouths of rivers. The alkali flats of the West are also places to approach with caution. If you can see large pebbles on the sand, it is likely to be safe, but if you are suspicious, probe with a pole or toss a stone into the area. If it sinks, beware.

Should you be surprised and feel your feet sinking in quicksand or in muck and find that trying to pull the foot out only seems to make it want to go deeper, get rid of any burden, such as a knapsack, that you may be carrying, then throw yourself full forward or backward and use swimming motions. Use a crawl, breast, or back stroke, or just roll over and over. The prone position gives more upward buoyancy from the material, whereas concentrating all the weight vertically while struggling only forces one down more rapidly. Make your strokes slowly and evenly until you move your body to more solid surfaces. You may lose a shoe and get good and mucky, and it may take you several hours to extricate yourself, but the greatest danger you will be facing is panic. If others are about, and not similarly entrapped, they can help by reaching out with a pole or rope, or they can build a pathway to the person using such objects as boards and brush that will distribute weight more broadly, as snowshoes do on snow.

KNOWING WHERE YOU ARE

The mountain men and other wilderness explorers were keen observers with phenomenal memories. It was their key to survival in combination with their skill in living off the land wherever they happened to find themselves. These are skills wildlife watchers might like to have today although few possess them. However, we have access to something the old-timers did not—detailed maps of almost anywhere in the United States.

The wise outdoorsman thoroughly studies topographic maps of any area he or she expects to spend time in. Flow patterns of streams, major land features, and highway patterns are all studied and put in the memory bank. The map itself is consigned to the day pack or knapsack to refer to when memory fails. With such preparation you may be temporarily disoriented but never lost.

Topographic maps are about 16½ × 20 inches in size and are drawn to scales that vary from one-half to two inches per mile. Most show contours in increments of twenty feet. Once you have become familiar with reading them you can form a mental picture of the hills, valleys, marshes, forests, rivers, and streams of the mapped area. These maps can be purchased at many sporting goods stores that cater to hiking and camping or hunting interests. They can also be ordered directly from the U.S. Geological Survey. Ask first for an index map that includes the general part of the United States that you will be exploring. This will show you all the quadrats available and their numbers. Locate the quadrat(s) that include the actual sites you will be exploring and order them by their number. For maps of areas east of the Mississippi, write Branch of Distribution, U.S. Geological Survey, 1200 South Eads Street, Arlington, VA 22202. For maps of areas west of the Mississippi, write Branch of Distribution, U.S. Geological Survey, Federal Center, Denver, CO 80225.

If you plan to explore National Forests write the U.S. Forest Service for maps of the appropriate forest. The address is Forest Service, U.S. Department of Agriculture, Washington, D.C. 20250. If you will be working around or on large lakes, request maps from the U.S. Lake Survey, Federal Building, Detroit, MI 48226. For Canada some topographic maps and general maps are available from the Map Distribution Office, Department of Mines and Technical Surveys, Ottawa, Canada. As with the U.S. Geological Survey, this office has general index maps from which you order the appropriate local maps. The Marine Sciences Branch of this office has hydrographic charts of Canadian waters for those who use the water and waterways.

Pack your maps in resealable plastic envelopes or bags, or laminate them with cloth backing and a clear plastic surface. A soggy map that is falling apart is virtually useless.

When you are in country with which you are not thoroughly familiar, carry a compass and know how to use it. There are several kinds available but those developed by Silva for the sport of orienteering are among the simplest, most reliable, and of reasonable cost. They work on the concept of the 360-degree circle rather than with the compass rose, which is a generally easier and more accurate method for people today to use. Most Silva compasses come with a good booklet on their use.

It is important to remember that a compass needle points to magnetic north rather than to true North. In only a narrow band running from the southeast corner of Georgia up through the Great Lakes region through a point above Lake Superior are magnetic north and true North essentially the same. East of this line the needle points west of true North and west of the line it points east of true North. The degree of the angle of variance from true North increases as you move away from the line up to about 25 degrees. Your topographic maps will have a declination symbol to tell you how many degrees of correction to make. This symbol is usually an acute angle marked with the degree of declination. One leg of this angle points to true North and the other to magnetic north. By using your compass you can orient your map to true North and then get your bearings on the map. Next you can set a direction of travel based on the key topographic features.

Don't set off with map and compass without some practice in their use on familiar terrain. Get a quadrant of a familiar area and practice using the map and compass to plot courses. If there is an orienteering club in the area join it, or meet some of its members who can give you some good instruction and guidance. Cross-country orienteering can be a great deal of fun in itself and is good not only for learning map and compass but also for physical conditioning.

BEING LOST

The chances of being truly lost are remote, but there are some parts of the country where the habitat is so uniform as to be almost featureless. If you are truly lost, the best thing to do is stay put, make yourself as comfortable as possible, and make some signal that can be spotted from the air by rescuers. If you must travel, beware of circling and be prepared to counter it.

To get a feel for your tendency to circle, go out into an open area and face a destination several hundred yards away. Now close your eyes and start walking. Don't peek. Walk at least fifty paces and more before opening your eyes. You will find you have veered to the right or left of your destination. It is worth doing this exercise several times to get an idea of how strongly you stray and in what direction. You will also find that your degree of tiredness affects this and that can be important to someone who has been in the field several hours before realizing that he or she is lost. Repeat the exercise and try to correct for your tendency to wander. How do you fare? How much can you improve your skill at correcting for your tendency to circle?

When actually lost you are essentially disoriented in the same way as if you were blinded. You will drift off course in the same way and tend to over-correct when you are aware of your wandering path. That is why it is best to stay put. If you must travel, set a route by sighting on a tree or rock dead ahead of you in the direction you want to go. Also mark an object where you are leaving from. Move to the object ahead and then sight back to the mark on the object where you were. Repeat this over and over to keep moving in a straight line. In most parts of the country you will intersect a road, path, or waterway within a few miles. If you intersect a waterway, follow it downstream. This will almost always lead to human habitation.

ELEMENTARY FIRST AID

Wildlife watching is much safer than most sports, but it does have its potential accidents. A first aid kit should routinely be carried in the field. This should be at least a single unit type with bandage, adhesive tape, gauze pads, tourniquet, scissors, and tweezers. It is useful to have antiseptic, eye wash, and ace bandage.

Injuries most likely to occur are puncture wounds, deep scratches, jammed fingers, and sprained ankles. It is prudent to take a first aid course or at least get and familiarize yourself with a good first aid book such as the *American Red Cross Standard First Aid and Personal Safety*. At the very least, become familiar with how to treat such injuries as listed above and others you might encounter in the field, particularly frostbite and hypothermia. These are valuable skills no matter what endeavors you may want to pursue. Usually the best way to avoid accidents and injuries is to be prepared to deal with them.

FURTHER READING

AMERICAN RED CROSS. *Standard First Aid and Personal Safety*, 2nd ed. Garden City, N.Y.: Doubleday & Company, 1979.
ANDERSON, BOB. *Stretching*. Bolinas, CA.: Shelter Publications, 1980.

ARNOLD, ROBERT E., M.D. *What To Do About Bites and Stings of Venomous Animals.* New York: Collier Books, 1973.

DOAN, DAN. *Dan Doan's Fitness Program for Hikers and Cross Country Skiers.* Somersworth, N.H.: New Hampshire Publishing Company, 1978.

FRAZIER, C. A., and F. K. BROWN. *Insects and Allergy and What To Do About Them.* Norman, OK.: University of Oklahoma, 1980.

GATTY, HAROLD. *Nature Is Your Guide—How to Find Your Way on Land and Sea by Observing Nature.* New York: E. P. Dutton & Company, Inc., 1958.

HALSTEAD, BRUCE W. *Dangerous Marine Animals.* Cambridge, Md.: Cornell Maritime Press, 1959.

KJELLSTROM, BJORN. *Be Expert with Map and Compass.* New York: Charles Scribner's Sons, 1976.

Royal Canadian Airforce Exercise Plans for Physical Fitness. New York: Pocket Books, 1976.

SHAEFER, V. J., and J. A. DAY. *A Field Guide to the Atmosphere.* Boston: Houghton Mifflin, 1981.

SHIMER, JOHN A. *Field Guide to Landforms In The United States.* New York: Macmillan, 1972.

WALLIS, EARL L., and GENE A. LOGAN. *Isometric Exercises for Figure Improvement and Body Conditioning.* Englewood Cliffs, N.J.: Prentice-Hall, Inc., 1964.

SOURCES

INSECT REPELLENTS
* Sportsman's Anti Insect Bands
Unit 405, 5300 N-A1A
Vero Beach, Florida 32960
(*impregnated elastic bands for pant and arm cuffs*)

CHAPTER 12

EXPLORING
SPECIAL GROUPS

THROUGHOUT THIS BOOK WE HAVE DISCUSSED generally the techniques of behavior watching, drawing examples from a broad spectrum of wildlife. This chapter is essentially a potpourri of comments about, and additional techniques for, working with specific groups of animals. Some groups are easy to observe, particularly those that are day active; others are far more difficult to observe because they are secretive, rare, nocturnal, and so forth. There is no attempt to be definitive or exhaustive but only to point to tools and directions that will trigger the reader's imagination and desire to launch investigations that will carry the sport of learning even further. You may be able to broaden general knowledge about any of a number of lesser-known species. In addition each section of the chapter suggests organizations of interested people you might wish to contact in order to find others who share your concerns and interests and who publish articles about the animals.

CREATURES BENEATH THE
WAVES

Until relatively recently, extended observations of aquatic creatures were largely limited to species that could be easily maintained in aquaria. Very few comprehensive behavioral studies of fish or aquatic invertebrates have been carried out in the wild. Today scuba equipment makes such studies much more feasible. Additionally armed with a mini-slate (see page 27) and underwater cameras, there is opportunity to see and record a great deal. In addition to custom housings for standard brand cameras, there are now both 35mm (Nikonos) Super and 8mm movie (Eumig Nautica) cameras that can be used in air or underwater without additional housings. The field is now wide open for underwater behavior watching.

Most North American native fishes that are not game fishes remain largely unstudied at least as far as their behavior is concerned. Many of these, particularly those of cold, flowing waters, do not do well in aquaria and thus cry out for field study. Modern wet suits take the chill off and make working in these waters more tolerable. Fish watching has attracted many people vacationing near the coral reefs of the world just because of the sheer beauty of the fishes that live there, but the habits and behavior of other fishes of other waters are often interesting, even bizarre, even if their colors are not gem-like.

Faced with polluted streams, rivers, and lakes, our fish fauna is increasingly being pushed out of the mainstream and into the backwaters. To save some of these species from extirpation we need to know much more about their habits. Their feeding behavior needs to be watched in considerable detail. Which species are opportunistic feeders; which are selective? How do different species interact with one another in the same stretch of water? What kind of substrate do they select for laying their eggs? How do stream fishes cope with annual flooding and scouring of the stream bed? Do given schools have territories or home ranges? Do members of schools interchange with other schools or do they always remain together except for those that suffer mortality? What factors in the environment cause a flight response? What factors elicit a color change, if any? The list can be extended on and on.

Laun describes the building of a very useful and simply constructed floating laboratory for use in aquatic studies (Figure 12.1). Essentially it is a plywood raft supported by three pine-sheathed, styrofoam floats. It has a very shallow draft and excellent stability although it is slow moving. It is excellent as a dive boat and with some easy modifications can have some glass bottom inserts that allow clear direct viewing from topside. The 8' × 16' boat will support a ton load and still draft only six inches which means that it can be taken into very shallow waters where young fishes and aquatic invertebrates may abound.

Figure 12.1.
Pontoon floating laboratory (after Laun).

For those even more ambitious, a two-hulled floating work station has been designed. The identical twin hulls can be used separately or joined to form the work station that is large enough for six people and their equipment. It is particularly useful for doing bottom sampling, seining, fish marking, and tagging. For more information contact: William C. Bullock, Head, Department of Industrial Design, School of Architecture and Fine Arts, Auburn University, Auburn, AL 36830.

For freshwater fish watchers there is an organization whose goal is "to encourage increased appreciation of native fish species through observation, study, research, and the restoration and appreciation of natural habitat; to assemble and distribute information about native fishes; and to promote practical laws for the preservation of natives both in the wild and the home aquarium." This organization is called the North American Native Fishes Association and it publishes a newsletter called *American Currents*. For further information contact: Jerry Corcoran, 1650 East Beach, Biloxi, MS 39530.

Our salt and brackish water fishes are similarly in need of detailed study. In many ways our coastal waters are as intriguing as coral reefs. Unfortunately the siren call of the reefs has too often blinded people to the near at hand. It is true that in our coastal waters fish concentrations tend to be more seasonal and nomadic but there are still many relatively sedentary species whose life histories and behavior are little known.

The invertebrate fauna—the crabs and crayfish, the mollusks, starfishes, and many others—have many interesting behaviors and can be studied fairly easily. Limpets, for example, have very definite home sites and marked individuals can be followed through the day and traced back to their "roosting" spot. Do they defend this spot? If so, how? Do other local mollusks demonstrate a like preference for certain spots? Do crayfish and lobsters defend shelters? Do apparently sessile creatures like anemones and hydra move about? Do clams and worms do anything down in the sand and mud?

There is an organization of people that explores questions such as these and many more. The members' focus of interest is on that zone of shallow water around our shores known to scientists as the littoral zone. They explore the life forms and the physical forces that exist in this area. Among their activities are several fish-tagging efforts. The organization is the American Littoral Society, which publishes a journal called *Underwater Naturalist*. Contact them at: Sandy Hook, Highlands, NJ 07732.

There are still limits to what can be done with aquatic observations in the field and there is a definite role for captive observation in the home aquarium. However, operating aquaria that can sustain healthy fish and/or invertebrates through periods long enough to watch normal behavior over a full cycle is a complex task. In the confines of a tank, chemicals concentrate that may be chronically toxic or may alter behavior. Anyone contemplating captive observations should develop basic skills in chemical analysis and aquarium management. Fortunately, there are a number of books on the market today to give fundamental guidance but often the native species will require even more special management, the nature of which you will have to discover through experimentation.

In recent years there has been a growing interest in marine mammals, as many species are fast dwindling because of overexploitation with modern technologies and disruptions to the habitat. A number of amateurs have teamed up with professionals to help gather the data that enlarges our understanding of these creatures and provides clues to needed management strategies to assure their continued survival into the future. Some people man lookout points along the coasts to spot and count migrating seals and whales. Others take photographs of the dorsal fins and the underside of the flukes of sounding humpback whales in order to help assemble "mug books" for identification of individual whales. There are also those who patrol the shores looking for any beached animals. Leatherwood, Caldwell, and Winn in their book (see the Bibliography) provide a listing of places to contact regarding whale strandings. Allied Whale, College of the Atlantic, Bar Harbor, ME 04609 will provide sighting and census forms for seals and whales in the Gulf of Maine.

There are some research vessels now that take on amateurs as crew and research assistants. The square-rigged sailing vessel *Regina Maris*, owned by the Ocean Research and Education Society, Inc., 64 Commercial Wharf, Boston, MA 02110, is one such ship. They have been following the various humpback whale populations in both the Atlantic and the Pacific adding to knowledge about breeding grounds, migration routes, feeding behavior, and population size.

In California, amateurs have contributed heavily to data gathering on the sea otter, an endangered species that has been making something of a comeback in recent years. This creature is observable from shore at many places along the Monterey coast, and its antics have captivated many. They, along with other marine mammals, are protected under rather stringent regulations by the Marine Mammal Protection Act. This act protects the animals not only from hunting but also from harassment. Harassment includes continued approach within the individual's flight distance. Sometimes whale-watching tours and some research vessels are guilty of such harassment which can interfere with normal feeding or breeding activities. Avoid the temptation to pursue animals in your own vessel unless you are fully aware of the law, are in compliance, and are sure you are in an area where the creatures are little pursued by others.

LAND MAMMALS

Certain groups of mammals—the hooved animals, the large carnivores, the primates, and the great whales—have received the bulk of the attention of the behavioral students. This is natural because most of these animals are under great pressure from mankind and their continued existence into the next century is questionable. To keep them with us we need to know as much about them as possible. They are also species with considerable "sex appeal" for the fund-raising needed for the ongoing professional research.

Other species have been largely ignored. Many are small and secretive; most are nocturnal, and thus, difficult to study. It takes time, commitment, and ingenuity, but there are great opportunities for serious amateurs to add significantly to our knowledge of these animals.

In North America the large predators are reasonably well known but the same cannot be said for the smaller predators of the weasel family. These animals, ranging from the diminutive least weasel to the wolverine, present a spectrum of small predators that are likely to be with us long after the wolf and the grizzly have vanished. The weasel clan tends to be wary and shy because they have been trapped relentlessly for their beautiful furs. Studying their behavior presents a challenge, although not an insuperable one. Much can be learned from tracking them in winter. Summer observations may be as much a matter of luck as skill but every so often it is possible to locate a den and observe the behavior there. I have learned a great deal from captive reared, human habituated individuals and slowly am gaining confirmation of the validity of such observations from sightings of wild individuals. If weasels are in your area, the multi-capture live trap for weasels described on page 81 may be useful so that you can individually mark them. A larger scale version might also work with mink.

Skunks are often the most common of the weasel clan and whereas they pose some potential problems they are actually quite easy to pursue and watch. They are extremely nearsighted so by keeping a respectful distance and moving quietly, you can follow along and observe detail with a binocular that has a good twilight factor. As long as you don't startle them there is little likelihood that you will be sprayed. On several occasions skunks that I was observing have come right up and sniffed my shoes or even nibbled on my shoelaces. Just remember that lifting the tail is an early warning of annoyance; stamping the front feet indicates that patience has about run out. Skunks are reasonably easy to live trap and they seldom spray inside an enclosure because they don't like the smell either. Specially constructed box traps of wood with a glass or plexiglass bottom are useful. Or use a commercial wire live trap covered with a tarpaulin and release the animal into a glass bottomed, wooden handling box. The transparent bottom lets you look up from underneath to determine the sex of the animal and perhaps read any toe clipping you might have done.

Skunks are often quite distinctive in the arrangement of white on black, therefore further individualization of a small population may be unnecessary. If you must mark, in preference to toe clipping, the animals can be tagged by using adhesive reflective tape with a nonreflective number painted on. This tag can be attached to the animal's tail where it can easily be spotted with a flashlight. Any handling of skunks must be done with extreme care, not only because of the scent, but more importantly because skunks are a major reservoir of rabies and any bite from one should be considered potentially dangerous. If you are bitten, do not release the animal but hold it captive for clinical observation.

Bats are often abundant but we have much to learn about their behavior. Bats have been banded extensively in the past, primarily in winter quarters, but their behavior during the summer months is far less frequently observed. As might be expected, those species such as the little brown and big brown bats that regularly use human structures to roost are better known than the others, particularly the migratory tree bats such as the red, the silver-haired, and the hoary. Denny Constantine showed that finding tree bat roots was at first a matter of luck and dogged persistence, but that after a few successes, patterns begin to emerge and one begins to think like a bat and predict what sites are likely to have bats roosting.

Mist nets have been used to catch bats, but they are a trial, for bats can get quite wrapped up in them, requiring considerable time and care to remove them uninjured. Constantine devised a bat trap composed of fine piano wires stretched taut with springs and spaced about an inch apart (Figure 12.2). The trap was placed in a cave opening and as bats came and went they hit the wires and slid down them into a container at the bottom. He then modified this trap into a smaller model that could be hung over a pond or other site that bats frequent. The size of the wires proved critical to the bat species caught. If 0.012-inch stainless steel music wires were used, the larger species such as red, hoary, and freetailed bats were caught, but the smaller *Myotis* species were able to use their sonar to successfully avoid the trap. When wires only 0.006 inch were used, some *Myotis* species were also caught.

Figure 12.2.
Left, bat trap; right, bat-holding cage.

Today it is possible to use monofilament nylon fishline instead of stainless steel wire, so the trap is more cheaply and easily constructed. It consists mainly of a sturdy frame (2" × 3") approximately six feet square. The strings are attached to screw eyes or nails at the bottom and then to springs at the other end. The springs attach to hooks on the top frame bar. Strings should be set at one inch apart. A permanent hardware cloth receptacle one foot wide, 18 inches deep, and as long as the trap, is attached to the lower part of the frame about four inches from the bottom. A 17-inch sheet of plastic is affixed around the inside of the receptacle to create a smooth surface that prevents the bats from climbing out.

When the trap is hung from a tree limb, a battery-operated light, or a plug-in light if you are near a dwelling, is attached to the frame to attract insects and thus ultimately the bats. With such a trap, summer captures for individual marking are more feasible. By using luminescent markers, or other identifiers (see page 103) you can determine if the same animal frequents the same hunting ground each night and whether or not a regular time sequence is followed. By hanging the trap with pulleys so it can be inspected easily, you can check the trap each hour and half hour to see if different species are using the same area in different time blocks. Use an insect light trap to capture flying insects in the same area and time blocks. Is there any correlation between insects flying and the bat species flying? Bats learn to avoid the traps after one or two encounters at a given location, so move the trap about often to maintain its efficiency.

A collecting container for bats is easily constructed from a tube cake pan, ¼-inch mesh hardware cloth, and a regular cake pan (see Figure 12.2). The two cake pans should be of the same diameter. The hardware cloth is rolled into a cylinder that will just fit inside the regular cake pan. The cylinder should be about 18 inches high and be attached securely to the bottom of the outside of the upside down tube cake pan. The bottom can also be attached permanently or held in place with the hooks and springs used to hold ironing board covers in place. Bats are put in through the center of the tube pan. They climb on the wire but can't climb the metal. If the bottom is removable rather than attached, it is easier to remove recalcitrant individuals.

A word of caution: Rabies is endemic in North American bats. Indeed, they seem to be the only animals that recover from the disease and then may act as carriers. I have handled many thousands of bats over the years with no problems. Most are too small for their teeth to break the skin, but some species can and do. If in handling bats you are bitten, hang onto that animal for clinical observation and seek medical attention. If bats turn out to be your passion and you intend to handle them frequently, you should investigate getting anti-rabies inoculations. There is an improved procedure for this today, but there are still some who are allergic to the serum and thus cannot receive the treatment.

Don't take unnecessary risks; rabies is no picnic. Just as with the handling of poisonous snakes, it is the bat handler who becomes overconfident and careless who is most at risk.

Among our smaller mammals, the shrews are good subjects for study. They are abundant, though secretive, and much remains to be learned of their behavior. Crowcroft wrote a delightful little book on the behavior of British shrews that is a model for studying ours, which are a different family of shrews from those in Britain. Shrews can be studied in the wild and under captive conditions and you may be quite surprised at what you discover. These little animals are insectivores and regularly described as voracious predators, yet I regularly watch the shorttail shrews at my bird-feeding station eating spilled sunflower seeds. These oil-rich seeds apparently substitute well for insects in winter. Shrews do better in captivity than the literature would suggest if plenty of water is available and the humidity is kept reasonably high. These animals actually are less concerned with light than adequate touch. I have kept them in hardware cloth sandwiches of tunnels with openings to the surface and they have remained very active even though they were quite visible (Figure 12.3). As long as they have touch contact with their surroundings, particularly from above, they appear to feel secure. I have kept the sandwiches on artifical sponges that are kept damp but not wet in order to maintain high humidity. So secure are the animals that they generally stay in the sandwich even when it is removed from the aquarium for cage cleaning. I have maintained animals for over twenty months in this arrangement. Shrew activity, in captivity and the wild, is one of the things that can be monitored with an automatic camera device triggered by an electric eye.

Another insectivore that the British have studied extensively is the mole. Our moles belong to different genera with different habits that have been far less intensively studied. Our moles seem to have distinct habitat preferences, although all spend most of their time below the ground. This presents some real challenges for observation. Undoubtedly some of the British techniques would be useful here and anyone wanting to investigate these creatures should read the books by Mellanby and by Gillian and Crowcroft (see the Bibliography). We can also try American ingenuity by taking acetate sheets, spraying them lightly with transparent red paint—or using red acetate if you can get it—and constructing elongated domes to replace segments of the tunnelways.

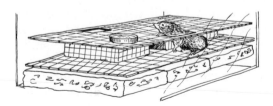

Figure 12.3.
Shrew enclosure.

This would permit observation of the animals as they shuttled about in the tunnel. Perhaps, as with shrews, touch is paramount and clear acetate would suffice. Only experimentation will tell. Another potential tool is a miniature upside down periscope to insert into the runway. The runway would then be lit with fiber optics attached to a light source and thrust into the walls of the tunnel. This device could let you discover what other life forms share the mole run. Figure 12.4 illustrates these theoretical devices. And who knows, such a runway-scope might prove useful in viewing into underground nests. And what about implanting a ceramic magnet just beneath the skin of the mole's back and plotting its position in its runways using a magnetic detector? What other approaches can you devise?

Moles can be live trapped by modifying a standard deadfall mole trap. The murderous tines are removed and the plunger is modified with an extender that has the tines at each end. When tripped these plunge downward to act as doors at both ends of the tunnel beyond the animal. The mole will have to be removed soon after the trap is sprung, however, or it will dig down and under. I have caught moles by noting where the tunnel was being heaved up, then plunging a barrier in the tunnel about eight inches behind the tunnel head. A shovel is then quickly put in beside the tunnel, pushed down, and lifted out. The divot will usually contain the mole. Some people slam the moving ground with the back of the shovel to stun the animal before digging. I have done this but find it is too easy to deliver a permanent injury this way.

Some of the suggestions for probing into the lives of moles and shrews can be modified for studying our mice. A good beginning to such a study is careful mapping of their tunnelways. The various voles, or meadow mice, in particular, like to keep their runways open and clear. Get down on hands and knees if need be and trace the tunnels and their offshoots. Locate nests and lavatory areas, favorite feeding spots, and so on. You will be amazed how much you can learn from this if you are patient and thorough. What other creatures use these runways? How do they interact with the mice? Can you set up observation points along the tunnelway for direct observations? Will a camera trap give good information? All in all there are many challenges awaiting those who will set

Figure 12.4. *Right,* commercial mole trap modified as live trap. *Center,* hypothetical mole-studying equipment; (A) viewscope; (B) fiber-optic; (C) penlight. *Left,* mole run with plastic cover.

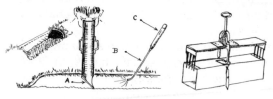

about systematically to learn about the behavior of our native small mammals. You may want to begin with the day-active squirrel clan and then move on to the more challenging groups.

Mammal watching has not attracted the fraternity that bird watching has, at least not yet, so there are not many mammal-watching organizations to be found. The major organization is the American Society of Mammalogists which is primarily an association of professional mammalogists, but they readily accept serious amateurs into the organization. For information write: American Society of Mammalogists, 1040 New Hampshire Street, Lawrence, KS 66044. Their quarterly is the *Journal of Mammalogy* and they have several other occasional publications related to mammalian species. The Wildlife Society is a similar group that focuses on game species—birds and mammals. Their publication is the *Journal of Wildlife Management*. For information write: The Wildlife Society, Suite S176, 3900 Wisconsin Avenue, NW, Washington, DC 20016.

BIRDS

Birds are probably the most looked at of all wild creatures. Largely day active and colorful, they have a strong attraction to many peoples throughout the world. Particularly in North America and Europe they attract legions of onlookers. Basically these fall into three categories: casual backyard feeders of birds, birders, and bird watchers. The first two are far and away the most abundant. The bird feeder puts out the food to attract in the locals and migrants, enjoys the activity, flashes of color, and song, but only takes casual effort to find out which species is which and what they do beyond the feeder. Birders tend to care little about what the bird is doing once they have checked the species off on their list. They are too busy charging off to find the next species to check off. Bird watchers do just that—they go slowly and watch what their subject is doing, sometimes for days or weeks. They tend to be among the *rara avis*.

Nonetheless, bird behavior has been studied in more detail than that for almost any other group. In fact, the science of ethology had its roots in the study of bird behavior. It would seem that there is little left to be explored. Not so. Certain groups such as the waterfowl have been explored in great detail while others remain only partially known. Even as common a bird as the eastern blue jay has behavioral mysteries to be unraveled.

It is interesting to note that whereas mammal observations have generated a number of species-specific books, most of the bird studies have ended up as shorter papers in journals. Indeed only a few of the monographs on particular species focus in detail on behavioral components.

For those who want to join the ranks of true bird watchers and particularly want to focus on behavior, the place to start is with Donald Stokes's *A Guide to the Behavior of Common Birds*. In this handy volume Stokes details what is known about the various visual and vocal displays and he also indicates some of what is not known. In addition to what is present in Stokes's book, there is also a lesson in what common species have not been included. (Many would have been in the book if the information had been available.) Be that as it may, the book is a great jumping off place for someone wanting to begin behavior watching. By studying these common species in the field and getting familiar with the actions that the book describes, you get a good basic feel for the structure of displays and how they function.

In addition to building behavior profiles, there are a number of other areas of field observations with birds. Various groups of bird watchers sponsor field studies that are greatly enhanced by broad participation from a number of observers.

One of the projects is a breeding bird census. This involves selecting a study site and undertaking a detailed description of the habitats on the site and precise locational definition of the site. It involves careful identification of all the species of birds that have established breeding territories on it. Once this is done a regular series of early morning visits is made to the site, and on each visit a detailed count of the individuals of each species by sight and/or sound is made. Breeding bird censuses are most valuable when the study area is censused year after year, the longer the better, for the data will provide evidence of the changes in both plant types and bird populations. For more details on participating in a breeding bird census write: Editor, *American Birds*, National Audubon, 950 Third Avenue, New York, NY 10022.

Some organizations have taken the breeding bird census a step further and undertaken a statewide breeding bird atlas that maps the breeding birds from census blocks throughout the state. To further encourage atlases the North American Ornithological Atlas Committee has been formed. Write: Dr. Miklos D. F. Udvardy, Department of Biological Science, California State University, Sacramento, CA 95800. Statewide bird atlases and longitudinal studies of population take both personal dedication and organizational talents so that data can be centrally filed and new observers trained to pick up the censusing of plots that others have had to abandon for any of a number of reasons.

Related to breeding bird censusing is the Nest Record Program sponsored by the Laboratory of Ornithology, 159 Sapsucker Woods, Ithaca, NY 14850. (The Laboratory produces an excellent annual publication called *The Living Bird* that usually includes good behavioral studies.) The Laboratory staff will supply free detailed instructions and data cards to those who are willing to report on nests they discover. Basically they are looking for data on nest location, number of eggs and young, time of nesting and related information. The pictorial guides to nests and eggs by Hal Harrison or the nest keys of Richard Headstrom will help the observer identify the nest if the parents are not spotted.

Spotting and observing nests is a tricky business. You should not remain near a nest for more than a very few minutes at a time because you may keep parents away from eggs or young at a critical time causing increased mortality. In addition, predators may follow your trail and be led to nests they might otherwise have missed. Once a nest is found you can mark its location with a strip of cloth or similar material. Place the marker a standard four feet to the right or left of the actual nest so that a casual passerby inspecting the marker will not disturb the nest. A tilting mirror on a telescoping pole is useful in getting a look inside nests above you without the disturbance created by climbing the tree. Always scan the nest area carefully with your binocular to see if the female is on the nest or if the parents are nearby before you approach more closely. Do not flush a bird from the nest unless absolutely necessary.

Some species have been expanding their range and this can be detailed through observation. There are always accidentals and wanderers which excite the birders, but species such as cardinals, titmice, and mockingbirds have been moving in permanently. Massachusetts Audubon has an annual winter census of these birds to determine what is happening to the population. Like the Laboratory of Ornithology, they supply free instructions and data cards. Herons and other species whose populations were decimated during the hard pesticide years have been increasing in numbers and documentation is needed for their breeding grounds and other areas of activity. The August migration of night-hawks is another phenomenon that is now being monitored by observer groups and bird-watching organizations around the country each tend to have their own pet observation projects.

Bird banding is also an interesting pursuit for the serious bird watcher. You will have to inquire around to find out who in your area is a licensed bander in order to begin learning by apprenticeship. If you have difficulty, write to the Bird Banding Office in Laurel, Maryland (see page 94). They can give you the address of the bird-banding association nearest you. These associations also publish journals you may wish to read. Of particular interest is the *Journal of Field Ornithology* (formerly *Bird Banding*), available from Membership Secretary, P.O. Box 797, Manomet, MA 02345. In time you may be able to gain your own permit and launch studies of your own.

Bird watching is a fascinating hobby and there are usually local interest groups, such as local chapters of the National Audubon Society, to be found in almost every region of the country. Check out these local groups before you join to determine if they really share your interests, because some are so dominated by the avid and competitive birders that they have little patience with the bird watcher who tends to slow them down in the field. If you are looking for the professional ornithologists and serious amateurs, the American Ornithologists' Union is the group, and its journal is *The Auk*. Write: c/o AOU Treasurer, National Museum of Natural History, Smithsonian Institute, Washington, DC 20560.

REPTILES AND AMPHIBIANS

For some reason it has become commonplace to link these two groups of animals together, even to lump them under the coined term "herptiles," even though they are quite different in anatomy, physiology, and behavior. They are discussed jointly here only because the major field guides to their identification, with one outstanding exception, deal with both groups between their covers.

For practical purposes we can say that amphibians are the frogs, toads, and salamanders. Behavior of these animals is largely stereotyped, although they are capable of simple learning. This means that when studying these creatures you have to be very alert to subtle changes in the environment such as light, temperature, and day length and the changes in behavior these may trigger. For example, feeding may take place only within certain temperature ranges or the amphibians may grab for unsuitable foods that move in certain ways while ignoring suitable food that is motionless. Amphibians tend to alternate periods of activity with long periods of inactivity and gear their activity patterns largely to physical conditions of the environment.

Generally, nighttime is the best time to go observing amphibians, usually between dark and midnight. In large measure this is because during this time period humidity is high and the air is fairly calm. Also for most amphibians, spring through early summer represents the breeding season when the most interesting behavior can be observed. Mild, rainy nights throughout the year seem to spark the greatest activity—thus wet gear and headlamps are almost *de rigueur* for amphibian watching. We need to learn a great deal more about these humble creatures because they may prove to be the "miner's canary" of our day. Sensitive to acid rain, the salamanders and probably some frogs are failing to reproduce effectively over broad sections of their range and in a few years may totally disappear from areas where they once were abundant. Declining salamander populations are an early warning that acid rain is taking its toll, ultimately for people as well.

Most amphibians are solitary except during the breeding season when they must gather together to reproduce. Frogs and toads seem to depend upon their calls to assemble breeding groups. As the first few males in an area start calling, the range of that sound increases, drawing in others from an even greater distance and attracting them to the focal point. Over how great a distance will an animal travel to reach its breeding pool? If placed equidistant between two breeding groups, which way will an animal travel? Do adults always go to the same breeding area year after year? If so, is it the one from which they hatched?

Some species gather all around the breeding pond, while others utilize only specific sections of the shoreline or water area. Do these areas remain the same from year to year? Do there seem to be any humanly recognizable cues that they use to choose a site?

Sex recognition in frogs is quite mechanical. Males tend to grab any passing object, including human fingers if available. If the object turns out to be another male, it will make noise and be released; if it remains silent, the male hangs on. There may be other cues that help the male distinguish its own species and these are grist for your studies. Are there size, shape, or textural cues? Occasionally there are mismatches and it is not unheard of to see something like a leopard frog firmly clasped to a female toad.

You may want to get into the game of recording frog and toad calls. This can be for more than collecting for its own sake. Since frogs rely heavily on sound for behavioral cues, you may discover some interesting behavioral relationships. Anyone contemplating such work should obtain the fascinating record and booklet developed by Charles M. Bogert, *Sounds of North American Frogs: The Biological Significance of Voice in Frogs* (1957), Folkway Records and Service Company, 117 W. 46th Street, New York, NY 10036 (Don't worry about the date. Folkway takes pride in keeping its records in print.)

Most North American frogs and toads have rather prosaic egg care habits, merely laying them and leaving them. But in other parts of the world, such as Europe, Africa, and Central and South America, there are species with rather bizarre habits such as building diked pools, building foam nests over water, and carrying the eggs in the vocal sac or in skin folds on the body. Travelers have an opportunity for some fascinating observations.

There is room for much data to be gathered on tadpoles and their behavior. Keys to tadpoles are very awkward to use and not very definitive. Currently available tadpole keys are primarily for mature tadpoles ready to transform but are virtually useless for earlier stages of development. New ways to identify them are needed. A promising approach to developing these lies in capturing known breeding pairs and hatching their eggs. Then careful data on the developing tadpoles and their behavior can be gathered and compared with that of other species. Do all species behave alike at some stages of development but differ at others? Can behavioral traits help identify various species at various stages of development? Does tadpole behavior change as crowding in a shrinking pool increases? What tadpole behaviors are environmentally altered and which are species-specific? The answers to such questions will have to be sought through both captive and field observations.

As indicated in Chapter 1, there is much to be learned about dispersion of both adults and newly transformed young from the breeding ponds. For the young, what species make up their primary foods? their enemies? What factors induce hibernation? What are the primary hibernation sites for the different species? How do they actually get into their hibernacula? For most toads and frogs we know most about their breeding behavior and least about these other activities. What is the average home range of a given species? How far do individuals wander? I am amazed at how many hints to answers I am gaining just from casual observation around a little backyard lily pool—and also how many new questions about frogs I am asking myself based on these observations.

A brief note about field equipment: For most work a headlamp is good since it frees your hands for note taking and photography; but for observations of congregations of animals, the beam is too concentrated. For that situation, a camplight with a fluorescent tube will put forth a broad illumination. Hang such a lamp around your neck and fasten it with a strap around your chest. This will put your head out of the glare, free your hands, and the light will obliterate your shape. If you are observing in a pond within view of a habitation, be sure you have the owner's permission. It also pays to inform the local police ahead of time about where you will be and what you are doing. People plotching about in swamps at night with lights tend to create considerable suspicion and, to non-naturalists, the answers to the questions that will be asked sound pretty far-fetched. Also a number of states have passed laws protecting amphibians from excessive commercial collecting for laboratories, so know the laws and be ready to prove that you are not violating them.

Frogs show little pain response and mutilation techniques of individually marking them are more acceptable. Toe clipping has been widely practiced by professionals; however, there is data to indicate that clipping hind toes impairs locomotion of frogs and that with some species, particularly toads, clipping foretoes interferes with stuffing food into the mouth. In leopard frogs, at least, this has been shown to result in weight loss. I have had some success with nylon thread looped through a fold of skin and tied off, as is done in rug hooking (see Figure 12.5). Various color combinations are possible. The animals seem to

Figure 12.5. Frog marking. Left, with numbered tag; right, with colored streamers.

shed around the threads without difficulty and it is easier to identify the animals out of water than with clipped toes which usually demand capture of the animal to accurately verify identity.

C. M. Breder tagged frogs by tying numbered waterproof tags around the frog's "waist." The tag is on the animal's back and is tied beneath. For smaller frogs a coded sequence of colored seed beads was used. Attaching the tags is basically a two-person operation that takes the development of a certain amount of deftness. The string must be tight enough so that it can't be slipped off but not tight enough to wear through the skin and cause sore spots and even embedment of the string in the skin.

For those who want to mark the frogs, and are willing to recapture for identification, they can use a butt-end bird band #1243, size 2½, fastened around the outer hind toe, or they can tattoo the frog's belly by scratching the skin with a #27 hypodermic needle to form the numbers and then putting India ink into the scratches.

Salamanders do not use their sense of hearing as frogs do. Their world seems to be one of chemo-reception. Their initial attraction to mates appears to be largely related to scent. Salamander coupling lacks the gross grappling of the frog world. Generally the male deposits a packet of sperm on the bottom of the pond or stream which the female must seek and pick up in her cloaca. Thus the salamanders tend to have more elaborate courtship rituals that induce the female to pick up the sperm packet. Courtship rituals of some species still remain largely unknown. For example, to my knowledge the courtship of the large aquatic siren has not yet been recorded in the wild and is a project for a dedicated skin diver in the South who is addicted to freshwater night diving with lights.

Students of salamanders would do well to learn basic water quality testing in order to chemically profile the breeding ponds or streams where they find the animals and to trace the chemical changes in these water bodies over time. Since these animals are so sensitive to chemical signals, these changes may alter their behavior or even their survival. Any attempts at captive rearing or mating will also depend on accurate recreation of the chemical environment. Also remember when trying to hatch frog or salamander eggs, that each egg is a living creature taking in oxygen and giving off metabolic wastes. Containers must be large enough so that each egg in the mass gets adequate dissolved oxygen and waste removal.

Some salamanders, such as the exceedingly abundant red-backed or woodland salamanders, lay their eggs on land and stay near them until they hatch, often curled around the egg mass. Is this just for moisture? Does the adult's slime have mold inhibitors? Are there other reasons for such behavior?

Among the first amphibians to venture forth in early spring are the various species of mole salamanders. They emerge during the first warm spring rains and head for their breeding ponds. These tend to be traditional sites and the animals will return again and again even if the pond is drained. Since they have life spans that may cover more than a decade, these annual migrations to nowhere can be a very sad and moving event. Assuming a more normal existing breeding pond, we still need to determine over how large an area the breeding population disperses. Are the animals truly fixed on this one site? Do they have any pattern of orientation in their movements to and from the ponds? To determine this pattern, you may wish to use a simple little trailing device as illustrated in Figure 12.6. You stick the spool holder in the soil, tie the thread around the animal's hips loosely, and release it. After several hours you can track the animal down by following the thread. Release the animal but leave the thread in place. Next day you can map the threads to determine any patterns of movement.

Unfortunately salamanders are difficult to individualize, although there is growing evidence that spot patterns on spot-marked species are individually varied. If your population is small a collection of photos may be useful in individual recognition. A close-up frame and a ring flash will be useful in getting consistent pictures of the same scale quickly. Toe clipping has been used for individualizing but the toes tend to regenerate in a few months. For individuals of species that you may not see again for a year this is not satisfactory.

Freeze branding is a very promising method for salamander marking. The branding irons can be made from insulated copper electrical wire. Remove about 1½ inches of insulation and shape the wire with needle-nosed pliers into one of the numerals 1 through 9. Fill a cylindrical styrofoam container, roughly 6″ × 10″, with chipped dry ice. Leave the brands in the container at least thirty minutes before use. Once the brand is used, reimmersion in the dry ice for thirty to sixty seconds is enough for repeat use. Apply the brand for about ten seconds. The brand mark should be visible in about twenty-four hours.

Once the breeding season is over the mole salamander adults disappear below ground and we know very little about adult nonbreeding behavior. Some ingenious wildlife observer will devise ways to learn more. Perhaps an underground viewing box would help provide an-

Figure 12.6. Spotted salamander with "follow string" and reel.

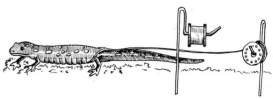

swers. How deep do these salamanders usually go? Apparently lacking specialized digging adaptations, how do they burrow about? Do they follow root channels in the ground? Are they limited to certain soil types and conditions? What are their primary foods?

The reptiles include the crocodilians, the snakes, the lizards, and the turtles. As befits their more complex evolutionary development, they often show more complex behavioral displays than amphibians. Alligators show some remarkable care-giving behavior for a reptile, not only building and guarding a nest but even picking up newly hatched young gently with their great mouths and depositing them in the water. Snakes engage in complex rituals often referred to as dances in which two individuals twine around each other. Originally thought to be courtship behavior, in almost all cases the two individuals have turned out to be males. What is the significance of such displays? Do they establish territory? Is there actually a female lurking nearby awaiting the outcome? The snakes do have actual courtship displays to be recorded. Turtles also have elaborate courtship rituals and nest-building behavior. Land turtles have been easier to study and are better known than aquatic turtles; but with ready access to snorkel gear it should now be possible to watch these turtles in their own element more frequently, thereby gaining more information on their feeding behavior, resting sites, and the like. Sea turtles need more observation as well. Fast disappearing due to overexploitation, their very survival depends on our learning more, and quickly. Once baby sea turtles hatch and return to the sea, they seem to disappear. They are not seen again until they are good-sized juveniles. They must breathe air and they have to go somewhere but the mystery of where remains. One theory is that they seek floating sargasso weed and similar flotsam and travel with it. Those who spend time at sea can regularly check all floating weed patches to see if they can find any of the young turtles.

The lizards are among the more poorly known of the reptiles as far as behavior is concerned. Some species are known to defend territories and even to show some dominance hierarchies within small colonies. There are displays using color patches on throat and/or flanks and other behavioral traits that make it surprising that they have not received more attention. Most lizards are day active but they do tend to be active during some of the hottest hours, making their observation a bane to those who shun the sun. Many lizards live in areas of little rain, so Robert Stebbins suggests individually marking such lizards with colored watercolor pencils. You need only wet the pencil and the lizard's scales with a little saliva and apply the color. It will last until the lizard next gets wet. It is not a long-term technique but it can be very helpful in short-term studies. Lizards can be caught by hand once you get the hang of it (and if you have good reflexes). For most, however, a thin pole with a fine wire or nylon monofilament noose is the best capture device

(Figure 12.7). The pole needs to be three feet to five feet in length (I prefer a telescoping fishing rod) so that you can stalk to just outside the lizard's flight distance. The noose is slowly worked over the lizard's head, and if you are lucky, one leg and then smartly pulled taut. This can be a frustrating activity on a breezy day when the wind refuses to let the noose be maneuvered in the directions you want. Noosing lizards can be quite sporting.

Marking individual snakes for field identification is difficult. Scale clipping is of little use unless you recapture. Recently, experimentation with freeze branding has shown promise although the marks aren't really seen until the shedding that follows the branding. Brands were cut from artificial sponges and glued to wooden doweling with silicon adhesive. These were then dipped into the coolant (liquid freon 12 or 22) until the coolant stopped boiling off the surface. The excess liquid was shaken off and the brand was then applied to the animal with enough pressure to squeeze the liquid coolant onto the skin for five to ten seconds.

Lewke and Stroud used just two brandings—a bar and an angle—to make all their numbers, using the angle numeration system devised by Farrell. With only a few more simple shapes you can use the more familiar Roman numeral system.

It would seem that it would be worth experimenting with this technique on lizards and turtles as well as snakes. Its main drawback is the manipulation of the coolant in the field. Dry ice and alcohol are awkward in the field and removing the freon from the cans in its liquid state is a technique that takes a bit of time to master. It involves inverting the pressurized can and releasing the liquid into an insulated container. At first it will boil off rapidly, but once the container reaches the temperature of the coolant, liquid will remain in the bottom.

There are a surprising number of amateur herpetological clubs around the country, particularly near major cities. A number are associated with museums, zoos, or nature centers. Many members are only interested in reptiles as pets but in every club there are those who are active field observers as well. There are two major professional herpetological groups in this country publishing journals on the biology of these animals suitable for interested amateurs. They are: Society for the Study of Amphibians and Reptiles, c/o Henri C. Seibert, Zoology De-

Figure 12.7. Lizard-noosing gear.

partment, Ohio University, Athens, OH 45701, which publishes *Herpetological Review* and *Journal of Herpetology;* and the Herpetologists' League, c/o Dr. Crawford G. Jackson, Jr., Department of Biology, University of California, San Diego, CA 92182, which publishes *Herpetologica.* Another special group of interest is the International Turtle and Tortoise Society, Inc., 8847 De Haviland Avenue, Los Angeles, CA 90045, which works to understand and conserve these creatures and publishes the *International Turtle and Tortoise Society Journal.*

INSECTS AND OTHER
INVERTEBRATES

The sheer abundance of insect species and their existence in virtually every major land and freshwater habitat assures subjects for wildlife watching to anyone seriously interested. However, insect watchers must first thoroughly understand that the perceptual world of insects is very different from ours. Mammals and birds have much in common with humans and even fish, amphibians, and reptiles share enough common ancestry that there is much perceptual overlap. However, insect eyes are constructed on a different basic plan than vertebrate eyes; the same is true of their hearing organs. Many taste through their feet and smell with their antennae. Some see wavelengths of light that are invisible to us. In short, the insect watcher must reorient his or her thinking about what is really being seen. An insect watcher must first carefully inform himself about the basic anatomy and physiology of insects.

Insect behavior is highly stereotyped. Modifications of behavior through learning are very limited. This does not mean that variations in behavior will not be seen because, since stereotyped behavior is essentially genetically programmed, normal genetic variations will regularly produce a percentage of variants.

The behavior of many species is influenced by environmental factors—light, gravity, temperature, humidity. The insect watcher must be constantly alert to such conditions. There must also be a good mix of field observation and experiments under captive conditions. In getting involved in the experiments some basic principles must be kept in mind.

1. The usual behavior of the insect must first be known if you wish to determine if the creature is doing something different.
2. The experiment must offer the insect a choice if it is to reveal preferences.
3. Variables must be controlled as much as possible.

4. Description of the experimental insect's behavior must be as complete as possible.
5. Assumptions should be based upon quantitative results if possible.
6. The experiment should be repeated several times.
7. Nothing should be done to the insect that would be harmful to it. This is not only humanitarian, but it also prevents biases in the results.
8. Your notes should clearly indicate all the methods and procedures of the experiment.

Most insects respond to a much smaller perceptual sphere than the vertebrates and thus permit much closer approach by people without flight. Whereas binoculars are standard for watching birds, good magnifying lenses are more likely to be useful for insect watching. There are, of course, shy species that do not allow such close approach—many butterflies and dragonflies fall into this category—and these are suitably observed with binoculars.

Insects are relatively easily marked for individual recognition with nail polish, airplane dope, acrylic paints, India ink, or by notched wings. Such marking is useful not only in recognizing specific individuals but also in marking a specific group of insects, such as all those found on a particular plant, in order to track their dispersal in the area.

The predominant focus of the study of insects has centered around their taxonomy. Relatively little behavioral study has been done. This is not totally inappropriate because before behavioral information is of much use, we must be able to know to which species of insect it belongs. However, the classification work is good enough in the area where most of the readers of this book will explore to encourage them to devote time to behavioral study. There are also now some reasonably useful field guides to the more common species. For those who want to dig a little more deeply into special groups such as the beetles or grasshoppers, useful pictured keys are available from the Wm. C. Brown Company, Dubuque, IO 52001.

Behavior of solitary wasps and honey bees has received considerable attention. A few butterflies have been studied in depth, as have aspects of dragonfly behavior. But even within these groups, a few species have been studied in detail while related species have received little or no attention. Even with those species that have been studied, the likelihood is that one particular aspect of their behavior has received attention while others have been largely ignored. Good comprehensive behavioral profiles of any species are rare.

In studying insects it is helpful to begin by watching the larger species with more spectacular behavior and then move to those where the action is more subtle. Dragonflies are a good beginning point. Note which species fly at what heights. Watch them hawk for mosquitoes and other small insects. Record their total feeding behavior. Which species form and patrol territories? How large are these territories? What forms of agonistic behavior do these insects exhibit? What happens when a female enters a male's territory? Do the different species have characteristic resting patterns? Can you determine intention movements to fly? And don't forget the equally fascinating aquatic larvae. They can be observed in aquaria or with water-scopes.

Butterflies often have fairly elaborate courtship rituals (these have not been studied for many species) and some are very aggressive not only to other butterflies but to other species as well. Some species are inclined to form aggregates, although these do not seem to be truly social. What kinds of interactions do occur in these aggregates? A number of butterflies show hints of territorial behavior but this needs much further exploration. Butterflies deserve more watching and less collecting. Indeed there is little need to collect them except to verify the identity or sex of individuals you have been observing.

Flies do not intrigue most people at first but once you overcome an initial aversion, you will discover that flies have a variety of interesting behaviors. The books by Dethier and Oldroyd hint at some of this diversity and point the way to further studies (see the Bibliography).

Beetles are the largest group of insects but the behavior of relatively few species has been studied at all. The grasshopper and cricket clan, also offers a rich field for study. Indeed almost any insect group offers broad opportunities for new discoveries.

In addition to looking at individual species' behavior, a fruitful field for observation lies in the study of those species that utilize a specific plant species, or even one individual plant. How does the behavior of each species affect their relationship to the plant? to other animals using the plant? Good subjects for beginning such explorations are milkweed, which has several distinctive species associated with it specifically, or a vine such as Virginia creeper, or woodbine, which harbors a host of insect life.

In studying insects begin by recording all the motions the species is capable of. In what sequence are the legs moved? If this varies, what stimulates the variation? What are its grooming rituals? Discover also where its sensory organs are. Then begin to determine its perceptual frame or *merkwelt*. Does it react to light? temperature? gravity? moisture? scents? colors?

Place the animal on a slanted surface. Does it move towards or away from gravity? What angle from horizontal does the surface have to be moved before the animal responds? How does the animal respond to walls and surfaces? Does it seek or avoid contact with them? Is food located by chance or by a food-seeking strategy? You can make a simple enclosure and place food inside. Place the insect inside and map its movement until it locates the food. Is there any apparent pattern to its actions? Can you determine what clues are being used, if any, to zero in on the food?

Various experimental setups have been used to determine color perception. Clear plates of shallow water with a few drops of detergent added are put out on different colored squares as one approach. The insects fly down to the color they prefer and are trapped and drowned. The different dishes are then censused for the number of each species attracted. Some species may show up only on one color; others will be found in several. Of course, this method eliminates those individuals from future study. You can also construct a chamber with the floor covered with different colored sections and release several insects of a given species into it for observation. Do they spend a significant amount more of time on one color than another? Is there a color they specifically avoid?

A most useful tool is a simple experimental chamber made from two jars interconnected by their lids which are joined together but have a section removed in order to permit passage from one jar to the other when both are connected to their lids (Figure 12.8). The two chambers are set up with your variables, that is, one is covered with dark paper, the other is open to light; or one with moist soil, the other with dry soil, and so forth. The insects are put into the chamber and allowed to settle down. Note the chamber they spend most of their time in over a series of observations.

Some creatures you may wish to observe, such as gall insects, pupae, and the like, may go through undetermined periods of dormancy. When the adults finally emerge most will head towards light. Using this behavioral trait, you can set up emergence boxes to aid in your study and to assure that your subjects don't fly away undetected. These are simply a box or jar, spray-painted black with a vial inserted in a hole in the side or lid. When the insects emerge they will make their way toward the light and end up in the vial. All you have to do is periodically check your containers to see if there is any action.

Insects are rather easily reared in simple containers for captive observations. A sampling of such containers is found in Figure 12.9. Simple water containers are made from vials partially filled with water and plugged with a piece of absorbent cotton. Insects get the water from

Figure 12.8. Insect environmental-preference test chambers linked together by interlocked lids with passageway (right).

Figure 12.9. Lower right, water phial for insects; upper right, insect emergence box; others to left are simple insect cages from common materials.

the cotton and as the water is used, air pressure will push the cotton down the vial.

The backyard wildlife watcher can really focus in on insects—even to the extent of developing "insect gardens." By this we mean something more deliberate than a poorly tended vegetable patch. Butterflies are often quite specific in their choice of food plants and a spare corner that can be given over to certain plants like thistle, milkweed, stinging nettle, and vetch will attract painted ladies, red admirals, blues, white admirals, monarchs, and other butterflies. Among cultivated plants, ragwort, michaelmas daisies, nicotiana, and buddleias all attract butterflies and a variety of other insect groups. Clumps of ivy will provide roosting sites for butterflies and moths, and some butterflies may even hibernate on evergreen vines. One of my friends lives in a heavily developed suburban area but maintains his yard as an insect sanctuary replete with such plantings, artificial "houses" for solitary wasps, and an active artificial clay pit as a source for mud dauber and potter wasps. Now well into his seventies both he and his wife find hours of satisfaction in studying the behavior of his miniature wild neighbors. His friend, the wasp expert Howard Evans, commented about insect watching: "We would do well, now and then, to stretch out on the good earth with notebook, camera, or sketch pad and chronicle the lives of some of our less self-important neighbors."

For those people seeking insect-oriented organizations and their publications, the following may be of interest:

1. American Entomological Society, Academy of Natural Sciences, 1900 Race Street, Philadelphia, PA. They publish a quarterly, *Transactions of the American Entomological Society,* and a monthly, *Entomological News.*
2. Entomological Society of America, 4603 Calvert Road, College Park, MD 20740. Their publications are both quarterlies—*Annals of the Entomological Society of America* and the *Bulletin of the Entomological Society of America.*
3. Entomological Society of Ontario, 1320 Carling Avenue, Ottawa, Ontario, Canada K127K9. Their *Canadian Entomologist* is a monthly.

4. Pacific Coast Entomological Society, San Francisco, CA. They publish *The Pan-Pacific Entomologist* quarterly.
5. The Xerces Society, c/o Teresa Clifford, Secretary, Department of Zoology, University of Wyoming, Laramie, WY 82071. This organization emphasizes the observation, study, and preservation of butterflies. Their publication, *Atala*, is biannual.

Spiders tend to be a highly neglected group of animals with a spectrum of interesting behaviors. The many patterns of web making, courtship behaviors, and hunting strategies are all fascinating. There are spiders that build webs under water, those that catch fish, and those that build silk-lined tunnels with trap doors. There are some that are sought by wasps to feed their young and interesting duels between these two species may be observed.

Other insect relatives such as sowbugs, pillbugs, crayfish, millipedes, and centipedes are all grist for the behavior-watching mill, as are such nonrelated invertebrates as snails, slugs, and earthworms. A little time spent in observing such creatures will reveal that they have interesting behaviors that you would never have expected.

OTHER SOURCES
OF COMPANIONSHIP
AND ASSISTANCE

In the various subsections above I have listed some of the organizations that might be of interest for that specialty. There is another organization that deals with all the groups through the commonality of behavior and that is the Association for the Study of Animal Behaviour, Biology Building, University of Sussex, Falmer, Brighton, Sussex BN19Q6, England. It publishes the journal *Animal Behaviour*. Another journal of interest is *Behaviour—An International Journal of Comparative Ethology*, E. J. Brill, Leiden, Netherlands.

Both these journals are prime sources for interesting studies on a variety of animal groups. To get at an overview of current articles in these and other publications you may want to start with *Animal Behavior Abstracts*, Information Retrieval, Inc., Fisk Building, 250 West 57th Street, New York, NY 10019.

For those looking for other naturalists throughout the world who share your interests, *The Naturalists' Directory and Almanac* is an excellent starting place. Indeed you may wish to be listed therein yourself. This guide is regularly updated and corrected. If a copy is not available in your library, or if you want to apply for inclusion in the next update, write directly to Ross H. Arnett, Jr., Editor, c/o *The Naturalists' Directory*, P.O. Box 505, Kinderhook, NY 12106. In addition, the same staff is introducing a magazine *Flora and Fauna* that includes news and notes along with updates to the current directory.

You may want to get a good semi-professional immersion into behavior watching and one of the best ways to do that is to participate in one of the combination working vacation-research assistant trips now being sponsored by several organizations. On the East Coast such an organization is Earthwatch Research Expeditions, 10 Juniper Road, Box 137, Belmont, MA 02178; on the West Coast contact University Research Expedition Program, Desk NH, University of California, Berkeley, CA 94720. Their prospectus of upcoming research expeditions almost always includes some that are involved with behavior watching. On these expeditions you pay your way and work as a field assistant to a professional scientist which provides an excellent learning opportunity.

The exploration of animal behavior provides material for several lifetimes of activity. It is a pursuit for people of all ages and the equipment needed is generally quite simple. Armed with the ideas compiled herein, you should be able to go forth to a lifetime of enjoyment and enrichment. Share your excitement and enthusiasm with others; help build a climate of concern for all forms of life that will prompt the necessary human actions to assure a place for all life on this most beautiful of planets.

> The materials and phenomena of nature as subject matter for study do not in themselves actually change; the continual and growing interest *in the same thing*, therefore must always be preserved.
>
> WILBUR JACKMAN, 1904

FURTHER READING

ARMSTRONG, EDWARD A. *Bird Display and Behavior*. New York: Dover Publications, Inc., 1965.

BARBOUR, R. W., and W. H. DAVIS. *Bats of America*. Lexington: University of Kentucky Press, 1969.

BAUGH, TOM. *A Net Full of Natives*. (Book #107) P.O. Box 487, Sierra Madre, CA: Freshwater and Marine Aquarium Magazine.

BROWN, J. L. *The Evolution of Behavior*. New York: W. W. Norton & Co., Inc., 1975.

BURKHARDT, D., WOLFGANG SCHLEIDT, and HELMUT ALTNER. *Signals in the Animal World*. New York: McGraw-Hill, 1967.

CALLAHAN, PHILIP. *Insect Behavior*. New York: Four Winds Press, 1970.

COUSTEAU, JACQUES-YVES and PHILLIPE DIOLE. *Octopus and Squid: The Soft Intelligence*. Garden City, N.Y.: Doubleday and Co., Inc., 1973.

CROWCROFT, PETER. *The Life of the Shrew*. London: Max Reinhardt, 1957.

EVANS, HOWARD E. *Wasp Farm*. Garden City, N.Y.: Natural History Press, 1963.

FREE, J. B., and C. G. BUTLER. *Bumblebees*. London: Collins, 1959.

GILLIAN, GODFREY, and PETER CROWCROFT. *The Life of the Mole*. London: Museum Press, 1960.

GREENHALL, A. M., and J. L. PARADISO. *Bats and Bat Banding*. Resources Publication 72. Washington, D.C.: U.S. Dept. of Interior, Bureau of Sports Fisheries and Wildlife, 1968.

JOHNSON, R. P. "Scent marking in animals," *Animal Behavior*, 21 (1973), 521–35.

KRESS, STEPHEN W. *The Audubon Society Handbook for Birders*. New York: Charles Scribner's Sons, 1981.

MELLANBY, KENNETH. *The Mole*. New York: Taplinger Publishing Co., 1973.

MORSE, DOUGLASS H. *Behavioral Mechanisms in Ecology*. Cambridge, Mass.: Harvard University Press, 1980.

PETERSON, ALVAH. *A Manual of Entomological Techniques*, 7th ed. Ann Arbor, Mich.: J. W. Edwards, Publishers, Inc., 1953.

SMITH, W. JOHN. *The Behavior of Communicating—An Ethological Approach*. Cambridge, Mass.: Harvard University Press, 1980.

SPOTTE, STEPHEN. *Fish and Invertebrate Culture: Water Management in Closed Systems*, 2nd ed. New York: John Wiley & Sons, Inc., 1979.

STOKES, D. W. *A Guide to the Behavior of Common Birds*. Boston: Little, Brown, 1979.

THUROW, G. "Aggression and competition in eastern Plethodon (Amphibia, Urodela, Plethodontidae)," *Journal of Herpetology*, 10 (1976), 277–91.

WELLS, K. D. "The social behaviour of Anuran amphibians," *Animal Behaviour*, 25 (1977), 666–93.

SOURCES

FREON
• Virginia Chemicals, Inc.
Portsmouth, Virginia 23700

BANDS AND TAGS
• National Band and Tag Co.
Newport, Kentucky 41071

WORKING OUTLINE FOR AN ETHOGRAM

Niko Tinbergen suggests that an ethogram is a comprehensive list of every action a species is capable of performing. Gathering such information is the wildlife watcher's first task because one should not even begin to analyze any one aspect of an animal's behavior until one is thoroughly familiar with the full range of the animal's activity, with each action described in detail.

The following outline flies a bit in the face of that advice because the very classification of the action into categories is itself a form of analysis and some of the questions asked imply an elementary type of analysis in the answering. Perhaps the outline is more precisely the building of a behavioral repertoire. In any case, there are so many species and they vary so magnificently, that no one outline for an ethogram will be satisfactory for all. This outline presents a number of basic questions whose answers can be sought in your observations and readings. You may well create additional questions under the various categorial headings depending on the peculiarities of your particular species. The format gives you a framework for organizing your notes and directing some of your observation.

SPECIES NAME: _____

INGESTIVE BEHAVIOR
- What special structures does the species have for securing food?
- How do these determine behavior patterns?
- Are there species-specific postures related to food and water procurement?
- Are there special behaviors that orient the species to the food or water?

- Are there intention movements that signal the initiation of feeding and drinking?
- What foods does the species eat?
- Is all food consumed at once or are there food storage behaviors?
- Are there special behavioral patterns geared to food or water scarcity?

ELIMINATIVE BEHAVIOR

- Are there characteristic postures for urination and defecation?
- Does the species randomly excrete wastes or is there a pattern of behavior to conceal wastes or to use them for social signaling?
- Are there times during the life cycle when body wastes are reingested?
- How is excess heat eliminated? Are there characteristic activities?

CARE-GIVING BEHAVIOR

- What are the distinctive postures associated with care giving?
- Under what conditions is care given to the young? other adults? other species?
- What vocalizations, if any, are associated with care giving?

CARE-SOLICITING BEHAVIOR

- What postures or calls induce care giving to young? other adults? other species?
- Under what conditions is care soliciting most effective?

MAINTENANCE BEHAVIOR

- What are the basic grooming actions?
- Is there a basic sequence of grooming actions?
- Are there special physical adaptations for grooming? If so, how are they used?
- Are there special activities associated with parasite removal?
- Are there special sleeping postures?

SHELTER-SEEKING BEHAVIOR

- How does the species respond to adverse weather?
- Does the species seek special sleeping or resting sites? If so, what are their basic characteristics?
- What conditions induce shelter seeking?

EXPLORATORY BEHAVIOR

- How does an individual of the species orient to new surroundings?
- Is the exploratory behavior of juveniles quantitatively or qualitatively different from that of adults?
- Does the animal regularly note changes in its surroundings? What are the clues it most responds to? Do changes in some objects evoke response while others do not?

AGONISTIC BEHAVIOR

- What postures of the species appear to denote aggression? What are the components of these postures? Can the intensity of the aggression be determined by these components?
- What structures does the species have for inflicting harm on others? How are these used? What behavioral defenses does another animal have other than submissive posturing?

- What postures of the species denote submission? What are the components of these postures? Can the intensity of the fear or submission be determined through these components?

SEXUAL BEHAVIOR

- What postures does the male use during courtship? the female?
- Can you determine if components of the courtship displays can be found in the postures of other behavior categories?
- What is the sequence of displays used throughout the sexual cycle for each sex?
- How do the displays of one sex synchronize the other partner for the next step in the sequence from courtship, pair formation, to copulation?
- At what age does sexual maturity occur? Are there behavioral changes to indicate maturity as well as physical changes?
- Are there behavior mechanisms to assure against excessive inbreeding?
- What behavior patterns are associated with nest and den building? Do these appear to be sexual or care-giving behaviors?

ALLELOMIMETIC BEHAVIOR

- Does the species exhibit allelomimetic behavior at any time during its normal life cycle? If yes, under what conditions?
- What behavioral signals trigger the movements of the group?

COMMUNICATIVE BEHAVIOR

- What calls, visual signals, olfactory signals, or other devices are used in communication?
- Under what conditions is each signal used?
- Are there two or more signals that are always linked together in a communication such as a postural display and an odor, or a call and a posture?
- What behaviors do given signals elicit in other members of the species?
- What other species respond to the species' calls or odor signals? Which signals do they respond to and in what ways? What signals do they ignore?

HOME RANGE AND TERRITORIAL BEHAVIOR

- In establishing home range and territory (if there is indeed a defended territory) components of what other behavioral patterns are employed?
- Are there activities that are unique to this function?
- Is there a difference in the behavior of the sexes in territorial defense?
- At what age does territorial defense begin?
- Are territories defended throughout the year or only at certain seasons?
- How are territory boundaries established?
- Are there neutral zones where several individuals who would fight on their own territory can and do freely and peacefully associate?
- Are the territories defended fixed geography or movable personal space?
- How are different parts of a home range utilized at different seasons?
- Do different sexes and age classes utilize different-sized home ranges?

HIBERNATION, EMERGENCE, AND MIGRATION

- Does the species regularly rest seasonally (hibernate or aestivate) or migrate?
- What conditions induce this behavior?
- What sites are chosen for hibernation or other seasonal resting?

- What provisions are made to meet basic physiological needs?
- What conditions induce migratory movement?
- Do various age classes migrate together or separately?
- What routes of migration are followed?
- What means of navigation are employed?
- Do certain weather patterns affect migration? If so, which ones and in what manner?
- What are the times and weather conditions that surround emergence from seasonal resting or initiation and return from migration?

DENSITY-DEPENDENT BEHAVIORS

- What behavior patterns vary significantly from normal under conditions of abnormally high or low populations for the habitat?
- What behaviors demand a given population density to be initiated and what seems to be that magic number?

SOCIAL BEHAVIOR

- Is the species basically composed of individuals that are loners except during the mating season, or is it a more social species that regularly consorts with others of its kind?
- If the species is social only at certain times of the year, what are these times and how does sociability help the species at these times?
- What are the normal social groupings—individuals, pairs, mother and young, kinship groups, large herds, or loose aggregates?
- Is there any form of dominance hierarchy?

ENVIRONMENTAL FACTORS OF BEHAVIOR

- Are there particular environmental factors that strongly affect specific behaviors of the species, as, for example, temperature range, relative humidity, amount of daylight, availability of water, presence or absence of certain other species, availability of certain nesting materials? If so, what behaviors do they induce or significantly alter?

APPENDIX B

OUTDOOR MANNERS

If wildlife observers are to be welcome on the world scene, they must observe a code of good outdoor manners. Increasingly, outdoor recreationists have become unmannerly. This has increased the number of No Trespassing signs and unfriendly attitudes of local landowners and has harbored a growing sense of disgust among other users of public lands as well. No group seems to be without its slobs—birders, hunters, snowmobilers, dirt bikers, photographers, cross-country skiers, and the full range of others. *Don't be an outdoor slob.*

- On land or sea, if you pack it in, pack it out (that means all candy wrappers, photo debris, food containers, and so forth)
- Whenever possible, seek permission to use private land.
- If you use gates, be sure that they are securely closed behind you.
- Never break through a fence. If you should accidentally damage a fence, take the time to repair it immediately or report it promptly to the landowner.
- Always walk the edge of tilled fields; never walk through crops or hay.
- Do not park your vehicles so that they block the passage of others.
- Be reasonably quiet in the field; don't frighten off wildlife that others may be trying to observe.
- If you are trying to view a rare wildlife visitor along with many other viewers, avoid pressuring the animal into actions it does not want to take and do not thoughtlessly trample the gardens and lawn of the landowner.
- Particularly in back country, leave a rough itinerary of your travels and an expected time of return with a responsible person who will know where to look for you if you are detained.

- Don't approach someone in a blind or on a stalk. Give them wide berth.
- If following predators or herd animals in a vehicle, do not press to the point of disrupting the animals' feeding.
- Do not press resting animals just to get them to "do something"; at zoos, do not poke at animals or bang on glass-fronted cages.
- If live trapping, always inspect your traps at least once a day.
- Never tamper with another's live traps, camera traps, blinds, or other equipment left in the field.
- Do not use recordings excessively to attract birds during the nesting season, particularly in areas where others are likely to be using such recordings also.
- Never press observation to the point of keeping wildlife away from their normal parenting duties.
- In order to get better viewing, never cut vegetation that normally provides shade and cover to a nest or den. If such vegetation is pulled back briefly for photographic purposes, be sure that it is returned to place.
- If you are traveling in a motor boat, reduce your speed drastically near shore so that the wake will not erode the banks or shore.
- Be alert for and honor diving flags.
- Never tamper with lobster traps or other aquacultural devices.

And finally, if you see someone being an outdoor slob, confront him or her civilly and explain how the action is offensive and may be hurting the chances of others who legitimately use the outdoors responsibly. Often the person is only acting out of ignorance or thoughtlessness, not with malevolence. For everyone's sake it is wise to begin with that assumption.

BIBLIOGRAPHY

FIELD IDENTIFICATION GUIDES

Wildlife watching has been aided immeasurably by the development of a number of good field identification guides. Several book companies have developed competitive guides and preference is largely personal. Some of the more satisfactory guides are listed below.

Mammals

BURT, WILLIAM H., and R. H. GROSSENHEIDER. *A Field Guide to the Mammals.* Boston: Houghton Mifflin, 1964.

DORST, JEAN, and PIERRE DANDELOT. *A Field Guide to the Larger Mammals of Africa.* Boston: Houghton Mifflin, 1970.

LEATHERWOOD, STEPHEN, DAVID K. CALDWELL, and HOWARD WINN. *Whales, Dolphins, and Porpoises of the Eastern North Pacific.* Washington, D.C.: National Marine Fisheries Service, 1972.

VAN DEN BRINK, F. H. *A Field Guide to the Mammals of Britain and Europe.* Boston: Houghton Mifflin, 1968.

WHITAKER, JOHN O., JR. *The Audubon Society Field Guide to North American Mammals.* New York: Alfred A. Knopf, 1980.

Birds

BOND, JAMES. *Birds of the West Indies,* 2nd ed. Boston: Houghton Mifflin, 1961.

BRUUN, BERTEL. *The Larousse Guide to the Birds of Britain and Europe.* New York: Larousse, Inc., 1979.

FFRENCH, RICHARD. *A Guide to the Birds of Trinidad and Tobago.* Wynnewood, Pa.: Livingston Publishing Company, 1973.

HARRISON, COLIN. *A Field Guide to the Nests, Eggs, and Nestlings of North American Birds.* New York/London: Collins, 1978.

HARRISON, HAL. *A Field Guide to Bird Nests* (east). Boston: Houghton Mifflin, 1975.

––––––. *A Field Guide to Western Bird Nests.* Boston: Houghton Mifflin, 1979.

HEINTZELMAN, D. S. *A Guide to Hawkwatching in North America.* University Park, Pa.: Pennsylvania State University Press, 1979.

KING, BEN, M. WOODCOCK, and E. C. DICKINSON. *A Field Guide to the Birds of South-east Asia.* London: Collins, 1975.

LAND, H. G. *Birds of Guatemala.* Wynnewood, Pa.: Livingston Publishing Co., 1970.

MEYER DE SCHAUENSEE, R. *A Guide to the Birds of South America.* Wynnewood, Pa.: Livingston Publishing Co., 1970.

MEYER DE SCHAEUNSEE, R., and W. H. PHELPS, JR. *A Guide to the Birds of Venezuela.* Princeton, N.J.: Princeton University Press, 1978.

PETERSON, ROGER T. *A Field Guide to Western Birds,* 2nd rev. ed. Boston: Houghton Mifflin, 1961.

––––––. *A Field Guide to the Birds,* rev. ed. Boston: Houghton Mifflin, 1980.

PETERSON, ROGER T., and E. L. CHALIF. *A Field Guide to Mexican Birds and Adjacent Central America.* Boston: Houghton Mifflin, 1973.

PETERSON, ROGER T., GUY MONTFORT, and P. D. HOLLOM. *A Field Guide to the Birds of Britain and Europe,* 3rd ed. Boston: Houghton Mifflin, 1974.

PROZENSKY, O. P. M. *A Field Guide to the Birds of Southern Africa.* London: Collins, 1970.

RIDGELY, ROBERT S. *A Guide to the Birds of Panama.* Princeton, N.J.: Princeton University Press, 1976.

ROBBINS, CHANDLER S., BERTEL BRUUN, and HERBERT ZIM. *A Guide to Field Identification: Birds of North America.* New York: Golden Press, 1966.

SERLE, W., G. J. MOREL, and W. HARTWIG. *A Field Guide to the Birds of West Africa.* London: Collins, 1977.

Reptiles and Amphibians

ARNOLD, E. N., and J. A. BURTON. *A Field Guide to the Reptiles and Amphibians of Britain and Europe.* London: Collins, 1978.

BEHLER, JOHN L. *The Audubon Society Guide to North American Reptiles and Amphibians.* New York: Alfred A. Knopf, 1979.

COCHRAN, D. M., and COLEMAN J. GOIN. *The New Field Book of Reptiles and Amphibians.* New York: G. P. Putnam's Sons, 1970.

CONANT, ROGER. *A Field Guide to Reptiles and Amphibians* (east). Boston: Houghton Mifflin, 1958.

SMITH, HOBART M. *A Guide to Field Identification: Amphibians of North America.* New York: Golden Press, 1978.

STEBBINS, ROBERT. *A Field Guide to Western Reptiles and Amphibians.* Boston: Houghton Mifflin, 1966.

Fishes

EDDY, SAMUEL. *How to Know the Freshwater Fishes.* Dubuque, Iowa: Wm. C. Brown, 1957.

GOODSON, GAR. *The Many Splendored Fishes of the Atlantic Coast.* Palos Verdes Estates, Ca.: Marguest Colorguide Books, 1976.

McClane, A. J. *Field Guide to Freshwater Fishes of North America.* New York: Holt, Rinehart & Winston, 1978.

―――. *Field Guide to Saltwater Fishes of North America.* New York: Holt, Rinehart & Winston, 1978.

Scott, W. B. *Freshwater Fishes of Eastern Canada,* 2nd ed. Toronto: University of Toronto Press, 1967.

Stokes, L. Joseph. *Handguide to the Coral Reef Rishes.* Philadelphia: The Academy of Natural Sciences, 1981 (*also includes coral and other invertebrates*).

Aquatic (Other Than Fish)

Campbell, A. C. *The Larousse Guide to the Seashore and Shallow Seas of Britain and Europe.* New York: Larousse, Inc., 1980.

Gosner, Kenneth. *A Field Guide to the Atlantic Shore.* Boston: Houghton Mifflin, 1979.

Klots, Elsie B. *The New Field Book of Freshwater Life.* New York: G. P. Putnam's Sons, 1966.

Meinkoth, Norman A. *The Audubon Society Field Guide to North American Seashore Creatures.* New York: Alfred A. Knopf, 1981.

Insects

Borror, Donald, and Richard White. *A Field Guide to the Insects of America North of Mexico.* Boston: Houghton Mifflin, 1970.

Chinery, Michael. *A Field Guide to the Insects of Britain and Northern Europe.* Boston: Houghton Mifflin, 1974.

Helfer, Jacques R. *How To Know the Grasshoppers, Cockroaches and Their Allies.* Dubuque, Iowa: Wm. C. Brown Co., 1953.

Jaques, H. E. *How To Know the Beetles.* Dubuque, Iowa: Wm. C. Brown Co., 1951.

Klots, Alexander B. *A Field Guide to the Butterflies.* Boston: Houghton Mifflin, 1951

Milne, Lorus, and Margery Milne. *The Audubon Society Field Guide to North American Insects and Spiders.* New York: Alfred A. Knopf, 1980.

Mitchell, Robert T., and Herbert S. Zim. *A Golden Guide: Butterflies and Moths.* New York: Golden Press, 1962. (*Illustrates caterpillars as well.*)

Maurier, Henri, and Ove Winding. *Collins Guide to Wildlife in House and Home.* London: Collins, 1977.

Pyle, Robert Michael. *The Audubon Field Guide To North American Butterflies.* New York: Alfred A. Knopf, 1981.

Swan, Lester A., and Charles S. Papp. *The Common Insects of North America.* New York: Harper & Row, 1972.

Spiders

Kaston, B. J. *How to Know the Spiders.* Dubuque, Iowa: Wm. C. Brown Co., 1952.

Levi, Herbert. *A Golden Guide: Spiders and Their Kin.* New York: Golden Press, 1968.

BEHAVIORAL STUDIES
OF SELECTED SPECIES
AND GROUPS

Mammals

ALLEN, DURWARD L. *Wolves of Minong.* Boston: Houghton Mifflin, 1979.

BAKKEN, ARNOLD. "Behavior of Gray Squirrels," *Symposium on the Gray Squirrel* (V. Flyger, ed.), Contribution 162, Maryland Dept. of Resource Education (1959), 393–407.

BARNETT, S. A. *The Rat: A Study in Behavior.* Chicago: Aldine, 1963.

CRAIGHEAD, FRANK C., JR. *Track of the Grizzly.* San Francisco: Sierra Club Books, 1979.

CRISLER, LOIS. *Arctic Wild.* New York: Harper & Row, 1958. (*Wolves*)

CROWCROFT, PETER. *The Life of the Shrew.* London: Max Reinhardt, 1957.

DARLING, FRANK F. *A Herd of Red Deer.* Oxford: Clarendon Press, 1937.

DEVORE, I., ed. *Primate Behavior: Field Studies of Monkeys and Apes.* New York: Holt, Rinehart & Winston, 1965.

DOUGLAS-HAMILTON, I., and O. DOUGLAS-HAMILTON. *Among the Elephants.* London: Collins, 1965.

DUBKIN, LEONARD. *The White Lady.* New York: G. P. Putnam's Sons, 1952. (*Little brown bat*)

ELTON, C. *Voles, Mice and Lemmings.* Oxford: Clarendon Press, 1942.

ERRINGTON, PAUL L. *Muskrat Populations.* Ames, Iowa: Iowa State University Press, 1963.

EWER, R. F. *Ethology of Mammals.* New York: Plenum, 1968.

FOX, MICHAEL W. *Behavior of Wolves, Dogs and Related Canines.* New York: Harper & Row. 1972.

GEIST, VALERIUS. *Moutain Sheep.* Chicago: University of Chicago Press, 1971.

GILBERT, BIL. *Chulo.* New York: Alfred A. Knopf, 1973. (*Coati-mundi*)

GODFREY, GILLIAN, and PETER CROWCROFT. *The Life of the Mole.* London: Museum Press, 1960.

HAFEZ, E. C. E. *The Behavior of Domestic Animals.* Baltimore: The Williams and Wilkins Co., 1963.

KITCHEN, DAVID W. *Social Behavior and Ecology of the Pronghorn,* Wildlife Monograph No. 38 (Washington, D.C.: The Wildlife Society, August 1974).

KROTT, PETER. *Demon of the North.* New York: Alfred A. Knopf, 1959. (*Wolverine*)

KRUUK, HANS. *The Spotted Hyaena.* Chicago: University of Chicago Press, 1972.

LAYNE, J. N. "The biology of the Red Squirrel *Tamiasciurus hudsonicus loquax* in Central New York," *Ecological Monographs,* 24 (1954), 227–67.

LINSDALE, JEAN M. *The California Ground Squirrel.* Berkeley: University of California Press, 1946.

MECH, DAVID. *The Wolf: The Ecology and Behavior of an Endangered Species.* Garden City, N.Y.: The Natural History Press, 1970.

MELLANBY, KENNETH. *The Mole.* New York: Taplinger Publishing Co., 1973.

MORRIS, DESMOND. *Man Watching: A Field Guide to Human Behavior.* New York: Harry N. Abrams, Inc., 1979.

Moss, Cynthia. *Portraits in the Wild: Behavior Studies of East African Mammals.* Boston: Houghton Mifflin, 1975.

Norris, Kenneth S. *The Porpoise Watcher.* New York: W. W. Norton & Co., 1974.

Ryden, Hope. *God's Dog.* New York: Viking Press, 1979.

Schaller, George B. *The Mountain Gorilla.* Chicago: University of Chicago Press, 1963.

―――. *The Serengeti Lion.* Chicago: University of Chicago Press, 1972.

Tunis, Edwin. *Chipmunks on the Doorstep.* New York: Thomas Y. Crowell, 1971.

Van Lawick-Goodall, Hugo, and Jane Van Lawick-Goodall. *Innocent Killers.* Boston: Houghton Mifflin, 1971. (*Hyaenas*)

Van Lawick-Goodall, Jane. *In the Shadow of Man.* Boston: Houghton Mifflin, 1971 (*Chimpanzees*)

Birds

Alcock, J. "Cues used in searching for food by Red-winged Blackbirds, *Agelaius phoeniceus,*" *Behaviour,* 46 (1973), 174–88.

Ficken, R. W. "Courtship and agonistic behavior of the Common Grackle (*Quiscalus quiscula*)," *Auk,* 80 (1963), 52–72.

Hochbaum, H. A. *The Canvasback on a Prairie Marsh.* Washington, D.C.: American Wildlife Institute, 1944.

Jackson, J. A. "A quantitative study of the foraging ecology of Downy Woodpeckers," *Ecology,* 51 (1970), 318–23.

Johnsgard, Paul A. *Handbook of Waterfowl Behavior.* Ithaca, N.Y.: Cornell University Press, 1965.

Lack, David. *Swifts in a Tower.* London: Methuen, 1956.

MacRoberts, M. H., and B. R. MacRoberts. "Social organization and behavior of the Acorn Woodpecker in central coastal California," *Ornithological Monographs,* 21 (1976), 1–115.

Meyerriecks, Andrew J. *Comparative Breeding Behavior of Four Species of North American Herons.* Nuttall Ornithological Club Publication, No. 2.

Nero, R. W., and J. T. Emlen. "An experimental study of territorial behavior in breeding Red-winged Blackbirds (*Agelaius phoeniceus*)," *Animal Behaviour,* 20 (1972), 112–18.

Nice, Margaret M. *The Watcher at the Nest.* New York: Macmillan, 1939.

Peek, F. W. "An experimental study of the vocal and visual displays in the Red-winged Blackbird (*Agelaius phoeniceus*)," *Animal Behaviour,* 20 (1972), 112–18.

Summers-Smith, D. *The House Sparrow.* London: Collins, 1963.

Stokes, D. W. *A Guide to the Behavior of Common Birds.* Boston: Little, Brown, 1979.

Tinbergen, Niko. *The Herring Gull's World.* London: Collins, 1953.

Amphibians and Reptiles

Goin, Olive B. *World Outside My Door.* New York: Macmillan, 1955.

Smyth, H. Rucker. *Amphibians and Their Ways.* New York: Macmillan, 1962.

THURROW, G. "Aggression and competition in eastern Plethodon (Amphibia, Urodela, Plethodontidae)," *Journal of Herpetology*, 10 (1976), 277–91.

WELLS, K. D. "The social behaviour of anuran amphibians," *Animal Behaviour*, 25 (1977), 666–93.

Fishes

BAERENDS, G. P., and J. M. BAERENDS-VAN ROON. *An Introduction to the Study of the Ethology of Cichlid Fishes*. Leiden, Netherlands: E. J. Brill, 1950.

MORRIS, DESMOND. *The Reproductive Behavior of the Ten-spined Stickleback*. Leiden, Netherlands: E. J. Brill, 1958.

THRESHER, RONALD E. *Reef Fish: Behavior and Ecology on the Reef and in the Aquarium*. Southfield, Mich.: Wonderland Books, 1980.

Insects and Other Invertebrates

ALEXANDER, R. D. "Aggressiveness, territoriality, and sexual behavior in field crickets (Orthoptera:Gryllidae)," *Behaviour*, 46 (1973), 174–88.

DETHIER, VINCENT G. *To Know A Fly*. San Francisco: Holden-Day, 1962.

———. *The Tentmakers*. Amherst: University of Massachusetts Press, 1980.

EVANS, HOWARD E. and M. J. W. EBERHARD. *The Wasps*. Ann Arbor, Mich.: University of Michigan Press, 1970.

LINDAUER, M. *Communication Among Social Bees*. Cambridge, Mass.: Harvard University Press, 1961.

LLOYD, J. E. *Studies on the Flash Communication System in Photinus Fireflies*. Miscellaneous Publications of the Museum of Zoology, University of Michigan, Ann Arbor, 1966.

OLDROYD, HAROLD. *The Natural History of Flies*. New York: W. W. Norton & Co., 1964.

STIMSON, J. "Territorial behavior of the owl limpet, *Lottia gigantea*," *Ecology*, 51 (1970), 113–18.

TEALE, EDWIN W. *The Fascinating Insect World of J. Henri Fabre*. New York: Dodd, Mead & Co., 1956.

URQUHART, F. A. *The Monarch Butterfly*. Toronto: University of Toronto Press, 1960.

VON FRISCH, K. *The Dance Language and Orientation of Bees*. Cambridge, Mass.: Harvard University Press, 1967.

WILSON, E. O. *The Insect Societies*. Cambridge, Mass.: Harvard University Press, 1971.

General Behavior References

ALLEN, T. B., ed. *The Marvels of Animal Behavior*. Washington, D.C.: National Geographic Society, 1972.

BARNETT, S. A. *Instinct and Intelligence*. Englewood Cliffs, N.J.: Prentice-Hall, 1967.

BURTON, MAUD R. *Inside the Animal World*. New York: Quadrangle, 1977.

EISNER, T. and E. O. WILSON. *Readings from Scientific American: Animal Behavior*. San Francisco: W. H. Freeman & Co., 1955–1975.

GRIFFIN, D. R. *Bird Migration.* London: Heinemann, 1965.

HINDE, R. A. *Animal Behavior.* New York: McGraw-Hill, 1966.

KOENIG, L. *Studies in Animal Behavior.* New York: Thomas Y. Crowell, 1958.

RHEINGOLD, N. L., ed. *Maternal Behavior in Mammals.* London: Wiley, 1933.

THORPE, W. H. *Learning and Instinct in Animals.* London: Methuen, 1963.

———. *Bird Song.* Cambridge, England: University Press, 1961.

TINBERGEN, NIKO. *Animal Behavior.* New York: Time-Life Books, Inc., 1965.

INDEX

Italic page numbers indicate where illustrations can be found.